# BACON

A BIOGRAPHY OF SIR FRANCIS BACON

BY
## CHARLES WILLIAMS

Copyright © 2019 Read & Co. Books

This edition is published by Read & Co. Books,
an imprint of Read Books Ltd.

This book is copyright and may not be reproduced or copied in any way without the express permission of the publisher in writing.

British Library Cataloguing-in-Publication Data
A catalogue record for this book is available
from the British Library.

www.readandcobooks.co.uk

# Charles Williams

Charles Walter Stansby Williams was born in London in 1886. He dropped out of University College London in 1904, and was hired by Oxford University Press as a proof-reader, quickly rising to the position of editor. While there, arguably his greatest editorial achievement was the publication of the first major English-language edition of the works of the Danish philosopher Søren Kierkegaard.

Williams began writing in the twenties and went on to publish seven novels. Of these, the best-known are probably *War in Heaven* (1930), *Descent into Hell* (1937), and *All Hallows' Eve* (1945) – all fantasies set in the contemporary world. He also published a vast body of well-received scholarship, including a study of Dante entitled *The Figure of Beatrice* (1944) which remains a standard reference text for academics today, and a highly unconventional history of the church, *Descent of the Dove* (1939). Williams garnered a number of well-known admirers, including T. S. Eliot, W. H. Auden and C. S. Lewis. Towards the end of his life, he gave lectures at Oxford University on John Milton, and received an honorary MA degree. Williams died almost exactly at the close of World War II, aged 58.

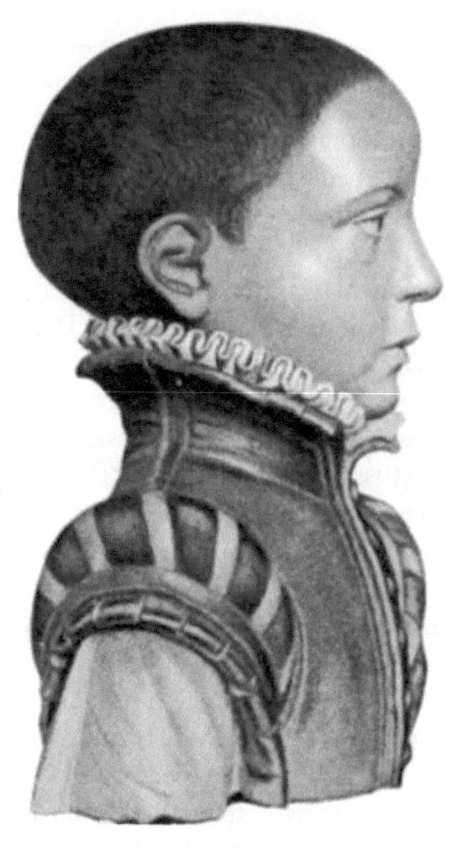

FRANCIS BACON AS A BOY

*NOTE*

*The following pages derive from a " Myth of Francis Bacon," written in verse for presentation at Downe House in July* 1932, *at the request of Miss Olive Willis. At that time it seemed that, in spite of the recent biographical flow, there was no convenient modern Life of Bacon, and the suggestion of Mr. Arthur Barker provoked my own inclination to attempt one. This book, therefore, was planned and partly written when the Life by Miss Sturt appeared. But the stresses here are quiet different from hers, and in any case Bacon is worth two, and will no doubt soon be worth at least ten, Lives. No one can be more aware than I how much there is in the Lord St. Alban which is not here, how many interests and how much interest. " He was, in parts, more than a man."*

*In view of Miss Rebecca West's recent book on St. Augustine, perhaps I ought also to say that the paragraph on St. Monica is derived from my own review of another (and much less interesting) Life published some years since.*

*C. W.*

*Easter,* 1933.

# CONTENTS

| CHAP. | | PAGE |
|---|---|---|
| I. | VOCATION | 1 |
| II. | THE SECOND ATTEMPT: BURLEIGH | 16 |
| III. | THE THIRD ATTEMPT: ESSEX | 39 |
| IV. | THE TURNING-POINT: THE HOUSE OF COMMONS | 103 |
| V. | "THE ADVANCEMENT OF LEARNING" | 138 |
| VI. | THE APPROACH TO GREAT PLACE | 151 |
| VII. | THE LORD CHANCELLOR | 213 |
| VIII. | THE "NOVUM ORGANUM" | 241 |
| IX. | THE REMOVAL OF PRESERVATION | 255 |
| X. | THE FINAL ENERGY | 286 |
| XI. | FRANCIS BACON | 302 |
| | A BRIEF CHRONOLOGY | 314 |
| | INDEX | 315 |

# CHAPTER I

## VOCATION

THE Fortune of Francis Bacon determined that he should be born on the twenty-second of January 1560/1, at York House in the Strand. It laid him in a cradle among the rulers of kingdoms; the names of empires were to be his daily business, but it interfused with them another and invisible empire which was to belong to his holidays and his nights, the empire of man over nature. His Fortune prepared in him an energy which has protracted itself through three centuries, saluted and studied by such men as Descartes and Leibniz, and (in another kind) Voltaire; an energy which, by the scope of its vision and the vital lucidity of its speech, was to make even his enemies his debtors. There was in his lifetime but one other power of equal and superior greatness; in the year of Francis's birth John Shakespeare was chosen to serve Stratford as a chamberlain, while Nicholas Bacon held the Great Seal of England. Men have been so astonished at the separate glories of the two children that they have refused to believe that the richness of God could put them in the world together. Yet the one is in a sense the measure of the other. The mortal greatness of Francis lacked but one thing—he was not Shakespeare; his judgment lacked but one intelligence—he would not have supposed the subordination was on his side.

His Fortune gave him energy and lucidity, but also a body troubled by ill-health. It set his cradle close by the Throne, but on the left side. There had been but recently another cradle on the right, in which the slightly deformed body of his cousin, Robert Cecil, had lain. Offices and powers loomed below the Throne and over the cradles that stood, for the future as for the present, so near the purple. Francis's father was Lord Keeper; his grandfather had been governor to royalty; his uncle was Secretary and presently to be Treasurer. The two cousins might look forward to succeeding to such offices, or (if they preferred) to accepting convenient titles, large estates, and enormous houses, now being built for them, such as Burleigh House or Theobalds. Gorhambury was begun two years after Francis's birth. His Fortune seemed to promise him everything he could want at the cost of a little industry. In fact, for all his unceasing industry, it kept him waiting for nearly fifty years for what he did want, providing him with unsatisfactory substitutes meanwhile, and having at last given it, immediately took it back again.

He emerged from his cradle into the world, a distracted and dangerous world, about which the rumours and uncertainties of a new reign ran thickly, through London, and to and from the ports, and overseas to other centres—The Hague, Paris, Madrid, Rome. He beheld the gardens of York House, and Whitehall away on one side; on the other, towards Saint Paul's, among similar palaces, Essex House, where his elder brother Anthony was to sit, thirty-five years later, writing and dictating letters to those other centres of diplomacy. He grew vividly aware of his brother, dutifully aware of his mother and his father, of great personages; among them, greatest of all, of the Queen. She was thirty-seven when he was born; one day, by his deceitful Fortune, he was led to her feet, and presented. She asked him how old he was. " I am three years younger than your Majesty's happy reign," he said, and maintained the same tactful " gravity and maturity " during his further youthful intercourse with her whenever she teased him with questions, so that she laughed and was pleased and called him "her young Lord Keeper." In Saint James's Fields, years afterwards, he knew of an echo; biography almost demands that he shall be supposed to have found it then, and that fancy shall invent and observe the young Lord Keeper listening to the echo in the Fields, as a mere convenient prophecy of his future as "privy councillor to King James and to Nature." "Probable conjectures," the *Essays* remark, "many times turn themselves into prophecies"; but any one who attended to the *Essays* could never write modern biography; let us pretend it happened. Add that there was, then or later, a conjurer, and all that was ever exposed of the Lord St. Alban's childhood is known.

The household in which the small Francis walked was industrious and serious, concerned with statecraft and religion. He inherited both, with a difference. His father, Nicholas Bacon, after the death of his first wife, had married again, as wives and husbands so often did then; hardly any period of history is fuller of those second marriages which contributed to the making of estates and the enriching of the Families. Sir Nicholas chose a lady as distinguished in her way as he in his, who became the mother of two sons—Anthony and Francis. She was Anne Cooke, the daughter of Sir Anthony Cooke, governor of Edward VI, the prince to whom Sir John Cheke, the brother of William Cecil's first wife, had taught Greek. Anne Cooke had herself been a tutor to the young Majesty. Her sister Mildred, William Cecil's second wife, was reported to be one of the two most learned women in England; the other was Lady Jane Grey. And as that group of Bacons, Cecils, and Cookes, with its connections, belonged to the learned among the learned, so they belonged also to the reformers among the Reformers, and to the rich among the rich. Nothing quite like it has been seen since among the governors of England : Gladstone, pious, well-read, well-to-do, is, of all people, the nearest example, and Gladstone had no brother-in-law or successor of his own rank.

Sir Nicholas himself was a political lawyer. He had been the son of the sheep-steward at the Abbey of Bury St. Edmunds ; he had received grants of monastic lands, had become one of the official class, had been used by Henry, Edward, and Mary, and on the accession of Elizabeth had been given the Seal by his brother-in-law Cecil. He often served Cecil in the office of an unofficial opposition. There was certainly no marked difference in their views, but sometimes their judgments differed, or it was thought convenient they should differ, and the brothers-in-law could afford a luxury which had its use in State affairs. He was one of the great men of the growing Civil Service ; he had drawn out a scheme by which some of the monastic revenues were to be spent on building a college for the sons of gentlemen where they could be trained for officialdom, some for foreign, some for home service. His father had been steward of the Abbey sheep ; Sir Nicholas enlarged and exalted in civil affairs a similar capacity. He was not alone. Pastors of all kinds were thronging or anxious to throng to England ; the hungry sheep were to be offered the most diverse food, and (but for the civil government) would have been considerably overfed. Mary's stoled priests were in possession, and in Flanders a Nuncio from the Roman Shepherd lingered. There was talk of the Council of Trent ; there was even a hinting at the removal of Elizabeth's bastardy. Unfortunately, before it could be removed, it would have to be implicitly admitted. The Queen's Majesty was not forward to admit her illegitimacy. At a Council held at Greenwich in May, while Francis still looked infantilely at the world, it was decided by his father, Cecil, and others, not to admit the Nuncio. But besides the stoles of those shepherds were the black gowns of others. The Marian exiles flocked back from Geneva, anxious to rebuild their fold. The Queen's Majesty had no liking for Geneva in her heart. Cecil and Sir Nicholas shepherded the pastors as far as they could— slightly Genevawards, and the mysterious religious emotion of the Queen assisted to preserve the mystical spiritual integrity of the Church of England.

But the official pastorate of Nicholas is a less vivid thing to us than the personal passion of Lady Bacon, who recalls an earlier mother of greatness—St. Monica. Over the all-but-fatalistic doctrine which was part of Augustine's contribution to Christian theology broods the all-but-fatalistic figure of the African matron whom her husband (setting an example to all English gentlemen) never struck, from whom her son was compelled to escape by deceit and stealth, who separated him from his paramour of ten years' love and their child, who proposed for him Christian marriage and the Catholic Church, and, rationalized into something as near predestination as orthodoxy will allow, still terrifies the metaphysics of the Church; which seems to be saved from her influence only by the still earlier mother in whom the humanity as well as the piety of Christendom has taken refuge, the silent maid of meditation who is the mother of the Divine Word.[1] But Anne Bacon found neither silence nor supremacy. She had always been religious; she was very much in her place in that group of governors. She was the kind of woman who could translate from its original Latin Bishop Jewel's *Apology*

[1] What would have happened to Christendom if her husband had ventured to beat Monica, as other African husbands beat their wives? to Luther, Calvin, Trent, and the doctrine of grace?

*for the Church of England.* And she did. But it was in her later years that religion became her realized passion, and it is by her later years that we know her best. She appears, from a letter of hers to Cecil, to have undergone some sort of emotional change in 1577 or 1578, when Francis was about seventeen, and near the time when her husband died. She speaks in that letter of having " found mercy," adding a pious acknowledgment of the fact that she has profited more by the opening of Scriptures in ordinary preaching during the last seven or eight years than for well-nigh twenty years in " odd sermons " at Paul's. Her grief was for her two sons, Anthony and Francis; not having Monica's genius, she had to content herself with lament and vain hope.

Modern biography suspects her of being the unknowing cause of her son's preference of atheism to superstition. " I trust they will not mum or mask or sinfully revel," she wrote of the Gray's Inn Christmas festivities. She was difficult with her household; a servant of Anthony's wrote to him that "nobody can please her long together," and again pathetically, " She made me to buy starch and soap to wash my linen withal: more than was wont to be: yet I care not so she would be quiet." It was probably what Anthony and Francis also wished. She complained of Anthony's vain-glory in buying horses. She objected to his lending his coach. She regretted the lack of Christian behaviour in Francis's cook. She was troubled by their personal habits. Anthony spent too much on coal when he was living at Essex House, and Francis at Gray's Inn sat up too late and then, when he did go to bed, lay musing on she knew not what (she was quite right) when he ought to have been asleep, and so got up late, " whereby his men are made slothful and himself continueth sickly." But for all her flurries and commands and entreaties and efforts after compulsion, she could not rule them. Anthony, angered by her treatment of his servant, once wrote: " However your Ladyship doth pretend and allege for reason your motherly affection towards us in that which concerneth Lawson ; yet any man of judgment and indifferency must needs take it for a mere passion, springing either from presumption, that your ladyship can only judge and see that in the man, which never any man yet hath seen ; or from a sovereign desire to over-rule your sons in all things, how little soever you may understand either the ground or the circumstances of their proceedings."

From his mother and his father, Francis went up in 1573 with his elder brother Anthony to Trinity College, Cambridge. It was two years since another young student had left that College ; Edward Coke, the son of an old Norfolk family, was by now reading law in Clifford's Inn. A long antagonism awaited its beginning. At Cambridge again Francis's life is hidden. He was ill ; he had his windows glazed and his stockings dyed, shoes were bought for him, and a bow and arrows, silk points, and a dozen new buttons ; a desk was put up in his study. That is all, except for one thing—he disliked the philosophy of Aristotle ; in fact, he fell in love.

It may have been slow or sudden, but when he was in London ten years afterwards he was engaged on the first work done for the sake of that love, and the dislike of Aristotle had, it seems, that same love for its cause. At a distance in time and person, many years afterwards, from the pen of his chaplain, we have his account : " Whilst he was commorant in the University, about sixteen years of age (as his lordship hath been pleased to impart unto myself), he first fell into the dislike of the philosophy of Aristotle ; not for the worthlessness of the author, to whom he would ever ascribe all high attributes, but for the unfruitfulness of the way ; being a philosophy (as his lordship used to say) only strong for disputations and contentions, but barren of the production of works for the benefit of the life of man ; in which mind he continued to his dying day."

Aristotle was still the master of those who thought. But Aristotle's own concern with existence had been turned through the centuries into a concern with Aristotle's method of thinking about existence, and even there the stress had been all on one side. As in religion texts had been used to prove opinions, so in natural science had facts ; as in religion texts, so in natural science facts, had been taken almost at random, certainly without examination, classification, or relation. An observed fact or a reported fable held almost the same worth ; for in argument they had the same worth ; each supplied a premise, and it was the premise that mattered. Induction, or the drawing of general principles from particular instances, provided the material for the far more important business of deduction, or the application of general propositions to particular instances. The world, and all the innumerable things and relations of things that make up the world, were taken anyhow in order that the necessary general propositions could be furnished to theorists, philosophers, or theologians. They were all food for the syllogism, sacks of manure on the mind in which the necessary crop of conclusions could be grown. But Francis Bacon objected to the world being used as manure.

It is impossible not to believe that he had seen the method in use in York House. No doubt religion was " rather different " ; in our modern phrase, it was not his subject. But the clash and challenge of text and text without examination of the context or consideration of the verbal intention had been going on, now this way, now that, for decades of years. Preconceived opinion, predetermined judgment, would seize phrases from Isaiah or Kings or St. Paul to prove what nothing would be allowed to disprove. The long examinations of heretics, under Mary or Elizabeth, meant only that in the end ; in the end, therefore, both Majesties or their governments were driven back on offering their prisoners the choice between changing their preconceived opinions or being put to death, that being, as all mankind knows, the only certain way of dealing with a preconceived opinion. Bacon was never anxious to put people to death unless their preconceived opinions were in danger of overthrowing civil quiet. Later he observed the universal peril—" Men create oppositions which are not, and put them into new terms, so fixed as, whereas the meaning ought to govern the term, the term in effect governeth the meaning." That was his note in the *Essays*, but in a paper on the controversies of the Church, while Lady Bacon from Gorhambury was unloading her heart, he let a similar warning sound: " The disease requireth rather rest than any other cure " ; " if we did but know the virtues of silence and slowness to speech "—O mother ! mother !—" a character of love more proper . . . than that of zeal," " peace, silence, and surceance."

But, though he observed it, dogmatic theology was not his metier. At Cambridge, however, he found the same thing. At York House they did not ask what a text *meant* ; it meant what their general principles needed it to mean. At Cambridge they did not ask what the facts *were* ; the facts were what were convenient for their general principles. Slowly or suddenly, he became aware of his business, but his business was not a mere contradiction of existing methods. He did not concentrate for fifty years on a hatred of degenerate Aristotelianisms. He had fallen in love, not (as do most young lovers) with the universe concentrated and manifested in a particular person, but with the universe in itself. A romantic passion filled him, no less romantic (as in other modes of love) for its realism: the particularities of space and time were to him as the particularities in which the universal form expresses itself to many by means of the form of the beloved. " Light-bearing experiments " were his method of wooing, and the light that disseminates itself for mortal lovers from the shape of their ladies was for him perceptible in the thoroughfares of the nature of the world. Emotional and intellectual at once, this thing that was as vivid as a person was as exact as a formula. Such mortal revelations remain, even in less great minds, as a centre of union; so, a man may suddenly and in a moment understand that space and time are one thing diversely manifested, or that eternity is a unique state and not a process of everlastingness. For most of us such flashes remain as a memory or a doctrine; our emotions and our minds live separate lives, and our spirits cannot or dare not follow the unity that is revealed. Francis Bacon's could and did; he fell in love and to the end of his life he remained passionately in love. He blamed himself sometimes for infidelity, but in fact his faithfulness continually filled and drove him, for he loved necessity.

The thing possessed him. The thing that was—fact—as distinct from words; the thing that was to be—knowledge—as distinct from fables; the thing that was to say it—truth—as distinct from argument. Man was still lost in subtle discussions, incurious, unlearned, accepting inaccuracy, rich only with insubstantial words. Words must be made substantial with truth; truth must be discovered by inquiry and observation, by rejection and selection. But to achieve that meant in fact nothing less than the entire reorganization of human thought. It seemed then that Francis Bacon must begin to reorganize human thought, must institute a great instauration of science. Back to observed fact, to right induction, to the world ! Man must gain knowledge, discover the true causes of things, extend human empire ; he must have certainty, not opinion ; he must rely on infinite experiment, infinite study, out of which certainty would arise. The method had not been used ; it had not even been tried ; nay, it had not been so much as shaped for trial. It was utterly without precedent. But it could be shaped, tried, used. He could proclaim it to men. The " delicate, lively, hazel eyes " (" viper eyes," Harvey called them, but Harvey did not love him), saw all possibilities open to the world of men ; there lay before them the universe of things, and its thoroughfares were already filled with " God's first creature, which is light." A ray of that light fell upon the road before him and his business on the road. He was to cry to mankind till they too saw it and ran to work and experiment and understand, and the vision should lie, palpable fact, before future ages. In such a moment a man understands his primal duty, and feels it already completed. Unrealized perfection exists within him ; his business is to preserve and define it.

York House, it may reasonably be presumed, would have displayed no intense feeling for the Great Instauration. The instauration of the Queen's safety and success was his father's business ; the instauration of Christ's kingdom on earth his mother's. Francis read law, and acceded to Sir Nicholas's intention of sending him to the Embassy at Paris. The proclamation of man's chief moral duty on earth must be made, but it must be made with authority. The more notable the place from which it was made the wider and more effective would be the call to mankind. Great men must be brought to take an interest, scholars and students. He was offered the beginnings of a career ; he accepted them. When in 1576

he went over to join Sir Amyas Paulet—another devout
Evangelical—in Paris, he stood at the opening of affairs,
and though on several occasions he was tempted to desert
them he never did, till he was thrown out with violence.
The reasons whereto (as he might have said), besides
the Great Instauration, were four : first, he held it to be
the duty of a man to serve the commonwealth ; second,
he thought himself peculiarly fitted to do so ; third,
it was to his immediate personal interest to do so ;
lastly, it was impossible for his imagination contentedly
to withdraw from the public activities of men. Many
poets and other creative minds do tend to occupy themselves so ; they cannot be content in retirement. To
retire from the world is to lose some part of their natures.
It was not by accident that Dante was a politician, or
Chaucer a civil servant, or Shakespeare a successful
business man, or Milton Latin Secretary. They feel a
summons not only to place but to great place ; they
desire to be among the chiefs. So very often does the
youngest clerk. But with those makers the demand is
more passionate, for men are part of that great whole
of Nature which is the stuff of their peculiar work. They
see things as a unity ; to reject a part of that unity is
to deny its true nature, therefore they desire to be
involved in that nature. " Why did he not retire ? "
asked Macaulay. For the same reason that Macaulay's
essays are less deep than his ; because the earlier mind
had a profounder and wider scope. It would be easy
for us to retire from the administration of government
to work at the Great Instauration ; that is one reason
why we could not have imagined the Instauration.

At Paris, or rather at Pont-Charenton, he found
another echo. " I did hear it return the voice thirteen
several times : and I have heard of others, that it would
return sixteen times : for I was there about three of the
clock in the afternoon ; and it is best (as all other echoes

are) in the evening. . . . I remember well, that when I went to the echo at Pont-Charenton, there was an old Parisian who took it to be the work of spirits, and of good spirits. For (said he) call *Satan,* and the echo will not deliver back the devil's name; but will say *va-t'en*; which is as much in French as *apage* or *avoid* And thereby I did hap to find that an echo would not return ' S,' being but a hissing and an interior sound."

It is the first example of the new method in contact with the old, directly and indirectly. Long afterwards Francis was to write in the *Novum Organum* of the leaping directly from the evidence of the senses to the most general principles instead of proceeding through middle axioms. The evidence of the senses was that the echo said " va-t'en " in reply to " Satan." The old method leapt directly to the principle of divine intervention, which is one of the most general principles possible. The new method, as eventually defined, would gather particulars of all echoes—St. James's Fields, Pont-Charenton, and the rest—and discover by careful comparison what echoes actually did do; that in fact, no echo ever said " S." In which case, it would be less probable that Divinity disliked the letter " S " than that the nature of an echo forbade the reproduction of sibilants. But indirectly also the thing ratifies a distinction. All the world around him was crying out " Satan " and hearing the answer of the Holy Spirit, " va-t'en "; only—or almost only—Francis conceived that the reply might be due to an incapacity for a particular interior sound; that, in short, the Holy Spirit could not hiss.

He did not succeed in finding an immediate explanation of another curious fact. He was troubled with one of the distresses of adolescence. " I had, from my childhood, a wart upon one of my fingers: afterwards, when I was about sixteen years old, being then at Paris, there grew upon both my hands a number of warts (at the least an hundred) in a month's space. The English ambassador's lady, who was a woman far from superstition, told me one day, she would help me away with my warts : whereupon she got a piece of lard, with the skin on, and rubbed the warts all over with the fat sides; and amongst the rest, that wart which I had had from my childhood : then she nailed the piece of lard, with the fat towards the sun, upon a post of her chamber window, which was to the south. The success was, that within five weeks' space all the warts went quite away : and that wart which I had so long endured, for company."

Between actual echoes and diplomatic rumours, warts on the hands and plots in the mind, conversations with studious Frenchmen and inventions of convenient ciphers, two years wore away, and the winter of 1578 was drawing to its close. One night in February he dreamed. He saw Gorhambury, the house that his father had built, plastered all over with black mortar. He might have been dreaming of the house of his own life, prophesied in his visionary mind of power, so covered with black. For the first separation between him and his end had begun ; unexpectedly, without his realization, the universe had intervened between him and his desire. His father had died suddenly. Francis, by that swift accident of an open window and a great thaw after heavy snow, was left without expected provision. Sir Nicholas had meant to purchase an estate for him as he had done for his other sons ; but now there was no estate and not very much money. He would have to work. In March he returned to England, bearing letters of commendation from Sir Amyas to the Queen ; and set himself deliberately to study law.

It was not, however, in law that he put his trust.

On the other, the more important, side of the Throne, to which his eyes were turned, stood his uncle. It seemed to Francis that nothing could be simpler than for the Lord Treasurer, who, as everybody knew, had the Queen's ear, to recommend his nephew to the Queen and find him some post under Government. He applied to him, writing youthful, solemn, respectful letters. He was to go on applying to him for a year, three . . seven . . . ten years. The Lord Treasurer continued to treasure his own council, and to lay up his powers for the use of the baby who had lain in the cradle to the right of the Throne.

## CHAPTER II

### THE SECOND ATTEMPT : BURLEIGH

IN 1590, towards the end of those ten years, a month or two after *Tamburlaine* had been first presented " on stages in the Citie " and a year or two before Shakespeare had certainly reached the way to the stages in the City, Edmund Spenser published, with the encouragement of Sir Walter Raleigh, the first three cantos of the *Faerie Queene*. He accompanied them with seventeen sonnets, addressed among others to Raleigh, Essex, Burleigh, Howard, and Walsingham. He described Raleigh as the summer's nightingale, with a compliment on the nightingale's verse. He invoked Essex as " magnific Lord," assuring him that this base poem was not worthy of his heroic parts, which it would later on more nobly celebrate. He assured Burleigh that at bottom it was a very serious poem and not as vain as it might superficially appear. Howard was an example to the present age of the heroes of antiquity, and Walsingham was Mæcenas.

The last unlikely comparison was used by another poet, William Harrison, who preluded with it verses commenting on " that anti-Christ at Rome "—a phrase which would have surprised the original Mæcenas. In fact Walsingham seems to have confined his patronal attentions to very minor poets, to Puritan scholars and divines, and to himself ; he made nearly twenty thousand pounds in five years, at the lowest reckoning, by farming the Customs from the Queen. But the fact that Spenser could address him with that rhyming and hopeful

untruth explains by accentuation the verbal music of
the age.  Verse is not so different from prose, nor public
dedications from private devotions, that Spenser can
be held guiltless of flattery if Bacon is to be blamed.
A few years afterwards Shakespeare was to assure
Southampton that " what I have done is yours, what I
have to do is yours, being part in all I have, devoted
yours." Such was the habit of writers to courtiers,
ministers, and great lords.

Beyond lords, ministers, and courtiers was the Queen
herself.  Every one is aware how poets and less intelligent people than poets " flattered " the Queen.  Fashion,
which denigrates so many reputations after death, has
had to wait three hundred years and more to have its
turn at Elizabeth ; it appears that it will soon console
itself for the delay.  But to her poets and servants she
was, what she was to Spenser, Glory.  She was all the
Goddesses, all the Muses, all the Nymphs and Graces,
the " imperial votaress," the " dearest dread," " the
bright Occidental star." To attribute deliberate insincerity to those voices is to misunderstand both their
imagination and their style.  They beheld, while they
shaped, the external world.  Their attitude towards
the Queen was voluntary and compulsory at once ; they
also, in that lesser thing, chose necessity.  They created
her, but they created what existed potentially.  They
formed her and believed in her precisely as we all form
images and believe in them.  They defined Royalty.

It is easy to believe they flattered, not so easy to
see that they flattered where they believed.  Yet the
whole similar tradition of romantic love illumines their
devotion.  The young lover believes that " authority
and reason " wait on his mistress ; that

> Wisdom in discourse with her
> Loses discountenanced, and like folly shows.

We have kept the one passion, because nature assisted

us ; we have lost the other, because—for the most
honourable reasons—the gentlemen of England took it
away. But in the days of Elizabeth it existed and it
was a power, producing interior as well as exterior
effects. It moved men's thoughts and beliefs not only
about the Queen but about themselves. There was in
the Majesty of Elizabeth a kind of fate, and when it
struck in anger men wondered if they were as guiltless
as they themselves had supposed, and saw, again as a
young lover sees in the averted face of the beloved, as
Dante saw when Beatrice denied him her salutation,
the wrath of the gods directed against them. She
might be mistaken ; she might be unjust. They protested against her injustice, but only as men protest,
with sighs or oaths, against the supreme injustice of
the universe.

No doubt in minds which were continually in close
contact with hers, or were themselves rather rational
than creative, this imagination flagged and disappeared.
The vigilance of Cecil worked from it as upon a hypothesis
justified by the results ; the violence of Essex despised it
as an offensive necessity. They controlled or attempted
to control her and fretted beneath her obstinacy, her
parsimony, her insatiable demands, and her secret fears.
That coldness and hatred came on them which (men
say) affects marriage and religion and all fulfilled
romantic dreams. No doubt also, in proportion as
sympathy with the Puritan fundamental of "no idolatry"
—of statues, miracles, transubstantiations, or living
men—grew stronger, the half-sacramental adoration
of the crowned figure grew less. The monarch was a
sinner, and his office at most but a necessary business
of a sinful world. John Knox had already exhorted,
rebuked, and denounced the Queen of Scotland. But
in England the deposition of the monarch had to wait
another thirty or forty years, and meanwhile to serve

the Queen was to serve reputed divinity. To make love to the Queen was—anyhow in its first stages—at once a convention and an excitement. The Queen might be old and ugly. But gods were different from their worshippers. Men who have quarrelled with their women have been thrown off their balance; men who have made love to queens have been in peril; but to make love and then to quarrel with this adorned, fantastic, earthy and unearthly Majesty was to run the risk of being flung into a whirling void of phantasms in which the only truth was the edge of the axe turned towards the condemned traitor as he was conducted from the court of his peers.

Of that last overthrow Francis Bacon was never in danger. He was never allured to such intimacies as Essex with Elizabeth or Somerset with James. But he felt and believed in the image of royalty, and therefore he believed in the powers and graces of royalty. It would be too much to say that he believed in Majesty rather than in himself; but he was always prepared to submit to Majesty, because Majesty, and those whom Majesty loved, were likely to be right. His imagination did continual homage to its own vision of the wisdom of the Crown. He did not merely pretend that a particular woman or a particular man was set by God in authority, but without any special capacity for the high office. He believed that God meant the King to rule and furnished the King with necessary endowments. Nobody, certainly, believes either to-day, in spite of the continual passionate entreaties of the Churches. But then our contemporary imagination hears the noise of the passage of the King rather as Mr. Perker and the Pickwickians heard the cheering round the Honourable Samuel Slumkey when he kissed the six babies at the Town Arms of Eatanswill. The whole of the sources, channels, and flood of that passion are hidden from us.

But in that Elizabethan poem which the Elizabethan Spenser laid at the feet of " the most High, Mighty, and Magnificent Empress, renowned for piety, virtue, and all gracious government . . . in all humility . . . to live with the eternity of her fame," [1] there is another figure, besides Gloriana, which illuminates the imagination of the age, and that is Prince Arthur. Prince Arthur was to marry Gloriana. And " in the person of Prince Arthur I set forth magnificence in particular, which virtue for that (according to Aristotle and the rest) it is the perfection of all the rest, and containeth in it them all, therefore in the whole course I mention the deeds of Arthur applyable to that virtue which I write of in that book." Magnificence in man was, no doubt, primarily a spiritual quality, but it had great earthly symbols. In that sense also Magnificence was a duty as well as an indulgence. A century earlier the Black Prince had been praised, in a poem written ten years after his death, for knowing well " the doctrine of largesse." Nowadays we praise the dead (if possible) for generosity, and do not mean the same thing. Great men, under Elizabeth, were still supposed to be wise in " the doctrine of largesse." Magnificence was to marry Glory, and all the earthly glories and magnificences were to attend on that supreme and superb bridal. Gloriana herself certainly was not much inclined to the doctrine of largesse ; nor was Burleigh. But that did not alter the fact that she approved it in others, and the imagination of her age approved it everywhere. Kings and great lords were not praised and admired for leading simple lives ; it would not have occurred to any one that they ought to lead simple lives. In 1599 Shakespeare's Henry V asked Ceremony what it was, but only after an intense appreciation of Ceremony,

[1] Compare the dedication of Robert Bridges's *Testament of Beauty* —" To the King." The change is not entirely gain.

"the farcèd title running 'fore the king, the throne he sits on, and the tide of pomp" that swells through so many of the plays.

Patrons were to behave magnificently to their clients. It was not an age of regular salaries. Men gave what they had and could; men took all that was offered. They took it in offices or houses or lands or money—money if it were possible. It is not likely that the Bishop of Durham to-day would send the Prime Minister £100 for favours received, but so much a former Bishop of Durham sent to Lord Burleigh. Bacon, writing in a fit of temper to Cecil, says that it is rumoured he has taken two thousand angels to help Sir Thomas Coventry to the Solicitorship. He obviously thinks Cecil has treated him very badly, but he does not think it a wrong or even improper act in itself. The ladies and gentlemen of that age, when they wanted anything, asked for it. They even let one another know of anything that was going which they could not themselves use. Francis wrote to his mother (18th February 1591/2) that Alderman Haywood had died, and that this would bring his son into the Court of Wards (of which the Lord Treasurer was Master). Lord Burleigh was often slow in disposing of his wards. It was hardly suitable for Anthony who had only just returned from abroad to ask anything of his uncle before they had met; Francis himself was reserving Burleigh's patronage to make his way with the Queen. Why should not Lady Bacon ask for the wardship of the young heir? but she had better be quick about it. We do not know if Lady Bacon acted.

The fact was that magnificence cost money, and as they were not ashamed of magnificence so they were not ashamed of money. They were not ashamed of asking for it, of getting it, or (even more extremely) of being refused it. The Queen, if she were in displeasure with any one, might decline a jewel. Austere precisians might prefer, if they were on bad terms with any one, to maintain the quarrel at the expense of their income. But the normal method was to make up the quarrel and ask for the advantage. The memoirs of the nineteenth and twentieth centuries read strangely to us after the letters of the sixteenth and seventeenth. Something is lacking in those later sedate volumes, some frank sound of human activity, of desire or necessity. If our later generations ask at all they do it in a quiet, dignified, self-respecting way—but how rarely they ask! The petitions of their fathers were not quiet, do not seem to us at all dignified, and hardly self-respecting. But self-respect has many modes, and quiet dignity is not certainly the chief virtue committed to man. The English had not then become proud of their reserve.

Ostentation as a virtue has disappeared from the galaxy, but in those days ostentation was the brightest of all. Whatever was kept secret was so hidden that even now we often cannot be certain of their motives and intentions. Whatever was shown was shown and spoken almost in the style of Tamburlaine himself. As artistic enjoyments meiosis and magniloquence are equal and opposite, and so as moral virtues. It is not certainly finer or wiser, though it may be safer, to say less than the truth than to say more. If the latter leads to looseness, diffusion, and insincerity, the former induces paralysis of speech and therefore often of thought. As in arts of decoration so in arts of expression, the Elizabethans were ostentatious. Rhetoric—even rant— was a courtesy—even a duty; they thought our simple tastes not merely rude but wrong. It is difficult, but healthful, to consider that they may have been right. Essex, while he was the Favourite of Elizabeth, meaning to assure James of Scotland of his devotion to the King's interests, wrote as follows:

" Most gracious and renowned prince,

" If I should only regard the weakness of mine own merit, without having an eye unto the exceeding bounty, whereby your majesty hath quickened me to make a present of all that service, which my poor ability may perform, I should have forborn to have made this paper witness of my boldness. But in what manner could I have framed a plea in excuse of inexpiable ingratitude, if I had not by some lines given a taste of the affections of my heart, which breathe only after the prosperous success of a king of so much worth, whose servant I am born by nature, and by duty am obliged to exercise all the powers both of my mind and body in advancing his designs ? Therefore such as I am, and all whatsoever I am (tho' perhaps a subject of small price) I consecrate unto your regal throne ; protesting, that what defect soever may be incident unto me, it shall appear more fitly to be set on the score of error than of wilfulness. And whereas I have presumed, out of the suddenness of my brain, to hatch a rude and indigested piece of work, most humbly I beseech your highness to overlook it with a favourable eye, and to conceive, that I took in hand to play the statesman rather out of the zeal I bore to so just a cause, than out of any overweening humour of mine own sufficiency. Neither do I doubt, that the minds of all my countrymen, being already in motion to betake themselves to a rightful cause, will jointly unite their hopes in your majesty's noble person, as the only centre, wherein our rest and happiness consist. I refrain from presenting thanks in lieu of full payment ; for I feel my forces unable to weigh with your highness's magnificence. Therefore in this behalf I will imitate Timanthes, who covered those parts of his picture with a veil which he could not express lively by the art of his pencil, esteeming it more commendable to refer them to the imagination of others, than to bewray his own imperfections in colours. In like sort, while I want apt words to reveal the thoughts of my grateful heart, I am determined to shadow them with the veil of silence, until some happy revolution of time shall turn my inside outward, and give a public demonstration of my loyalty. In mean season I please myself with this hope, that being unable to present more, your accustomed grace will accept of my good will, which offers all that it can.

"Your majesty's most humble and affectionate servant. "7.
"LONDON, *May* 17."

Nor did ostentation apply only to politics; it applied to everything, intellectual or emotional. Bacon filled his speeches with his knowledge, as the pious filled theirs with quotations from the Bible. The Queen made an angry and impromptu speech in Latin to the Polish ambassador. Drake dined to music. They displayed their feelings. The Bishop of Lincoln wept in the House of Lords when he was accused by the Commons. Sir Edward Coke wept when he left the Court of Common Pleas for the King's Bench, and so did his brethren and subordinates. Men exhibited their glory, their learning, their pathos; so also their cruelty and their hate. They made a display of pain, and where they could not display it, they confessed, formalized, and announced it. Few men at any time are not willing to cause pain to others in order to achieve their desires. But in our age the ostentatious causing of physical pain has, very fortunately, gone out of fashion. The pain we cause is normally interior, secret, and only half-acknowledged. It is always possible to explain that one's victim has misunderstood a verbal cruelty, however exquisite; and even possible, so deceitful and transitory are the hellish moments of man, to believe that it was not meant. But it is hardly possible for executioner or victim to misunderstand the fire put to the bundle of wood or the steel that searches the entrails. The torch and the knife are meant for pain ; if they are justified or defended, excused or forgotten, it is still as pain and only as pain.

The ostentation, not of pain—or that only in one instance—but of speech, concerns the movement of Bacon's mind. Words themselves are ostentation, a showing forth, and he was a master of words. But, as all masters must be, he was to an extent the instrument of that which he controlled. Men capable of great phrases are, by their inevitable nature, sometimes subordinated to those phrases. We have thought so much of realism, of writing with " the eye on the object," that we have forgotten that, though the eye may be on the object, the mind is elsewhere. It is, in fact, a truth which is only half the truth. To mean to put a thing in words is to mean, at most, to create an image of the thing, with the life of the image and not of the thing itself. It—whatever " it " is—is discovered only by its creation in words, and the exterior thing is but a nourishment or a medicine for the other more obscure life. One word thrusts another into being. But the care which a man will take over his creation if he means it to come before the world he may neglect in a familiar letter. He will not therefore be insincere. What is true of the poets and Majesty is true of any writer in passion. He creates, in writing, the thing in which he believes ; it is desire manifested and fulfilled. That the outer world destroys it does not prove it untrue. In his great moments it is the last intelligence of man to be able to believe that a thing, so defined and created, is true eternally and yet may seem to change.

The privilege of those moments brings its corresponding falsehood, as all such moments do, casting not only their glory but their shadow on customary life. Where that customary life itself exists in a high style of rhetoric and imagined abandonment, the disproportion between the phrase and the thing grows more marked. The mind of Bacon may have seen a phrase as false even while he wrote it: was he singular? Yet where he wholly or partly wished it to be true, to strike it out would be to hasten its denial. He was content to lie—as all the servants of imagined devotion, in prose or poetry, have lied, and he prepared for himself—as they do—the future vengeance of the universe. Poets can write business letters; they can be commercially sincere. But where they need not be, they suffer for their inevitable and creative falsity: vicarious in their pain for the world that is nourished on their power.

Against the glory and ostentation of that age there was already present an enemy without and an opposition within. The first was an austerer power, soon to increase, a witness (as it declared itself) to another glory. The passion that, for no mortal gain, extinguished the lights on the altars, and tore the copes, and even the surplices, from the celebrants, and checked dances and revelry and merrymaking, and banished plays—all to give clear room to that sacred darkness in which the uncreated light could spiritually shine; the passion that abolished the ritual and denied the mystery of the Mass, and pierced the ensuing void with the sound of solitary voices preaching and praying, and either way proclaiming to men the awful Presence which no idolatrous mummery might pretend miraculously to control and enshrine—Puritanism was coming. The Puritan was a moment of man's existence; his strength was that he was a moment of man's experience of reality; his weakness that his own reality could not prolong that transcendant fact. But he was a witness to a glory inexpressible among earthly things: the least flash of the least diamond on mitre or stomacher was an offence to the bareness which alone properly reflected divinity

The creed rose into angry fanaticisms of destruction, as the creed it opposed had sunk into corrupt lethargies of superstition. It strained after the mystical abolition of man before Deity, and the secret knowledge of the saints was demanded as a profession of experience from the youngest in those aspiring schools. The illumination of Christendom has been more tender and more slow ; as by a subtle working, without his own knowledge, the newborn child has been decoyed on to the heavenly way ; the love of a man's heart and the desire of his eyes have been touched with the soft light of eternity. But the few seconds of mortal life were too short for such tardiness in the minds of men who inherited the harsher side of the tradition of the Middle Ages, and the Limbo to which the Church consigned unbaptized children or the hell with which it threatened stubborn heretics brought forth a deeper darkness and a fiercer flame of spirit to consume its own branches. The purity of that fiery knowledge was often mingled with earthlier flame. Walsingham did not lose by his antagonism to Rome nor the City merchants diminish their greed by their creed. The Puritanism of Cecil was no nobler than the Catholicism of the Earl of Northampton, who was his chief rival. But where it existed in its integral devotion it was possessed by a vision of unearthly glory, and it despised as it opposed the glory of a king.

Those terrible antagonisms were to pass. The Church remained ; the Puritan remained. But after centuries, in a less ostentatious age, the Church was to deprecate the acts of her ministers, and the Puritan to admit the beauty of holiness in his opponents. Meanwhile, however, they made more bitter the national warfare which was beginning—warfare between the nations and warfare within nations. It was not enough that men should promise not to do things ; they must promise not to believe things. The preoccupied voice of Bacon proposed that the Roman party should be relieved from penalties if they would swear not to bear arms against the Queen. But no one took any notice. Saints and sinners under every Monarch died for their beliefs. Sir Thomas More and the holy monks of the Charterhouse years before had gone as the principals of a whole university of martyrs; doctors, masters, and scholars of agony following them for a century. The Kings of Europe smote their philosophical enemies with torment and death. It may at least be said for them that though they used they did not invent the habit; that also had come from of old.

In that war Magnificence, and the Magnificence of England, became a maze to protect itself. Treacheries were reduplicated till treachery had lost its own intelligence. Men grew uncertain whom they betrayed. The privacies of their ostentation coiled through every kind of duplicity. The secret service of Walsingham and the secret service of the Roman Church were intermingling in a subtle dance of conspiracies, martyrdoms, assassinations, and executions. In 1576, when Bacon went to Paris with Sir Amyas Paulet, Don John of Austria was sending an ambassador to the Queen to ask for shelter for his troopships if they were driven into an English port by storms, and at the same time proposing to use the troops to dethrone Elizabeth and free Mary Stuart; of whose marriage with Don John, Paulet wrote to Walsingham that he had heard by sounding the secretary of the Duke of Guise. The marriage of Alençon with Elizabeth, the intrigues in Scotland, occupied Paulet's attention. With these there is nothing to show that the young Bacon had any direct business. But the English embassy at the Court of the Medici cannot have led even a junior member of its staff to think that great place was without its keyholes, its privy stairs, and its secret whispers.

On the edge, as it were, of Magnificence, figures remote from Gloriana and Prince Arthur, moved the obscure persons of Anthony and Francis Bacon. The death of their father left each of them to make his own career, with such aid only as their kindred would give them or they could procure themselves by proving their value. Anthony had one advantage over Francis: he had possessions and revenues—in Hertfordshire, the manors of Abbotsbury, Minchinbury, and Hores, of Colney Chapel, the farm of the manor of the priory of Redbourne, the site and demesnes of the manor of Redbourne, the farm of Charings; in Middlesex, the woods in Brent Heath, Brightfaith Woods, Merydan meads, and the farm of Pinner-stoke. He had therefore the possibility of determining his activity. He determined on foreign travel. Francis had returned to England in March. Anthony left later in the same year. He was abroad for some thirteen years, till February 1591/2. It is only after that date that the purpose, or at least the result, of his activity becomes clear. He returned to take up the direction of an English secret service abroad.

His travels took him to Paris, Bruges, Geneva, Toulouse, Lyons, Montpellier, Marseilles, Bordeaux, Montauban. At Bordeaux he was said to have contracted a friendship with Montaigne, to whom after his return he wrote. Unfortunately Montaigne died before he could answer the letter, and a correspondence of the most fascinating possibilities for us was cut short. At Geneva he lodged in the house of the famous Theodore Beza, who admired Lady Bacon so much, either on her son's report or from her translation of Jewel, that he dedicated an edition of his *Meditations* to her. To him also Anthony wrote after his return, but apparently on his mother's account. Lady Bacon would have sympathized more strongly than her son, especially a son who wrote to Montaigne, with Beza's horror at discovering that there actually were people who wondered whether " that body which had antichrist for its head " might not be part of the true Church. But in those days the Pope felt the same almost physical horror at those who thought the body which had Elizabeth for its governor might be. At Bordeaux again Anthony was denounced by three priests—probably justly—on an accusation of being in the centre of Huguenot discontent, and using his pen and person to assist it ; he was protected by the Governor—we dare not believe at Montaigne's instigation. At Montauban he fell into a more serious difficulty ; he made the wife of Philip de Mornay, the Huguenot leader, angry, partly by persuading her husband to send fifteen hundred crowns to a gentleman in England, partly by supporting the principal minister of the town, who had annoyed the lady (her name was Charlotte Arbaleste) by " censuring her scandalous excess in head-attire." The breach which Charlotte Arbaleste caused between de Mornay and Anthony compelled him to borrow a thousand crowns from the friendly Bishop of Cahors. The bishop had heard favourably of Anthony from the great Marshal de Biron, and in some compensation for the thousand crowns got him to write to Burleigh asking for the release of two priests, then imprisoned at Westminster. Unfortunately, the only result was that a Mr. Lawson, Anthony's servant, who carried that and other letters, was promptly imprisoned as well, largely at the urging of Lady Bacon, and kept in prison for almost a year.

Lady Bacon indeed was by this time furious with her son. He was consorting with Papists ; he was endangering his soul. " My mother," wrote Francis to him, " through passion and grief can scant endure to meddle in any your business." Anthony got a soldier-friend of his to visit Burleigh and intercede for the unhappy

Lawson. Burleigh sent him to Gorhambury, where Lady Bacon let herself go. "She let not to say that you are a traitor to God and your country; you have undone her; you seek her death; and when you have that you seek for, you shall have but a hundred pounds more than you have now. . . . She said you are cursed of God in all your actions, especially since Mr. Lawson's being with you. . . . She wished you had been fairly buried, provided you had died in the Lord. In my simple judgment she spoke it in her passion and repented immediately her words." It was perhaps excusable. According to her own showing Lady Bacon had spent her jewels and borrowed from "seven several persons" in order to send her son the money he kept begging for his necessary expenses, and (Mr. Beza apart) all she could see for it was commerce with Papists and servants suspected of Papistry coming with intercession for imprisoned priests. "Mr. Lawson is in great necessity, and your brother dares not help him, in respect of my Lady's displeasure." So Mr. Lawson remained in prison, a victim of a mother's religious passion as was the paramour whom Monica, centuries before, had torn from Augustine and sent back to Ostia.

Anthony, however, had other correspondents— Nicholas Faunt, Walsingham's Puritan secretary, and occasionally Walsingham himself. Certain of his letters were shown, secretly, to the Queen, who commended "his care and diligence." Mr. Faunt wrote at length concerning state business, and at greater length concerning the displeasure Christ would no doubt show at the way the archbishop and others were treating the professors of the Word. He alluded picturesquely to those who, "having the mark of the beast, it is impossible they should know the necessity of that sweet food of the gospel"; he seems to mean the bishops. He entirely approved of Lady Bacon: "the Lord raise up many such matrons." The loving-kindness of the Lord, however, goes even beyond Mr. Faunt's guess; he limits the number. With Francis Mr. Faunt was not intimate. He called on him in Gray's Inn, but was told he was not at leisure. "This strangeness" caused Mr. Faunt "to doubt that he greatly mistaketh me"; in a sentence of Elizabethan volubility running to eighty-nine more words Mr. Faunt explained his friendship. That he simply bored Francis stiff does not seem to have occurred to him.

Yet that was the growing division between the two types of mind. Neither Anthony abroad nor Francis at home spoke Lady Bacon's language or Mr. Faunt's. Anthony might lodge with Beza, or Francis go with his mother to hear Puritan lectures at the Temple. But their hearts were not in the quarrel between the religions. Francis's God certainly was "the Father of lights," but the two candles which burned upon the altar in the Queen's chapel at Westminster and shocked the earnest professors of the Word were neither here nor there in that glory of descending revelations. We do not know much about Anthony's God, but we know that he was concerned not with theology but diplomacy. The two brothers inherited war, but (as they saw it) it was a war of this world and not of another, or if of another then merely *ex hypothesi*, and the hypothesis was official, so that the supernatural argument was rather *ex officio* than anything else. Anthony wrote to one of his secret service correspondents (who was himself then a Roman) that certain rigours in a bill against recusancy were " of many misliked, namely, of us brothers, who will do our best against them." It might certainly have been his correspondent's religion which evoked this placability, but it is likely that Anthony was more preoccupied with the setting up of throne against throne than of altar against altar.

Francis was occupied with a work in which neither the ardent Protestant nor the devoted Papist would have felt much interest, despite its title which was, quite simply, *Temporis Partus Maximus, The Greatest Birth of Time*. After all, with an entire new revelation all of his own, Francis, young, passionate, and ambitious for his design and himself, could hardly be expected to do more than acknowledge the revelations of the past. Like that other young genius, now feeling his feet on the London stage, and about to hear his lines uttered aloud by his fellows, Francis wanted civil order and a quiet life, anyhow in externals; although Shakespeare, being perhaps himself *temporis partus maximus*, did not trouble to write anything so-called. Francis preceded him a little; it was about 1584 that he was devising this first study of the new idea; it was not till 1592 that Robert Greene complained of the "shake-scene" who was strutting in peacock's feathers. The new young prophet, in the intervals of making a living, was busy in shaping the great new instauration: as the young imagination always attempts directly to do, and discovers only by experience at what a distance, by what unexpected methods, and in what different language, the thing as eventually done has to come about. He was then twenty-four or so, and there he was sitting down to announce the Greatest Birth of Time. Something of the solemn concern he felt with it had crept into his manner. Some one, perhaps several some ones, told Burleigh that his nephew was "stuck-up." Burleigh, on ethical principles no doubt, but principles possibly accentuated by his own feelings about Francis, passed on the statement. Francis, in a stately and solemn letter, accepted the admonition, saying that as a matter of fact if he had a fault by nature it was being too bashful, and if there was anything that he hadn't, it was arrogancy and overweeningness. If he thought well of himself at all, it was in being free from anything of that sort. No doubt his bashfulness had produced the lamentable misunderstanding. And he would mend his ways in future so that he appeared what he really was. And he remained his lordship's most obedient, etc. etc.

The two things are not, in fact, incommensurable. Many young men think they are geniuses. Francis certainly thought he was. A conviction of genius does not, in the real genius, necessarily mean a personal arrogance, nor need it have done in Francis. But it probably did mean that he had no time to waste on people like Nicholas Faunt, and no hesitation in believing that his concern was more important than theirs. That he happened to be right was simply their ill-luck; they could not then know that so much of what they—Faunt and Burleigh and their like—did and said would have to be perpetually explained and excused through "future ages." They could not know that future ages spoke to them in Francis's slightly alien voice. It also meant that no one at that time was accusing him of subserviency; certainly not the great man's great man, the Secretary of State's secretary, who was turned away from the door of the unknown lawyer in Gray's Inn.

It must not, however, be supposed that Burleigh had neglected his nephew. He had, it is true, been more occupied with helping on Edward Coke, who had by now gained a great legal reputation, without any nonsense of contemplative studies, had made a marriage which had brought him £30,000, and had in 1592 (he was then forty) become Solicitor-General. But Burleigh had also done something, if not so much, for Francis. In November 1584 he appointed him Member of Parliament for Gatton and also had him chosen Member for Melcombe, in Dorsetshire. This was almost a matter of course. In February 1585/6 he seems to have lent his influence to have him advanced among the lawyers at

Gray's Inn, apparently out of his due time. There is a paper on which Burleigh has noted Francis's advantages; it is impossible not to think that the Lord Treasurer contemplated these privileges with satisfaction as showing that goodwill which (he assured Lady Bacon) he felt for his nephew. Indeed, they are considerable, especially in eyes which are used to the careful distinctions of a slow advance at Court. They are:

" Specially admitted to be out of commons; sending for beer, victuals, wine.

" Admitted of the Grand Company, whereby he hath won anciety of forty, being but of three years' continuance.

" Utter Barrister upon three years' study.

" Admitted to the high table, where none are but Readers."

What more could the boy want? However, five years afterwards, in 1589, the Lord Treasurer procured for his nephew if not a post at least the promise of a post. Francis was appointed to the reversion of the Clerkship of the Star Chamber. It is true the then occupant held it for another twenty years, during which time " it was like another man's ground buttailing upon his house, which might mend his prospect but it did not fill his barn." But such as it was, there it was.

All this was not what was wanted. About 1592 Francis addressed another letter to his uncle.

" My Lord,

" With as much confidence as mine own honest and faithful devotion unto your service and your honourable correspondence unto me and my poor estate can breed in a man, do I commend myself unto your Lordship. I wax now somewhat ancient; one-and-thirty years is a great deal of sand in the hour-glass. My health, I thank

God, I find confirmed ; and I do not fear that action shall impair it, because I account my ordinary course of study and meditation to be more painful than most parts of action are. I ever bare a mind (in some middle place that I could discharge) to serve her Majesty ; not as a man born under Sol, that loveth honour ; nor under Jupiter, that loveth business (for the contemplative planet carrieth me away wholly) ; but as a man born under an excellent Sovereign, that deserveth the dedication of all men's abilities. Besides, I do not find in myself so much self-love, but that the greater parts of my thoughts are to deserve well (if I were able) of my friends, and namely of your Lordship ; who being the Atlas of this commonwealth, the honour of my house, and the second founder of my poor estate, I am tied by all duties, both of a good patriot, and of an unworthy kinsman, and of an obliged servant, to employ whatsoever I am to do you service. Again, the meanness of my estate doth somewhat move me : for though I cannot accuse myself that I am either prodigal or slothful, yet my health is not to spend, nor my course to get. Lastly, I confess that I have as vast contemplative ends, as I have moderate civil ends ; for I have taken all knowledge to be my province ; and if I could purge it of two sorts of rovers, whereof the one with frivolous disputations, confutations, and verbosities, the other with blind experiments and auricular traditions and impostures, hath committed so many spoils, I hope I should bring in industrious observations, grounded conclusions, and profitable inventions and discoveries ; the best state of that province. This, whether it be curiosity, or vain glory, or nature, or (if one take it favourably) *philanthropia*, is so fixed in my mind as it cannot be removed. And I do easily see, that place of any reasonable countenance doth bring commandment of more wits than of a man's own ; which is the thing I greatly affect. And for your Lordship, perhaps you shall not find more strength and less encounter in any other. And if your Lordship shall find now, or at any time, that I do seek or affect any place whereunto any that is nearer unto your Lordship shall be concurrent, say then, that I am a most dishonest man. And if your Lordship will not carry me on, I will not do as Anaxagoras did, who reduced himself with contemplation unto voluntary poverty: but this I will do; I will sell the inheritance that I have, and purchase some lease of quick revenue, or some office of gain that shall be executed by deputy, and so give over all care of service, and become some sorry book-maker, or a true pioneer in that mine of truth, which (he said) lay so deep. This which I have writ unto your Lordship is rather thoughts than words, being set down without all art, disguising, or reservation. Wherein I have done honour both to your Lordship's wisdom, in judging that that will be best believed of your Lordship which is truest, and to your Lordship's good nature, in retaining nothing from you. And even so I wish your Lordship all happiness, and to myself means and occasion to be added to my faithful desire to do you service. From my lodging at Gray's Inn."

There is nothing to show whether Burleigh took any notice of this or not; he had another piece of advancement in his mind. One that was nearer unto his Lordship, his son, Robert Cecil, was being inducted into Burleigh's position. Walsingham was dead, and Robert Cecil was Secretary in all but name. Francis might send assurances that he would not compete; Burleigh did not suppose he would. But the mere assurance, and the taking all knowledge for his province, and the desire for place in order to command more wits, and the suggestion that action in such place was less trying to the health than Francis's ordinary course of study and meditation—Burleigh's lecture on arrogance did not seem to have produced any result.

But two things had happened by now. Francis had grown intimate with the Earl of Essex, and Anthony had returned to England. The combination deflected the young philosopher on to his third effort. His first movement had been thwarted by his father's death; his second by his uncle's indifference; his third was to end in division, antagonism, and destruction.

## CHAPTER III

### THE THIRD ATTEMPT: ESSEX

(i)

THE title of Favourite was in those days almost that of an office of State. The Favourite was not intruded upon a constitution ; in so far as there was any constitution, in our sense, he was a part of it. He was ostentatiously the Prince's friend, and the ostentation was publicly recognized. He and every one else used his title not by any means as if it were something slightly shameful, but naturally or magnificently, as one might say General or Admiral, Secretary or Treasurer. Essex wrote to Anthony : " I am as much distasted with the glorious greatness of a favourite as I was before with the supposed happiness of a courtier." He was not, of course, or only for a moment, being later extremely angry when the glorious greatness disappeared, but he used the word quite simply. " You are now Favourite," wrote Francis, years afterwards, to Villiers, and in the *Essays* he speaks of Favourites with a similar casual recognition. This fact conceals itself in the apparition of Elizabeth's lovers ; they were not unusual but usual. The intimacies might—or might not—be more extreme than those James permitted, but the principle was the same. To hope to be a Favourite, to intrigue and fight for it, was as natural to that age as to ours is the hope, the intrigue, and the fight, for Cabinet office ; it was indeed a civil office that was in dispute. The method of approach was different from the approach to a post in the ordinary civil service, and the necessary qualifications, mental and physical, were different. That was because it was approached not through the Monarch's political needs but through his personal taste. But success, once achieved, exalted the holder of the office in business as in delight. The amount of leisure left for orgies—of whatever indescribable sort the un-describing histories suggest—must, to judge from even those historical accounts, have been very limited.

This public recognition of a public position, however, involved a corresponding disadvantage. If the Favourite fell, he fell indeed. It was not only unwise and dangerous to be devoted to a fallen Favourite; it was something near a monstrous disloyalty. The Favourite stood where he did at the will of Majesty; if Majesty overthrew him Majesty did but destroy what Majesty had raised. To support him was to insult Majesty with a theme stolen from its own prerogative. Petitions, suits, presents, and subservience, were offered to the Favourite because the Monarch chose. What the Monarch designed, the Monarch could break, and the duty of the subject was to obey the King. We admire—in men of the past—devotion to the man in himself. But it would never have occurred to any one to admire Villiers for himself: he was admired because the King wished: "*le Roi le veult.*" If that formula changed into "*le Roi s'avisera,*" all others advised themselves also. It was unfortunate for the fallen officer, but it involved no moral disorder in the client. In all loyalty to the sacred Majesty, *on s'avisera.*

Elizabeth's temperament made things in her reign more uncertain, especially now when the drama of Favouritism was played between an old, intelligent, and suspicious woman, and a young, rash, and grasping male. But it did not alter the fundamental facts. Nothing but the most extreme personal devotion would justify a man in supporting the Favourite against the Queen ; nothing at all, if the fallen Favourite should think to take up arms—that would have been, as it were, two treasons at once. The difficulty, under Elizabeth, was generally to know whether and when the Favourite was fallen. It was not merely a matter of self-interest but of morality, public and private. And that morality was also of immense importance to the self-interest of all the Court.

Robert Devereux, Earl of Essex, of noble blood, attractive, enthusiastic, cultured, intensely egotistical, was in 1591 twenty-four years old, and had been Favourite for some four years. The indulgence which Elizabeth had allowed herself in these relationships demanded from their victims an extreme strain by which their rank or possessions profited. The high imagination of Spenser and Shakespeare, the religious devotion of Bacon, became in these interchanges between the Queen and her subject almost a horrible mimicry of itself. It is nothing against the imagination itself that it should be so ; all imaginations, of any kind of love, have their peril of perversion. If Elizabeth had been merely foolish, things might have been easier, but she was not. Her demand for flattery may easily, in her earlier years, have been partly a desire for reassurance in the dangerous throne she occupied, and partly a pure enjoyment of phrases, for she was a woman of great culture. But the unchecked demand had grown, and was combined now with a further demand for a complete surrender on the part of her Favourites, a surrender which she on her side neither could nor would allow. She required of others, as so many do who are not hampered as she was by her physical nature, her ill-health, her royalty, her peril, that which she would not or could not give from herself. She blamed them for refusing it. It is a trick morality has ; when it is not allowed to illumine ourselves, it illumines others, and we see our sins on their faces.

Yet, all their angers and hatreds allowed, they fought for her favours. Essex drove Raleigh from the Court, and Raleigh joined with Cecil to destroy Essex. Alike to noble and ignoble fancies and desires she was the Queen, and they sought everywhere for means to gratify her, though at the same time they cheated and dared her. Their emotions, as well as their greed, were touched; they blasphemed, but they blasphemed a living goddess, and their guilt sometimes haunted them. Only perhaps the Cecils' emotions were untouched; if so, it is why they won through.

When Francis first met Essex we do not know, except that it was before 1592, for then Anthony, returning with his gathered knowledge of Europe and his capacity for directing an organized secret intelligence, found them intimate. Francis's own account was given years after in a small volume published in 1604 under the title of *Sir Francis Bacon his Apologie in Certain Imputations concerning the late Earle of Essex*, and addressed to Mountjoy, Earl of Devonshire, a friend and colleague of and all but a conspirator with Essex. There he asserted that he had dedicated his travels and studies to the Earl's service, not for his own advancement, but because "I held my Lord to be the fittest instrument to do good to the State." The pure abstract judgment of this later phrase was probably coloured at the actual time, more than twelve years before, by personal and philosophical considerations. But though they coloured they did not create it. Francis did believe exactly that, though he probably also believed that Essex was the fittest instrument to do good to the Great Instauration by means of Francis Bacon also. We have, unfortunately, no comment of Essex on the great work, but he was young, full of intellectual as well as military zeal, and no amount of learning mixed with love came ill to the Queen. It is not likely that Elizabeth would ever have taken much interest in the entire reorganization of science. But it is very likely that she was pleased to be Pallas as well as Aphrodite; her stomacher was set with diamonds, but also with sapphires.

Francis threw himself whole-heartedly into the promising relationship. He thought afterwards that he had " in some sort " neglected not only his fortune but his vocation in order to labour at the Earl's. But then the Earl short-circuited the Cecils ; here was access and interest. He gave himself, and he also gave his brother. Anthony is a very important person in that quadruplex of himself, Francis, the Favourite, and the Queen. He had returned with the purpose of putting his accumulated knowledge at the disposal of the Government in the persons of the official ministers. The official ministers, however, were now Burleigh and Robert Cecil. Burleigh took anything that Anthony offered and gave him nothing but polite thanks. " On the one side," Anthony wrote in 1596, " coming over, I find nothing but fair words, which make fools fain, and yet even in those no offer or hopeful assurance of real kindness, which I thought I might justly expect at the Lord Treasurer's hands, who had inned my ten years' harvest into his own barn without any halfpenny charge. And on the other side, having understood the Earl of Essex's rare virtues and perfections, and the interest he had worthily in my sovereign's favour, together with his special noble kindness to my germain brother, whereby he was no less bound and in deep arrears to the Earl than I knew myself to be free and beforehand with my Lord Treasurer ; I did extremely long to meet with some opportunity to make the honourable Earl know how much I honoured and esteemed his excellent gifts, and how earnestly I desired to deserve his good opinion and love, and to acknowledge faithfully my brother's debt, presuming always that my Lord Treasurer would not only not dislike, but commend and farther, this my honest desire and purpose."

It is charming to think of Anthony writing the last sentence. Francis, with a greater mastery of language, could hardly manage that malicious innocence. The portrait of Burleigh commending and farthering the Favourite's command of a whole rich source of foreign information is incredible, and Anthony knew it. But Anthony stood with Francis and Francis with Anthony, and Burleigh had been remotely avuncular with both of them. They both "took up with" the Favourite, laying their capacities at his disposal and receiving unashamedly everything that he could give. They had themselves different gifts to offer; in the course of the next ten years it became clear whose was the gift of which the Favourite could make most. Francis was lucid with his own divine vision of human knowledge, but Anthony was lucid with the latest intelligence from France and Scotland, Rome and Spain. It was Anthony who grew in importance, and Francis who, if he did not decrease, at least retired. The Favouite was willing to do all he could for Francis, since the two held so closely together that to do it for Francis was to do it for Anthony. He had known Francis first, and still admired him. But it was Anthony who was offered and accepted rooms in Essex House, and Francis who was given a remoter piece of land.

The greater fame of the younger brother has hidden from us the more immediate importance of the elder. Letter after letter to Anthony concludes with some such words as "Commend me to your brother. I will write to him to-morrow." It was Anthony to whom the Earl's secretary Reynolds applied when he was discontented at the engagement of a fifth secretary; it was Anthony of whom Reynolds says, " No man shall go before me (in his lordship's service) but Mr. Anthony Bacon." It was Anthony of whom Essex in a secret dispatch to the same Reynolds wrote: " When I say in the beginning of my letter, that this is only for your own eyes, I exclude all men but Mr. Anthony Bacon, who in all these things is to me as the hand with which I write this. Commend me unto him a thousand times." It was Anthony to whom the brother of the deceased Bishop of London applied to move the Favourite's intercession with the Queen for the Bishop's children. It was Anthony to whom the wife of the Lord Howard the Vice-Admiral wrote, when she feared her husband would miss his fair portion of the plunder of Cadiz. It was Anthony on whom his aunt Lady Russell called (she was Burleigh's sister-in-law) to tell him how much " the kind old nobleman " (Burleigh) loved him, though, to be sure, Anthony busied himself with matters above his reach, " as foreign intelligences and entertainment of spies." That she ventured so much without Burleigh's connivance is hardly believable. It was then Anthony to whom the Treasurer thought it worth while to extend a possible hand; Francis was mentioned by his brother only, and that only by the way. To Anthony, Robert Cecil protested an absolute amnesty and oblivion of all misconceits passed, with a willingness to do anything he could with the Queen, with his father, or of himself, which, as Anthony said (he was writing to his mother) was so much the more comfortable that it was God's working and not his own seeking. But Anthony had no use for Cecil. " By God, he is no ass," Lady Russell had said in their interview. " Let him go for a mule then, madam," Anthony had answered, " the most mischevious beast that is," and so seems to have reckoned him. It was Anthony to whom Sir George Carew

applied, protesting devotion to the Favourite. It was
Anthony who wrote to Essex when his brother's *Essays*
were to be published, presenting him "the first light
and taste of such fruits." It was to Anthony that the
Lord Eure opened first a proposal of a marriage between
his son and the Favourite's niece, and on Anthony that
Eure's brother " called daily, to know the Earl's pleasure
and resolution "; to Anthony again that Eure first
applied for relief when he grew tired of his office in the
marches of Scotland. It was, finally, Anthony to whom
the Kings of Scotland and of France wrote autograph
letters.

At first certainly the three worked together. In
1592 Francis invited to his lodge at Twickenham not
only Lancelot Andrewes, the future bishop, but also
Mr. Thomas Phillipps, the cipher expert who had added
to the last letter of the Queen of Scots a postcript asking
for the names of the six gentlemen chosen to assassinate
Elizabeth. At this time there was going on a secret
correspondence with agents abroad : " with which there
were acquainted the Queen's Majesty, the Earl of Essex,
Mr. Francis Bacon, Sir William Waad, and Mr. Phillipps."
But the two great personages here used discretion ; the
others were not acquainted with everything, but used
" every man in his turn, as the Queen and the Earl would
employ them." The Favourite on one occasion asked
Francis to draw up a draft Instruction to agents at
Rheims and Rome ; suggesting that he should consult
Phillipps on Walsingham's custom in such matters.
In such correspondence and occupation Francis was
gradually less used. The Cecils did not want him at all,
however glad they would have been to detach from the
Earl's service that other subtle mind which from Essex
House itself went on writing to agents in Scotland, in
France, in Spain, in Venice, in The Hague, encouraging,
urging, and criticizing their work. Francis was a lawyer ;

he was turned on to the examination of prisoners and suspects. He toiled carefully; he gave good advice. He contributed to the Masques which the magnificent Earl presented at Court. He was among the Learned Counsel Extraordinary to the Queen, and was used "on matters of State or Revenues." But he had no official position, no appointment, and no salary. The Queen "knew her strength so well as she looked her word should be a warrant," which meant in effect that he had all the difficulty and none of the security of her service. Francis, who believed that God had set the Queen's Majesty to rule, and believed also that God meant him to assist the Queen's Majesty, not unnaturally thought that God also meant the Queen to recompense him. Unfortunately, however, he hampered this divine intention (if it existed) by making a speech.

He had first been appointed to the House of Commons by Burleigh in 1584. He had been shifted to various boroughs, to Taunton, and to Liverpool, and in 1592/3 was brought in for Middlesex. Very early he took a part in the business of the House; in his first session he was one of a Committee to which a Bill concerned with Common Informers was referred. In his second (1586/7) he spoke on Mary of Scots, with whose destruction the House was eagerly concerning itself, was again member of Committees, and was even the first-named of thirty on a Committee concerning a benevolence to be offered to the Queen. In the next Parliament (1589/90) he was still more to the front; he provided "a note in writing" on subsidies which was read and approved by the House, and "the said Mr. Bacon appointed to repair to the learned counsel charged with drafting the Bill for the further proceeding therein with them."

This growth in reputation he owed no doubt partly to his father's reputation, partly to his legal capacity, partly to his own genuine tact in dealing with the House, a tact he retained through very difficult periods as long as he sat in it. And this arose from the fact that he felt with and in the Commons; he was a House of Commons man. Only to be a House of Commons man under Elizabeth was to have an intense feeling for a body that was supposed to be one of the aids to good government, and good government was exercised by the Crown. It was a Committee, largely appointed by the ministers of the Queen, called together that it might be of use to the Queen. Few of its members had then realized how much use it might be to itself and the class it represented. Twenty years were to pass before the last Parliament of Elizabeth became obnoxious over monopolies; thirty before James was refused subsidies; sixty before the power of the House defeated the King in arms. Bacon's idea of revolt against the Crown might have included a wild rising of the populace or the outbreak of a great lord. But, at least in 1583 and 1593, even he is not likely to have imagined the actual future; no one ever does. The curve of life always runs out of sight round the edge of our blinkered eyes.

He gave himself freely therefore to the maintenance of the Commons' privileges. He knew that his intellect subordinated itself to the will of Majesty, and he must have been emotionally clear that he desired to do nothing to offend Majesty. There is nothing to suggest that even the possibility of offending Majesty entered his mind.[1] But he may have felt, once or twice, that in the Commons at least he could meet Robert Cecil on equal terms.

Parliament met on 19th February 1592/3. The Queen came down to the opening. The Lord Keeper made a speech. The Government—that is, the Crown—

---

[1] There has been talk of his " showing independence." But to oppose the Crown would not, to Bacon, have been showing independence; it would have been to deny government. He would have regarded himself almost as an Anarchist.

needed money, and needed it at once. The King of
Spain was building ships, better than those of the
Armada ; the King of Spain had control of harbours in
Brittany ; the King of Spain was sending money into
Scotland, and gaining friends there ; the King of Spain
would come down on England, by land from the north,
by sea from the south. The Houses were not to bother
about making laws ; there were too many laws already,
and an abridgment was very desirable. They were
not to sit long—they would be needed back in their own
places. They were to vote the necessary money and go.

It was true that the Crown was finding itself, and
was to continue to find itself, in serious financial difficulties. For its revenue remained largely fixed, and
the value of money was going down. The cost of
executive government had widened and heightened at
once. Subsidies, said the Chancellor of the Exchequer,
did not yield above half what they yielded in Henry VIII's
time. The Crown had been selling land, which brought
in ready money but lowered its regular income. It was
compelled therefore to have more frequent resource to
the Lords and Commons for extra money.

The debates opened. Francis came to his feet. The
Lord Keeper had said there were too many laws and
hinted at abridgment and codification. He was delighted
to hear of this proposal. He was not himself privy to
questions of war and money ; he was not in the secrets
of Government. (Cecil, listening, must have thought it
was not through his cousin's modesty but by his own
and his father's caution.) But about law he did know
something. As the laws stood at present they were far
too many. The common people could not half practise
them nor the lawyers half understand them. (Edward
Coke, then speaker, must have thought this was Bacon's
inefficiency ; he himself could understand them perfectly well. If any one wanted to know anything

" he may apply to me.") An abridgment would be to her Majesty's eternal praise. The Romans . . . the Athenians . . . Louis of France . . . reform . . . from which digressions he came back to end with treasure ; if the Queen wanted money, she must have it. He sat down. He had come to the right conclusion, but in the eyes of Ministers he had taken a long while about it.

The Commons had got as far as proposing a certain supply—two subsidies, with four fifteenths and tenths—when they were interrupted by a message from the Lords, who sent to say they had before now expected to hear from the Lower House and they proposed a conference. The Commons assented and appointed a Committee to confer—Cecil and Francis both being on it. Cecil's father, the Treasurer, told them that not less than three subsidies were needed ; at another conference he would explain further.

On the next morning Cecil reported the conference to the House, and, without making any motion, sat down. It seems almost as if a subtle attempt were in progress to remove the decision on the amount of taxation from the floor of the House to the smaller committees and conferences. The Government were already beginning to feel the inconvenience of extracting treasure from the gentry, merchants, and lawyers. But the moment Cecil was down Francis was up. He agreed to the subsidies, but could not to the conference. " The custom and privilege of this House hath always been to make offer of the subsidy. . . . I wish . . . we should proceed as heretofore we have done."

With this lead given them the Commons broke into discussion and decision. They would not confer ; they would vote by themselves. The Lords were shocked and demanded to hear the precedents. The Commons refused to tell them, and—by now we reach Saturday—adjourned till Monday.

On Monday there were further arguments. Sir Thomas Heneage and Sir John Wolley moved that Saturday's decision should be reversed. It was explained that the precedents did not really apply. Sir Henry Unton moved that the House should confer, " but not in any sort to be conformed " to the Lords. Cecil explained that no one had ever meant that the House should confer about a subsidy ; certainly not. They would just confer. Sir Walter Raleigh moved for a general conference with the Lords, which was unanimously voted for the next day. Sir Thomas Heneage, reappearing, asked, rather rashly, what they were to confer about, for " either we must conform to somewhat they will say or else we must deliver them somewhat that we will say . . . we desiring their conference." It was objected that the House did not desire a conference. It was answered that Sir Thomas had been misunderstood. And eventually the House again resolved to confer by a committee, but for the committee not to conclude anything without referring back to the whole House.

The conference took place : the Lords uttered further alarms of war. The Spanish king had sent another fifty thousand crowns into Scotland, and so on. On the Wednesday afternoon the Committees were ordered to meet to discuss the actual subsidies. The Government proposed to allow four years for collection of three subsidies. A Mr. Heale was anxious to give an even larger grant. And after him Bacon rose again.

He had talked of the laws instead of the money ; he had delayed the money by talking of custom and privilege ; and now he proposed to delay the money still further. To the three subsidies he agreed, but he demanded six years for the collection (as, in fact, had been the usual custom—the collection of a subsidy being spread over two years). Mr. Bacon alluded, as he very well might, to the poor, meaning the small landowners. " The poor man's rent is such as they are not able to pay it . . . the farmers must sell their brass pots . . . we are here to search the wounds of the realm, not to skim them over. . . ." And so on. Eventually Mr. Bacon's proposal was put by, and three subsidies, with six fifteenths and tenths, were voted for the next four years. The Queen sent a message of thanks, with an allusion to some " persons . . . who had . . . made their necessity more than it was, forgetting the necessity of the time." And the Houses were left to anything else they liked to do.

It is clear from all this that Bacon, from the point of view of the Queen and the Government, had been a perfect nuisance. He had wanted law and privilege and customary method—the Romans, the Athenians, and Louis of France—reform of law because of the common people and delay in collection because of the farmers. He had delayed the business, embarrassed Cecil, and possibly inconvenienced the Lord Treasurer. He had put himself in a position of something very much like opposition to the Court. He had done and said nothing out of accord with his principles. He had a real concern for the abridgment of the Laws ; it was one of his earliest and latest dreams. He had a real concern for the poorer men ; he had already moved an Act against enclosures. He had a real concern for the privileges of the House ; he always believed they were easily and beautifully reconcilable with the full-moving Prerogative of the sacred Throne. " With all wise and moderate persons," he had said, " custom and usage obtaineth that reverence as it is sufficient manner to cause them to stand and discover and take a view ; but it is no warrant to guide or conduct them ; a just ground, I say, it is of deliberation, but not of decision." The Government, however, had not wanted to discover and take a view. Could Francis have been aware that he was—what in modern slang is called—" showing " Cecil ? He was always a House of Commons man, whereas Cecil to the end of his life never was ; eighteen years afterwards Francis was bitterly to criticize his cousin for incompetence in the same necessity of tactful dealing. Cecil had refused to make him " privy to great matters " ; very well, Cecil should feel that his cousin was not so negligible as he thought. Cecil thought—did he ?—to slip behind the custom and privilege of this House. It was not by such sly means that the ancient houses of Parliament were to be reconciled with the awful authority of the Prince.

But he had gone farther than he thought ; he had brought anger on his head and prepared trouble for his feet. Cecil was (no doubt) friendly, he always was friendly ; but the Queen and the Treasurer were very angry. Burleigh let him know it, perhaps expecting submission, apologies, promises. He did not get them. He received a letter saying that his nephew conceived he had spoken properly and desired to be properly taken.

" It may please your Lordship,
" I was sorry to find by your Lordship's speech yesterday that my last speech in Parliament, delivered in discharge of my conscience and duty to God, her Majesty and my country, was offensive. If it were misreported, I would be glad to attend your Lordship to disavow anything I said not. If it were misconstrued, I would be glad to expound my words, to exclude any sense I meant not. If my heart be misjudged by imputation of popularity or opposition by any envious or officious informer, I have great wrong ; and the greater, because the manner of my speech did most evidently show that I spake simply and only to satisfy my con-

science, and not with any advantage or policy to sway the cause; and my terms carried all signification of duty and zeal towards her Majesty and her service. It is true that from the beginning, whatsoever was above a double subsidy, I did wish might (for precedent's sake) appear to be extraordinary, and (for discontent's sake) mought not have been levied upon the poorer sort; though otherwise I wished it as rising as I think this will prove, and more. This was my mind, I confess it. And therefore I most humbly pray your Lordship, first to continue me in your own good opinion : and then to perform the part of an honest friend towards your poor servant and ally, in drawing her Majesty to accept of the sincerity and simplicity of my heart, and to bear with the rest, and restore me to her Majesty's favour."

Burleigh's displeasure was a difficulty, but, now that the friendship with Essex was flowering, might not have been final. But Burleigh told him that the Queen was highly displeased. Still obstinate, still astonished that so obvious a matter of order and high regard for decency could anger the Majesty, still conscious that he could have spoken very differently if he had chosen, he wrote again. Actually he could not have chosen; it was always impossible for Francis Bacon to go back on any firm principle he had once laid down. To methods, to policies, to personalities, he would conform wherever possible, but some things were not possible. He imagined his honour involved. He wrote again to Burleigh and to the Queen :

" My Lord,
" It is a great grief unto me, joined with marvel, that her Majesty should retain an hard conceit of my speeches in parliament. It mought please her sacred Majesty to think what my end should be in those speeches, if it

were not duty, and duty alone. I am not so simple but I know the common beaten way to please. And whereas popularity hath been objected, I muse what care I should take to please many, that taketh a course of life to deal with few. On the other side, her Majesty's grace and particular favour towards me hath been such, as I esteem no worldly thing above the comfort to enjoy it, except it be the conscience to deserve it. But if the not seconding of some particular person's opinion shall be presumption, and to differ upon the manner shall be to impeach the end, it shall teach my devotion not to exceed wishes, and those in silence. Yet notwithstanding (to speak vainly as in grief) it may be her Majesty hath discouraged as good a heart as ever looked towards her service, and as void of self-love. And so in more grief than I can well express, and much more than I can well dissemble, I leave your Lordship, being as ever,

"Your Lordship's entirely devoted."

"Madam,

"Remembering that your Majesty had been gracious to me both in countenancing me and conferring upon me the reversion of a good place, and perceiving your Majesty had taken some displeasure towards me, both these were arguments to move me to offer unto your Majesty my service, to the end to have means to deserve your benefit and to repair my error. Upon this ground I affected myself to no great matter, but only a place of my profession, such as I do see divers younger in proceeding to myself, and men of no great note, do without blame aspire unto. But if any of my friends do press this matter, I do assure your Majesty my spirit is not with them. It sufficeth me that I have let your Majesty know that I am ready to do that for your service which I never would do for mine own gain. And if your

Majesty like others better, I shall with the Lacedemonian be glad that there is such choice of abler men than myself. Your Majesty's favour indeed, and access to your royal person, I did ever, encouraged by your own speeches, seek and desire ; and I would be very glad to be reintegrate in that. But I will not wrong mine own good mind so much as to stand upon it now, when your Majesty may conceive I do it but to make my profit of it. But my mind turneth upon other wheels than those of profit. The conclusion shall be that I wish your Majesty served answerable to yourself. *Principis est virtus maxima nosse suos.* Thus I most humbly crave pardon of my boldness and plainness. God preserve your Majesty."

By now another matter had arisen to which that letter refers. Elizabeth had refused to know anything of the sincerity and simplicity of his heart. She refused him access to her person and to the Court. She might almost have said of him what, about that time, Robert Greene was writing of Shakespeare : " peacock's feathers " . . . " conceive himself the only shake-scene in the whole country." Anthony referred the resolution of the trouble to God (he was writing to his mother) : " whose (Francis's) speech being so well grounded and directed to good ends, as it cannot be denied but it was, I doubt not but God in His mercy will in time make it an occasion of her Majesty's better opinion and liking." In time, no doubt ; but the infinity of time which lies before operating Providence seems to make it occasionally a little unconscious of our own need for swiftness. Providence, forgetting or ignoring the difficulty Francis was in, had chosen that moment to call to itself the then Master of the Rolls, Sir Gilbert Gerrard, on the 4th of February 1592/3. The Attorney-General, Sir Thomas Egerton, was promoted to fill his place. The Solicitor-

General then was Edward Coke. Coke, like every one else at that time, was still a Royalist. But he was not the easiest man to get on with, and he was already developing his passion for law. The Monarch and her ministers were in matters of law more concerned with the thing proved than the thing that proved. But Coke was concerned with the thing that proved. It was but a difference of stress, but that difference was taken up by two separate harmonies. Coke was always capable of producing statutes, maxims, and precedents, to show what the law permitted, but they were Coke's interpretation of precedents and maxims. "I am afraid," said one of his successors, "we should get rid of a good deal of what is considered law in Westminster Hall if what Lord Coke says without authority is not law."

Even if Coke had been obviously the ideal man for the Attorneyship he would probably have had to wait. Elizabeth, as always, dallied with the problem, and "smiling put the question by." Nothing was done, and then it occurred to one of the Essex House group that something quite different might be done. Why should not Francis be appointed? It is unfortunate that we do not know on whom first the brilliant possibility broke. Once recognized, the opportunity drew them to attempt it. There was the vacant office, there was Francis, there (for that matter) was the Queen. Why not? The Earl knew that his rather disheartened client was talking of abandoning the Court and returning to study. To remedy this, make his own man Attorney, check the Cecils, strengthen his power at Court and in the courts, would be delightful. Francis always thought himself a better political lawyer than Coke; he admired the other "with a difference," and the difference sometimes hampered the admiration. Somehow the idea got put into words. But the unfortunate business in the Commons was seriously in the way. In May Francis was approaching the Cecils, certainly not without Essex's assent. The Cecils, obviously, were in a difficulty. Francis was the Favourite's man but he was their relation. He pressed the relationship once more. He wrote to Burleigh's eldest son, Sir Thomas Cecil, asking him to intervene with his father; he wrote to Robert Cecil to the same effect. Robert Cecil answered charmingly—with something of the malicious innocence Anthony had earlier used. Let his cousin make it up with the Queen and secure access; let him press the Earl, "who hath true love towards you and the truest and greatest means to win it of her Majesty. From the Court, this 7th of May 1593. Your loving cousin and friend, Rob. Cycell." "The truest and greatest means" —Essex certainly thought he had. Robert Cecil sweetly agreed. No doubt the Earl, if properly pressed, would procure the appointment. By July the Queen, also properly pressed, had been brought to the point of saying that when she had dispatched the Scottish and French ambassadors she would be able to attend to home affairs. But she thought Bacon was young and untried. In August the Earl wrote to Francis that he had had a full audience, and had pressed his demands—absolute amnesty and access. But the Parliament speech was rankling still; the Queen refused; the Earl expostulated. "Her humour is to delay." Burleigh emitted assurances to Lady Bacon that he looked "to do his nephews good." The world thought he had more power than he had. He wished their health was better, but, as he remarked, "none are, or very few, *ab omne parte beati*; for such are not elect, but subject to tentations from the highway to heaven." On his nephew's behalf he chanced the risk of temptations sufficiently in September as to name him (so he said) for "a fit man" to the Queen.

The thing swayed to and fro continually. In

December the Earl quarrelled with the Queen; it was said that he had gone to Dover thence to pass to the Continent. But "this lewd and false bruit" turned out to be "a monstrous scandal." The Queen had been agitated by the rumour. "Thereupon," wrote one of Anthony's correspondents, "was 6589 greatly altered, and resolved to have sent after him, if the same night he had not come as he did." Francis's chances rocked on such disturbing waves of emotion; they sprang a leak when Anthony heard, by the beginning of the next February, that Burleigh was pressing 6589 for Coke to be Attorney and Robert Cecil officially Secretary. Francis himself about that time delivered his first pleading in the King's Bench with sufficient success for his uncle to send messages of congratulation. He followed this up with another delivery, some days afterwards, when the learned Judges "paid him respect"—so wrote another young lawyer. His arguments were spangled with unusual words, "rather gracious for their propriety than strange for their novelty.... All is as well as words can make it, and if it please her Majesty to add deeds, the Bacon may be too hard for the Cook." With such culinary jests the world at large watched the contest, and the jest is a proof that the contest had become clear to the world. It was not therefore merely on Francis's own behalf that the Favourite was deeply engaged and at times enraged. On 30th January the famous coach interview had taken place between him and Robert Cecil. In that exchange Cecil suggested the Solicitorship instead; that might be of easier digestion to the Queen. "Digest me no digesting," said the Earl Elizabethanly, "for the Attorneyship I must and will have for Francis Bacon; and in that I will spend my uttermost credit, friendship, and authority against whomsoever, and whosoever goes about to procure it to others, it shall cost both the mediators and the suitors the setting on before they come by it.¹ And this be you assured of, Sir Robert, for now do I fully declare myself; and for your own part, Sir Robert, I do think much and strange both of my Lord your father and you, that can have the mind to seek the preferment of a stranger before so near a kinsman; namely——" And he went on to say again what a fine fellow Francis was.

No doubt he was, but Francis's merits—even had Cecil believed in them—were not the central point. The challenge which the Earl had issued was explicit in meaning, if not (to us) in language : " it shall cost both the mediators and the suitors the setting on." It was implicitly accepted, and it failed. By 10th April 1594 the Queen had raised Sir Edward Coke to be her Attorney, and Essex's reputation was stained : " a thing," wrote Anthony's friend to him, " as much bringing this great man's credit in question as any other he had managed all this time." Francis, disappointed at the result, anxious at the method, hurt at the publicity, thought that no man had received a more exquisite disgrace than himself. But the disgrace was only half accomplished. The Essex House group now tried for the Solicitorship, vacant by Coke's promotion. Another year of applications, delays, approaches, repulsions, interviews, letters, hope, disappointment, and disgust went slowly by. The Queen was a little kinder. She would not be gracious but she would deign to use him in her own business. She thought he was not deep in law; all that he showed was all that he knew, though he had " much other good learning." The Favourite pressed and failed, and demanded and was denied, but of course there were many other affairs—of many different kinds —between the aged Majesty of Elizabeth and the

¹ In the report the last phrase is in the conditional tense. But the Earl must have spoken in the present, and the reporter mingled direct speech with oblique.

flaunting Lordship of Essex. The Cecils professed that they consistently did all they could; the Bacons did not believe it.

At the beginning of 1595 Lady Bacon, assisting the Divine Providence, had an interview with Sir Robert, and found him "all kindly outward." He was sure all would be well. Lady Bacon said that there was very strange dealing somewhere; everybody was shocked at the way Francis had been treated. Sir Robert remarked that experience showed her Majesty's nature was not to resolve but to delay. Lady Bacon said that some people believed that if the Lord Treasurer had really been in earnest, "it had been done," which produced from Sir Robert what he said was a verbatim narrative of a conversation between his father and the Queen, in which Burleigh had assured her that the Judges would accept Francis, and every one expected it. Sir Robert himself thought that Francis ought to carry himself wisely, as if he made no doubt of the place —as he himself did in regard to the Secretaryship.

Francis was not at all clear that all would be well. There was something very curious in the Queen's language. She was said to have complained that "she had pulled him over the bar"—"note the words (he wrote to his brother), they cannot be her own . . . what the secret of it is *oculus aquilæ non penetravit.*" The eye of the eagle, however, could penetrate the fact that at these particular cross-roads there had been very dubious work. Within the next few weeks he sent a note to his cousin, telling him how rumour said he had been bought with two thousand angels to support another applicant. This (of course) Francis did not believe; only he suspected that he had been carefully praised by some one to Elizabeth for the wrong things. There was a word "speculation" in the Queen's mouth—it had no doubt been used as a commendation which should discommend

—" I am not ignorant of these little arts." He half apologized to Burleigh for believing " such idle hearsays " later on, but the whole business fretted and worried him ; not merely in himself, but because of the shadow of suspicion it threw on all his actions. Any service he did would be thought " but lime-twigs and fetches " to place himself ; he was like a piece of stuff in a shop, and if her Majesty would not take it, then it might be sold in bits and pay better. Yet he could not lightly be willing so to dispose of himself : "*primus amor* will not easily be cast off."

Once something nearly came of it. On a certain Sunday afternoon the Favourite had a kind of appointment to discuss and conclude the matter with the Lord Treasurer. He came ; the Lord Treasurer, an old man, was asleep, and his servants hesitated to wake him. The Favourite went on to play tennis ; the Lord Treasurer woke, heard of it, and sent messages after him. Essex, following Drake's example, thought there was time enough to go on with the game, and did ; in spite of his gentleman-in-attendance, who, " while I gave him drink," urged him to act. But at first the Lord Treasurer had been asleep, and now the Earl was at tennis, so nothing could be done, and nothing was done. The Great Instauration of the knowledge and power of man sat on the doorstep and waited till—if ever—the wakefulness of the old and the leisure of the young should agree.

Its prophet, however, had his own obstinacy. Burleigh, at intervals, told him that the Queen, so many months after, was still ruffled over those speeches in the Commons, but that he was explaining them. Francis said he was sorry the Queen was still upset ; he was glad to hear his uncle was explaining. And there he stayed. He never went any further in apology or explanation ; he never sang any kind of palinode. He

would say or do anything to show that what they meant
was loyal, but he would not alter what they meant—
it was part of the thing he called *primus amor*. He used
that phrase privately to Fulke Greville, and again in a
letter to Essex which may have been meant for the
Queen's eyes. " Having now these twenty years made
her Majesty's service the scope of my life, I shall never
find a greater grief than this, *relinquere amorem primum*."
He was then asking for leave to travel ; he had told his
brother that " her Majesty's nature " would not care
" though the whole surname of the Bacons travelled,
nor of the Cecils neither." It was, however, one thing
for the Queen not truly to care what he meant, and
another for her to grant him licence to go ; when it
came to the point he did not risk an application.

The prolonged and difficult vigil of his mind went
on. He watched his friends with a certain bitterness.
He did not trust the Cecils. He did not wholly trust
Essex either. He did not believe that Essex would
discommend him in subtle praises to the Queen. But
he did think that his affairs might become a mere
appendix to some suit Essex had to the Queen, and
appendixes to matters between Essex and the Queen
would depend entirely on the particular relations at any
particular moment between Essex and the Queen—an
unsafe reliance. His *primus amor* depended on an
entirely different kind of *amor*, and the knowledge did
not make him happy.

Was the phrase itself insincere ? Hardly, perhaps,
if the young child in Sir Nicholas's house is remembered
—" my young Lord Keeper." But assuredly a greater,
if not an earlier, love lay in Bacon's heart : the revelation at Cambridge. And yet that was not so much the
thing that was loved as the thing that loved ; it was
more his than any other duty or affection. All his life
that strange shadow lay over him : he offered himself,

and men were shy of the offer, for he brought with him something that might easily become a terror. Men like Bacon are not easily loved or used; something terrific exists in them, however humbly they speak. Perhaps, of all the great people he knew, only Elizabeth and Essex were for a while capable separately of understanding that vision. But each of them had other preoccupations. The learning of James had little aspiration within it; the aspirations of Buckingham had little learning to balance them. None of all of them would do much to hasten the nuptials upon which Bacon brooded, " between the mind of man and the nature of things."

There was during these tiresome months a Christmas which is more noteworthy to us than to Bacon. In 1594 the young lawyers of Gray's Inn prepared for their Christmas revels to turn the Inn into " the shape and order of a peopled kingdom," under a monarch who was called the Prince of Purpoole. They gave him ministers and officers, gentlemen and guards; and sent invitations to the friends of the Inner Temple to send an Ambassador to this high solemnity. On a December evening the Ambassador with his train arrived, was received in great state, and introduced to the Prince. There was to have been acting, but the hall grew so thronged and there was such tumult that at last the Ambassador in discontent retired. The revels continued, however, and as a conclusion to that evening the players were brought in, and performed the *Comedy of Errors*. But the evening was regarded as a misfortune, and, to atone, on 3rd January another " grand night " was held, at which the Prince and the Ambassador were present in their several states, and after other entertainment six councillors made speeches to present, both lightly and seriously, the port to which " the ship of our government should be bounden." The speeches were Bacon's and they made compensation for the Night of Errors.

In the early comedy the imagination of Shakespeare was already opening ; the lyrical beauty and the violence and the laughter are his yet unformed matter. But in the after speeches that other imagination was shaping itself—" I will wish unto your Highness the exercise of the best and purest part of the mind, and the most innocent and meriting conquest, being the conquest of the works of nature ; making this proposition, that you bend the excellency of your spirits to the searching out, inventing, and discovering of all whatsoever is hid and secret in the world."

Once more, but not in aspiration or delight, those two great powers were to approach each other in their separate progress through this troublesome place we call the world.

(ii)

About the end of October or the beginning of November 1595 the Favourite came one day from Richmond, where the Court then lay, to Bacon's lodge at Twickenham. He came in disappointment and some disgust, to make his own reparation to his client for the failure of his suit. Serjeant Fleming had at last been chosen for the Solicitorship. Bacon received him with respect and affection, but also with something of hesitation and foreboding. Lady Bacon had written in August, " Though the Earl showed great affection he marred all with violent courses." Francis's own judgment was not very different. The whole had precipitated into definition his general feeling of the character of Essex, as such personal episodes must do. It was one thing to hold that Essex was in general too rash and violent with the Queen ; they had always differed on the best way to take with her. But now that method had resulted in a definite and spectacular failure. Francis had been pushed on and pushed back, fought for and fought

against and fought over, in front of the whole Court
and all the gossip-writers of the day. The sacred
Majesty of Elizabeth was beyond criticism. But the
ostentatious patronage of Essex and the more delicate
ostentatious assurances of the Cecils had led to this—
that he whose heart's life was the renovation of human
thought was left like the dregs of a cup of wine in a
drinking-wager. He believed that his friend had done
his best, but that is small consolation when your friend
has failed in your affairs through his own folly, especially
if the friendship itself is dwindling to something of the
second order. Essex was annoyed, on his dog's behalf
and his own, that his dog had not won the race. He
petted and consoled it ; he gave it a bone, a good meaty
bone ; there were plenty more in the Royal larder, from
which he could have what joints of that kind he chose
at the expense of a little trouble with the old woman
who owned it. But he had other dogs. The dog,
though he needed the bone, would have preferred that
Essex had not quarrelled with the handicap. The
separation between Francis Bacon and that great place
which was to be the means of his desired end, a separation begun by the death of his father, continued by the
indifference of his uncle, was now widened by the violence
of his friend. The Favourite had failed, and failed by
something inherent in him. Favourites who failed thus
in their clients' business might come to fail more lament-
ably in their own. Intelligence for a moment became
prophecy ; friendship hovered over the abyss in which
it was to sink. The Earl, handsomely grieved, most
generously produced his bone. He insisted on a compensatory gift ; Francis must accept a piece of land
from him. Bacon reminded him of the Duke of Guise,
who had given away all his fortune to friends, turning
his estate into " obligations " ; an unwise method, for
friends often did not pay back obligations, and the Earl

might be left with many bad debtors. The rashness, though Bacon did not say so, was all of a piece—handsome or ugly at different times. The Earl tossed the warning aside, and pressed the gift. Bacon, half-reluctantly, half-gratefully, accepted. He did not really want land; it was convenient financially, of course, but he did not *want* it. He wanted high office—for himself, for the State, for the proclamation of truth. However . . . " My lord, I must be your homager, and hold land of your gift, but. . . ." But all homage in law was " with a saving of his faith to the King and other lords "; all homage Bacon could pay must be with those " ancient savings." Essex went off, magnificently and centrally Essex, to recover ground with the Queen. Bacon, unchangeably and centrally the Great Instauration, prepared to set to work again.[1] But he was not ungrateful to Essex, only anxious. He wrote to him to say so.

" It may please your good Lordship,
" I pray God her Majesty's weighing be not like the weight of a balance; *gravia deorsum, levia sursum.*

---

[1] Francis was not, one may pause to note, the only unfortunate. In 1597 Sir Thomas Bodley, returning from the United Provinces, hoped to be given office by the Cecils. But Essex, according to Bodley's own account, was anxious to attach the unoccupied diplomat to his own foreign office. He began, as with Francis, to make violent recommendations to the Queen, who, as with Francis, resented it. The Cecils also resented it; Robert afterwards told Sir Thomas that at first a joint Secretaryship had been thought of, but that they grew determined to prevent, as far as they could, the rise of any man whom the Earl " with such violence . . . had endeavoured to dignify." Sir Thomas, having lost their favour, decided that he dared not trust to " the slender hold-fast " that Essex had upon the Queen, especially in view of " his perilous, feeble, and uncertain advice, as well in his own as in all the causes of his friends." He withdrew, therefore, and founded the Bodleian, for which Essex presented him with the captured library of the Bishop of Algarve. The gift was more relevant than the land that went to Francis.

But I am as far from being altered in devotion towards her, as I am from distrust that she will be altered in opinion towards me, when she knoweth me better. For myself, I have lost some opinion, some time, and some means; this is my account: but then for opinion, it is a blast that goeth and cometh; for time, it is true it goeth and cometh not; but yet I have learned that it may be redeemed.

"For means, I value that most; and the rather, because I am purposed not to follow the practice of the law: (If her Majesty command me in any particular, I shall be ready to do her willing service:) and my reason is only, because it drinketh too much time, which I have dedicated to better purposes. But even for that point of estate and means, I partly lean to Thales's opinion, That a philosopher may be rich if he will. Thus your Lordship seeth how I comfort myself; to the increase whereof I would fain please myself to believe that to be true which my Lord Treasurer writeth; which is, that it is more than a philosopher morally can digest. But without any such high conceit I esteem it like the pulling out of an aching tooth, which, I remember, when I was a child and had little philosophy, I was glad of when it was done. For your Lordship, I do think myself more beholding to you than to any man. And I say, I reckon myself as a *common* (not popular, but common): and as much as is lawful to be enclosed of a common, so much your Lordship shall be glad to have.

"Your Lordship's, to obey your honourable commands, more settled than ever."

But "my Lord . . . had a settled opinion that the Queen could be brought to nothing but by a kind of necessity and authority." The great words illuminate relationships far beyond the single pair of whom Francis used them; they define a high, ideal, and infrequent beauty between man and woman which Milton, seventy years afterwards, struck out also in the too-often-misunderstood line " He for God only ; she for God in him." Had such a profound union as to justify those awful words been possible between the Queen and her Favourite, Essex would have been justified. But as he was not in the end for God but for Essex, so she was not in the end for Essex but for Elizabeth. They were great personages ; they were far more intelligent than Lady Bacon, fussing at Gorhambury, half-bothered and half-comforted by her religion, obeying it and possessing it, directed by it and imposing it. Yet Lady Bacon was dealing with a mystery to which those others were then strangers. Much more, in its own deliberate intention, did it dominate her greater son—that thing of which necessity and authority are separate and equal definitions, from which springs all the perfection of man's life, and to which—as to necessity and authority—we return.

It may be that those two great persons found, in the fantastic and tragic conclusion of their lives and their love, the thing they had missed in their conscious interchange. Death is no more alien to it than life, nor anguish than joy. Beyond mortal knowledge they may have discovered finality. " Little man, little man," the dying Elizabeth is said in one tale to have cried to Cecil, " *must* is not said to princes." She taunted Essex with her royal power to say *must* to him, and he rebelled. He said *must* to her, and she slew him. But in neither of their hearts did so perfect a knowledge say *must* as to the servant of the one and the client of the other in the desired vision of the secret causes of things.

Francis abandoned—of course he did—his idea of renouncing the practice of the law. His financial affairs were too difficult to permit it, and his only hope of settling them, sort of an official position and fixed salary, was to increase his practice. Money matters had been a trouble for years and were to be for more years. He and his brother were both in debt, trying to borrow money, to sell land, to pledge land. In 1593 Francis wanted to sell an estate, but first apparently he had to procure his mother's consent. Anthony wrote to her pointing out that, if she refused, his brother would have to dispose of his reversion of the Star Chamber clerkship. Lady Bacon in reply let herself go over Francis's friends and servants in general, " cormorant seducers and instruments of Satan "—and over one of them, a certain Henry Percy, in particular, " he keepeth that bloody Percy . . . as a coach companion and bed companion— a proud profane costly fellow, whose being about him I verily fear the Lord God doth mislike and doth less bless your brother in credit and otherwise in his health." There was another who never loved him and was " thankless though bragging "; there was another who was " a filthy wasteful knave." However, she offered her help, but on condition that Francis himself asked for it, that he gave her a note of all his debts, and passed over to her the receipt of all his money for his land. She would then see that he was discharged. We do not know what Francis answered; but we know it must have been in his most careful and involved style, for she wrote again the next day, and again to Anthony. " I send herein your brother's letter. Construe the interpretation. I do not understand his enigmatical folded writing. O that——" and so on. Francis had hinted that she would make of him only a ward—" a remote phrase to my plain motherly meaning." She broke suddenly into agreement—it was all the fault of his servants : " God bless my son. What he would have me do and when for his own good, as I now write, let him return plain answer by Fynch. . . . I send the first flight of my doves to you both, and God bless you

## THE THIRD ATTEMPT: ESSEX

in Christ.—A.B." All seems to have gone satisfactorily. But there was much riding to and fro in those days between Gray's Inn and Gorhambury.

A year afterwards, however, things were still very bad. Francis had borrowed and was borrowing from Anthony, and Anthony was borrowing wherever possible for both their needs. He noted "My brother coming to me after a fit of the stone, and falling into talk of the money he ought me as principal debt, he acknowledged to be due to me £650; whereof £200 I borrowed of Mr. Mills and paid it him again; £200 of the money I had of Alderman Spencer——" and so on. These odd shadowy figures appear in the dim light around the brothers and their Court affairs. Mr. Mills may have been the Mr. Mills whose occupation of the Clerkship to the Star Chamber kept Francis from it. Alderman Spencer had been concerned in buying an estate of Anthony's. There was "my uncle Killigrew" (Sir Harry Killigrew), who "uncled" Anthony with "a frivolous excuse"; and Mr. Sugden, when Francis "had rather have brought payment than allegation"; and a certain "man in the City" by whose "strange slipping and uncertain or cunning dealing" Francis was driven to have resource to two of his private friends, Henry Maynard and Michael Hickes, the two secretaries to Lord Burleigh, offering them what he would not offer to any but private friends, the lease of Twickenham, his pleasure and his dwelling. There was Mr. Nicholas Trott, of Gray's Inn, who in 1594 was applauded by both brothers as being of the utmost kindness, but to whom somehow as the years went by Twickenham Park had got mortgaged (if Maynard and Hickes had had it, it had been redeemed) and by November 1601 was likely to pass finally. Anthony by then had died, and Francis, in a desperate effort to save himself, again had recourse to the two secretaries and to the final arbitrament of the

Lord Treasurer Buckhurst. The paper Bacon submitted is worth giving in full, because of the almost pathetic vagueness which a mind that had " taken all knowledge for his province " was showing of the small hamlet of knowledge which his own money affairs involved.

> " The state of the account between Mr. Trott and me, as far as I can collect it by such remembrances as I find; my trust in him being such as I did not carefully preserve papers ; and my demands upon the same account.

| | |
|---|---|
| About 7 or 8 years passed I borrowed of him upon bonds . . . . | 200L. |
| Soon after I borrowed upon bond other . | 200L. |
| Upon my going northward I borrowed of him by my brother's means . . . | 100L. |
| But this was ever in doubt between my brother and me ; and my brother's conceit was ever it was twice demanded, and that he had satisfied it upon reckonings between Mr. Trott and him. | |
| About a twelvemonth after, I borrowed of him, first upon communication of mortgage of land, and in conclusion upon bond . . . . . | 1200L. |
| But then upon interest and I know not what reckonings (which I ever left to his own making) and his principal sum, amounting to 1700L. was wrapped up to 2000L., and bond given according as I remember. | |
| And about August xlii$^{do}$ Rnae I borrowed of him upon the mortgage of Twicknam Pk. | 950L. |
| So as all the monies that Mr. Trott lent at any time amount to the total of . . . . | 2650L. |
| Of this sum he hath received, about 5 years since, upon sale of certain marshes in Woolwich . . . . . | 300L. |

## THE THIRD ATTEMPT: ESSEX 73

| | |
|---|---|
| He received about 4 years since, upon sale of a lease I had of the parsonage of Redbourne . . . . . | 450L. |
| He received about 3 years since, upon sale of the manor of Burstone . . . | 800L. |
| He received about 2 years since, of Mr. Johnson of Gr. Inn, being my surety for 200L. principal . . . | 233L. |
| He received of my cousin Kemp, another of my sureties, at the least . . . | 100L. |
| He hath received in divers small sums of 40, 30, 10L., computation of interest | 210L. |
|     So as the sums which he hath received amount to the total of . | 2093L. |
| He hath now secured unto him, by mortgage of Twicknam Park . . . | 1259L. 12s. |
|     Upon my cousin Cooke's band . | 210L. |
|     Upon Mr. Ed. Jones's band . . | 208L. |
|     Upon mine own band . . | 220L. |
|     Sum total . . . | 1897L. 12s. |
| He demandeth furder for charges and interest till the first November 1601 . . | 138L. 4s. 8d. |
|     So the total sum of the money he now demandeth is . . | 2035L. 16s. 8d. |
|     So as the whole sum of principal and interest amounteth to . | 4128L. 16s. 8d. |
|     Deduct out of this the principal, viz. . . . . | 2650L. |
|     Remaineth in interest grown . | 1478L. 16s. 8d. |

" Upon this account I demand the abatement of some part of the interest, considering he hath been beholding to me, and his estate good and without charge, and mine indebted. And this I demand because upon every agreement and renew of assurance he made faithful promise (as himself confessed before my Lord Treasurer) that he would submit the interest to arbitrament of friends. And divers of my creditors that made no such promise, and are less able and more strangers to me, have in friendly manner made me round abatements.

" But absolutely I demand the abatement of interest

upon interest, which no creditor that ever I (had) did so much as offer to require. And this cannot be so little as 400L.: for his manner was upon every new account to cast up interest and charges, and to make it one principal, as appeareth by his last account and other writings.

"Thirdly, I demand the abatement of 400L. which he hath no conscience to demand, for his colour is that because my Brother sold him land charged with a rent of 4L. (as I remember by the year) more than he sayeth he intended, therefore I should pay the value of the inheritance of this Rent.

"Fourthly, I demand the abatement of 100L., by his own agreement to be defalked upon his mother's death (as by his indenture appeareth), and though it were conditional if I paid it by a day, yet it is all one, for if I paid it not, it is accounted for.

"So as I will make him this offer, if he will discharge the three bonds and the interest since, I will pay him down his 1259L. 12s. for the redemption of Twicknam Park."

Eventually the matter was settled, on payment apparently of something under £1800, and Twickenham Park was safe.

In 1598, so difficult were things, Francis was even arrested for debt. He had been to the Tower, he and Mr. William Waad, on course of his usual duty as one of the Learned Counsel, to examine a prisoner. On his way home he was seized at the suit of a goldsmith named Sympson, to whom he owed £300, though, according to Francis, Sympson had agreed to take payment a fortnight later. By the intervention of one of the Sheriffs, to whom a message was sent, Francis was carried to a private house near by and not to prison. Messages were also sent to Mr. Sympson begging him to come and treat; he refused. Francis was compelled to write to Sir Thomas Egerton (by that time Lord Keeper) asking him to intervene. "I humbly desire your Lordship to send for him . . . to bring him to some reason; and this forthwith because I continue here to my further discredit and inconvenience, and the trouble of the gentleman with whom I am. I have an hundred pounds lying by me which he may have, and the rest upon some reasonable time and security; or, if need be, the whole; but with my more trouble." He also pointed out the boldness of the obnoxious goldsmith, who had presumed to have him arrested while on her Majesty's service: " Mr. Sympson might have had me every day in London," he wrote in a short note to Cecil. The angels of the sacred Throne were not to be so treated while on their errands.

The actual errand was curious enough, though it has no direct relation to Francis except to show how some of his time was passed. He was engaged in a long examination of various prisoners and suspects concerning a plot to murder the Queen. A certain Edward Squire, first a scrivener, afterwards in some employment about the Queen's stables, at last went to sea with Drake and was taken by the Spaniards. In Spain he became known to a Jesuit, Richard Walpoole, who carried " a waking and waiting eye upon those of our nation," and Walpoole engaged him in a plan to poison the pommel of the Queen's saddle. The poison was given him in a double bladder; Squire, when a convenient time had come was to prick the upper part full of holes, and, carrying it within the palm of his hand covered by a thick glove, to squeeze it upside down on the pommel. He was also, if possible, to poison the Earl of Essex, for which he could use the rest of the stuff. " Conveniently moneyed," Squire came to England, and carried out his part, laying his hand upon the pommel of the saddle and crying out in a familiar and cheerful manner, " God save the Queen." He then went to sea with Essex, and used up the poison on the Earl's chair. But God saved both the Queen and the Earl; nothing happened. The other conspirators, being very angry with Squire over this and the convenient monies which he had had—on account, as it were, caused information to be conveyed to the authorities, who at first thought it was a counterfeit accusation, and that Squire was an honest man; however, " as it was a tender matter," he was sent for, examined, thought he had been betrayed, and confessed—" without torture or show of torture." He was thereafter executed.

In the examination of such fantastic tales, whether faery or actual, whether mere invention or religious frenzy or ineffective deed, Francis spent some of his time. He was used in the better-known and more complicated, but not essentially different, accusation of the Queen's physician Roderigo Lopez, for conspiracy and treason. This had been earlier, and was, so to speak, Essex's own plot as against the Cecils'. Elizabeth was always being saved from plots; and in that " obscure sequestered place " of conspiracies within conspiracies, evils masquerading as virtues, and virtues as evils, of religion losing its scruples, and policy inventing devotees, it is impossible to say what in truth ever happened. But that slow examination and cross-examination and re-examination of fanatic or mercenary or innocent did not carry the genius of Bacon much nearer to the height of his hope.

After the great refusal of the two Law Offices, he was in 1596 a little better treated. Elizabeth, having snubbed Essex and disappointed Bacon, became reconciled to the one and courteous to the other. For a little the three of them vibrated to each other almost as fixed points—the Queen and the Earl close together, Bacon beyond the Earl but not quite in a direct line, so that there was a space for relationship along the old path established many years before, obscured by troubles since, but soon to some extent to be re-illumined. By July 1596 Bacon wrote to his brother; "I do find in the speech of some ladies and the very face of this Court some addition of reputation. . . . The Queen saluted me to-day as she went to chapel." There was in that year some effort to get him made Master of the Rolls. Egerton having been made Lord Keeper, but it failed, Essex had no opportunity to press it strongly; he was going off to take Cadiz, which with great bravery and glory he did. On his return, Francis sent him a long letter (4th October 1596), welcoming him, admiring him, but (its Elizabethan phrases of rhetoric made substantial with truth) putting his danger as strongly as could be dared. Francis justified himself by claiming that whenever Essex had followed his counsel it had always been advantageous. He stressed the present peril, imagining himself in the Queen's place—" How is it now ? A man of a nature not to be ruled ; that hath the advantage of my affection and knoweth it ; of an estate not grounded to his greatness ; of a popular reputation ; of a military dependence : I demand whether there can be a more dangerous image than this represented to any monarch living, much more to a lady, and of her Majesty's apprehension ? " He urged the means to appease such danger—among other things let the Earl, if he praised the Queen, do it familiarly, not formally, *oratione fida* not *adornatis verbis*; let him always have certain particulars afoot which he might abandon upon the Queen's opposition, as recommending some to places now void (which was a handsome enough proposal, considering the Mastership of the Rolls was still vacant), or pretending private journeys to his estates, but not great foreign journeys of employment, or at the lowest matters

of habit, apparel, gesture, etc. ; let him avoid seeming to
grasp at the show of military command, the substance
of which would come to him naturally upon other greatness ; let him choose the place of Privy Seal rather than
Earl Marshal or Master of the Ordnance ; let him also
bring in some other martial man to be of the Council,
or at least pretend to do so ; let him keep as much
popularity as he could get, for this reason avoiding
monopolies, but by all means denounce popular courses
to the Queen and blame them in others ; let him show
himself careful of his estate and not a possible charge to
the Queen. And as for the matter of affection—if those
other impressions were destroyed in the Queen's mind,
that could not hurt ; but joined with them, " it maketh
her Majesty more fearful and shadowy, as not knowing
her own strength " ; let him therefore be always ready
to give way to some other Favourite, so only that the
new man held no dangerous aspect towards him. For,
that secured, " whosoever shall tell me that you may
not have singular use of a favourite at your devotion,
I will say he understandeth not the Queen's affection
nor your Lordship's condition. And so I rest."

An austere, and for that matter a not particularly
austere, moralist might quarrel with this advice as
involving hypocrisy and insincerity. But it was certainly a lucid statement of the best way for a Favourite
to take, and the way most men, if intelligent enough,
would and do take. It is extraordinary how nearly,
in the ordinary affairs of life, we all behave, whenever
possible, as Bacon knew that men desirous of advancement or safety will. We are all intuitive Baconians.
But the fact that he saw and said what was the wise
thing to do has enabled his readers to feel superior to
his advice while following it badly. Incapacity is the
mother of pride, and often of morality also, in the many
marriages she makes with men.

At least Essex did not follow the counsel. In the next March, within six months after this letter, after a quarrel with the Queen about an appointment to the Wardenship of the Cinque Ports, he threatened to leave the Court. His carriages were ready; at the last moment the Queen sent for him, and he came from a private interview appeased by his own appointment to be Master of the Ordnance, which Francis had begged him not to take. In May he got himself made commander-in-chief of a great new expedition against Spain. He sailed after doing Bacon the last kindness he was to have the power to do, recommending him as a suitor to a lady whom he contemplated marrying, the widow of Sir William Hatton and the daughter of Sir Thomas Cecil, Burleigh's son by his first marriage. It would have been a marriage for money, but many marriages under Elizabeth were marriages for money. Estates were bound together so, and parents arranged unions with that in view. Essex, in the midst of all his preparations, naval and military, stopped to write charming letters to Sir Thomas Cecil and his wife on behalf of Bacon's suit. He spoke of his client's " virtues and excellent parts," and said that his love for him was " exceeding great." He told Sir Thomas that Francis was " likely to rise in his profession "; he told Lady Cecil that Francis was " worthy of very good fortune." They are handsome recommendations, but there is no smallest hint that Essex himself has anything to do with Francis's future. One does not say of a friend with whose good fortune one has charged oneself that he is " likely to rise in his profession." " If I had one as near me . . . I had rather match her with him than with men of far greater titles." No doubt. But this is not the tone in which the Queen's Favourite would have preferred an intimate. The proposal came to nothing. The lady married Sir Edward Coke, " the

Huddler" (Bacon called him), and years afterwards was to come banging at Bacon's bedchamber door with her complaints.

It was the last cool kindness Essex was to do Francis; what kindness remained, an obscure and suspected kindness, was to be on the other side. There grew, after his return from the Island voyage, an alienation between them. The great expedition was a failure. Results were small; the tempers of all the commanders were ruffled; the temper of the Queen was frayed. Essex, still popular, still loved, still violent, asked for no more advice from the Queen's Learned Counsel. There was "a discontinuance of privateness . . . between his Lordship and myself; so as I was not called nor advised with, for some year and a half." But what happened to the other Bacon, the sick man who sat in his rooms at Essex House conducting the foreign correspondence of the Queen's lover? Up to the end of 1597 a mass of it remains; afterwards none. There are no more letters between Anthony and the Earl. Anthony remained in Essex House till he was expelled by the Queen. He must have seen his brother often enough, for they loved each other more perhaps than either of them ever loved another living person. Or did that alienation come between them also? It must have done if Anthony was still serving the Earl in his darker secrets and Francis knew nothing of it. If it did not, if they still talked freely, then either Francis knew much more of the Earl's emotions and schemes than it is easily credible that he did, or else Anthony himself knew nothing, which is even less credible. It seems more likely that the two brothers also fell a little apart, and as earlier Anthony had, but in no ill sense, come between the Earl and Francis, so now the shadow of the Earl lay between Francis and Anthony. If this were so, it was indeed an alienation, and the Queen's

Counsel, as he went to and fro on his learned business, must have felt that the rash folly of the Favourite had separated him from something more intimate than great place.

In the early part of that year, about the beginning of February, he had published the first edition of the *Essays*—a small volume containing ten essays, and also *Colours of Good and Evil*, and *Meditationes Sacræ*. The book was dedicated to his brother, who had wished it to be dedicated to the Earl, and immediately sent him a copy.

By October, after the unfortunate return from the Island voyage, the relations between the Favourite and the Queen had grown more dangerous. Essex (so Bacon noted that " a great lord " had said) had " but one friend and one enemy ; and that one friend is the Queen and that one enemy himself." But now that opposition approached a subtler alteration. The whirlwind that was Essex was drawing the Queen into its orbit ; she was infected by the dangerous temper he had in himself, and he, seeking his own safety, became a treacherous friend. The wild balance between them was trembling more dreadfully every week ; yet still she loved, and he permitted love. But she had, beyond that, one great advantage—he lived, and it was she who permitted life. It is possible that this knowledge lay more keenly close to both their hearts than later ages realize, and added a terrible background to their disputes. Essex, in daring her anger, dared her to destroy him, and as his position grew more dangerously uncertain he was driven in secret to provide against her accepting that challenge, by making preparation in turn to destroy the means she could use to execute it. Into such a base material conclusion was the high spiritual truth of necessity and authority which operates everywhere transmuted in their minds.

He returned to find that Cecil had become Chancellor

of the Duchy of Lancaster, and that the Lord Howard, who was Lord Admiral and had shared the Cadiz adventure with Essex, was now Earl of Nottingham, thus ranking above Essex. He sulked, kept himself in, insisted on having Nottingham's patent altered, and talked (or others talked for him) " of combat against either the Earl of Nottingham or any of his sons or any of his name." He remained aloof for some six weeks or so ; then the Queen again yielded. She would not alter Nottingham's patent, but she made the obstinate Favourite Earl Marshal, an office which ranked above the Lord Admiral's. Thereafter the Earl of Essex allowed himself again to be seen in public. It was the second office which Francis had warned him not to hold.

" She yielded " ; in effect she never did. She had her own way, but she had continually to compensate Essex for letting her have her way. Whatever appointment she made she had to appease the indignant Favourite by new honours, to buy back his favour with fresh bestowals. Gifts she might have made freely became bribes to recover him. It might not have mattered to a milder temper, though even a milder temper would have found it tiresome never to be certain of having its own way. Even Queen Anne tired of a Duchess. Elizabeth found it something more than tiresome. In December Essex had been placated with the Earl Marshal's staff ; in the next June or July a more furious quarrel than ever broke out. The troubles in Ireland were becoming serious ; at a small meeting of the Council, where Cecil, Nottingham, Windebank, and Essex were present, the Queen proposed to appoint Sir William Knollys, his uncle, Lord Lieutenant. Essex, for reasons of his own, wanted Sir George Carew away from Court and insisted that he should be " kicked upstairs " to the Lieutenancy. The Queen refused, Essex, " *sui immemor et obsequii negligens, incivilius, quasi ex despicentia,"* abruptly turned his back upon her. In a burst of rage, the old woman struck him. He wheeled, his hand on his sword; the Admiral flung himself between; Essex swore that he could not and would not bear such treatment—not from Henry the Eighth himself. And "*fremens ex aula se proripuit*"— "raging he precipitated himself out of the room."

The breach was more or less vaguely covered by October. Francis heard of it what all the Court heard—rumours. He grew more and more doubtful of the Earl's prospects, and when the apparent reconciliation was effected, he wrote Essex a letter in which he touched again on the order of his own allegiance.

"It may please your Lordship,

"That your Lordship is *in statu quo prius*, no man taketh greater gladness than I do; the rather, because I assure myself that of your eclipses, as this hath been the longest, it shall be the last. As the comical poet saith, "*Neque illam tu satis noveras, neque te illa ; hoc ubi fit, ibi non vivitur.*" For if I may be so bold as to say what I think, I believe neither your Lordship looked to have found her Majesty in all points as you have done, neither her Majesty percase looked to find your Lordship as she hath done. And therefore I hope upon this experience may grow more perfect knowledge, and upon knowledge more true consent; which I for my part do infinitely wish; as accounting these accidents to be like the fish *Remora*; which though it be not great, yet hath it a hidden property to hinder the sailing of the ship. And therefore as bearing unto your Lordship, after her Majesty, of all public persons the second duty, I could not but signify unto you my affectionate gratulation. And so I commend your good Lordship to the best preservation of the Divine Majesty.

"From Gray's Inn."

The Queen, according to report, said that Essex "had played long enough upon her, and that she meant to play awhile upon him, and to stand as much upon her greatness as he had done upon his stomach." But in September Burleigh died. Whatever Elizabeth's private view of Burleigh may have been—whether that of affectionate mistress or thwarted dupe (historians take both sides), she was thus left, as an old woman, without the presence, advice, and perhaps direction of a man who had been by her for forty years. By the 18th of October Essex, having made some kind of submission, was again in favour; by the 20th it was rumoured that he would himself go to Ireland; by the end of the year it was certain. The Favourite was to be Lord Deputy. But, in her angrier moments, the very title may have sounded a strange threat to the ears of the Queen, and a stranger promise to the Earl's.

The Court was shaken by conflicting suspicions, rumours, fears, and hopes. It was understood that Essex had himself prevented the appointment of Lord Mountjoy, a friend of his own, on whom the Queen and her Council had first fixed for Deputy. It was known that Essex was to have a huge force under him, that he was making extreme demands on the Government, that he was going rather to please himself than the Queen. At the beginning of March he was still reported to be highly dissatisfied with the terms of his commission; he was even supposed to be playing on the Queen's fear rather than her affection. "Fearful and shadowy" the two great personages passed in and out of their private chambers. "He goeth not forth to serve the Queen's realm but to humour his own revenge . . . we do sometime think one way and sometime another . . . the Queen is not well pleased, the Lord Deputy may be pleased now but I sore fear what may happen hereafter," wrote a friend to Sir John Harington, who was proposing

# THE THIRD ATTEMPT: ESSEX

to go on the same expedition, and was to be secretly warned of the true way in which things were setting. " There are overlookers set on you all, so God direct your discretion." On 27th March the Earl set out. He was still popular outside the Court ; it was to no hostile audience that the actor of the Chamberlain's men was, within a few weeks, to declaim the expectant and victorious lines :

> "Were now the general of our gracious empress,
> As in good time he may, from Ireland coming,
> Bringing rebellion broached on his word. . . ."

But at Nonesuch and Westminster the feeling was very different.

How far and where Essex had consulted Bacon during these agitated six months does not appear. In the account of his relations with the Earl, published four years afterwards and addressed to Mountjoy himself, which, since Mountjoy had been intimate with Essex, is at least presumptive in favour of a general truth he said that the Earl " expressly and in set manner " asked him his opinion, and that he vehemently protested against the whole project, as being " ill for her, ill for him, and ill for the State." " It is not nor it cannot come to good " ; neither the Queen nor he could possibly be contented nor countenanced. " I did as plainly see his overthrow chained as it were by destiny to that journey as it is possible for any man to ground a judgment upon future contingents." A man like Essex, with an army in freedom . . . but one could not tell that to the Earl, and even the worst project never looks quite as bad before as it does after. Looking back, Bacon saw the whole dreadful chain of cause and effect, inevitably linked. Looking forward, he could not see so much. There was always a possibility that he might be wrong ; some chance *might* go right, the Earl *might* succeed, the Queen *might* be pleased. . . . He wrote to him once more, " as one that would say somewhat, and can say nothing, touching your Lordship's intended charge for Ireland."

It was a letter as well shaped to encourage Essex in the right way as ever he wrote, but one word runs through the first part of it with a continuous insistence —the word " peril." ". . . A service of great merit and great peril . . . the greatness of the peril . . . no small consequence of peril . . . whole charges of peril . . . the greater peril of your fortune . . . the peril of that State . . . the peril of England. . . ." It is a great service, but let Essex " cure himself "—" obedience is better than sacrifice " : " observe the due limits of instructions," for fear of " a dangerous disavow." In short, no doubt everything would go right, but Essex had better be very careful that everything did not go disastrously wrong, whether he won or lost, and Bacon had by now little hope that Essex would be careful. " Obedience is better than sacrifice " ; he did not add that disobedience was likely to mean another kind of sacrifice. The Queen, though none knew it, had made her last compensation ; she had, at the Earl's will, thrust him forward to be as herself. Between " as herself " and herself there opened the abyss which was to swallow him.

While during five months in Ireland he marched and countermarched, wasting time, wasting his army, achieving in the end nothing but a poor talk with Tyrone and other secret talks with his friends on the possibility of striking some great stroke in England, the Queen brooded and loved and despaired in her palaces. Her mind altered ; the fire burned within her, and she spoke of it to many, passionately. " My Lord's proceedings— contemptuous—some private end of his own." The words which were privily in others' mouths were publicly in hers. It was the private end that pleased or terrified others, and shook the Majesty itself. He was there with an army : what might come to be ? She spoke of all that might be ; she spoke of it once to Bacon at Nonesuch, when he was in attendance on business. She knew it ; he knew she knew it, and he had to answer : he had too much intelligence and tact to be merely good-humouredly casual about it ; besides, he was not in a position to be casual in the Presence—that method had to be left to men in great place, not adopted by one of the Queen's Learned Counsel Extraordinary. He allowed it, allowed that with arms and power the Earl might prove cumbersome and unruly, and he fell back on his old solution ; let Essex be at home, an honour and ornament in the eyes of the people and foreign ambassadors.

The next thing Bacon and such outsiders knew was that he was home indeed. He came, riding in haste across England with a band of friends, breaking in upon the Queen, at ten one September morning, welcomed and then relegated to his chamber, amid general uncertainty. The expedition had been a failure ; the Lord Deputy was back at Nonesuch—in favour, in disgrace. Bacon wrote to him, and again the letter opened on the old monotonous note. At that moment nobody knew whether the Favourite was still Favourite or not, whether the Queen's pleasure was to have him still recognized, admired, and served, or to have him cast out of her grace and therefore of all men's. The old agitations were beginning with threefold violence. Bacon repeated himself. He supposed (he wrote) that Essex had come in the person of a good servant to see his sovereign mistress ; it would be hard for Bacon to find him ; he would not try ; he would merely send the salutations of " him that is more yours than any man's and more yours than any man." He concluded by saying that no doubt " your Lordship's wisdom and obsequious circumspection and patience will turn all to the best." Essex *might* be intelligent; whatever had gone wrong might yet be remedied. He turned the phrase in his letter and sat back to wait. He had done what he could; if only Essex would believe him, and be humble and wise. . . . But if Essex was determined to destroy himself then Bacon had no intention of being destroyed with him; that would have been foolish to himself and treasonable to the Queen. He went so far —and in the circumstances it was going very fairly far— as to call upon him, and offered him still the same advice. " Do not make much of the Irish result; admit it was not fortunate. Do not press on the Queen the necessity of your return to Ireland; leave it entirely to her. Seek access; seek access by all means." The Earl shook his head, and said little.

He had arrived on the Friday, 28th September; on the Monday he was committed to the custody of the Lord Keeper at York House. Stories were abroad of his return, and of the temper of the six gentlemen who rode with him from London to Nonesuch; he had brought "a great number of captains and gentlemen" with him from Ireland, but most of them remained in London. One of them, Sir Christopher St. Laurence, seeing an "enemy" (Lord Grey of Wilton) passing them on the road, offered to kill him at once and the Secretary when they reached the Court. Essex, "detesting impiety," forbade it. The Queen, gracious at first—in that first sudden shock of seeing the beloved form— had now retired herself and caused the Earl to be relegated to the custody of the Lord Keeper Ellesmere. With him from October to March he remained, brought to the Council and sent back again, but prevented from the access Bacon advised and he desired. The Queen having him as semi-prisoner at her will and within her reach, could afford to nourish and indulge her emotions.

While she did so, Bacon suffered the not infrequent peril of being consulted by her, whenever he had occasion to see her on ordinary legal business of State. He was only one of her learned counsel, not a minister or one of her personal circle. But he had been intimate with the Earl, and Elizabeth, perhaps for that reason, talked to him. It was, from any point of view, a dangerous privilege, not only for Essex but for himself, not only for himself but for Essex. To press the Earl's faults too far or not to press them sufficiently was equally fatal, and a word might be too far or a word not far enough. The Queen knew more than Bacon did about what had happened in Ireland; she knew that Sir William Warren had reported how Tyrone had sworn that within two months there would be a great and strange alteration, that Tyrone hoped before long to "have a good share in England." She knew that Essex was still harping on the fact that he was the only person who could deal with Tyrone. Bacon knew that she knew things he did not know. He knew that her mood was changeable and her temper uncertain. And he knew that he was being blamed by outsiders for incensing her against the Favourite. If he did not know he seriously suspected that the Queen was encouraging this view of his responsibility. He had been twenty-five years old when the wretched Davison had been flung from office to prison because the Queen chose to lay on him the responsibility for the execution of Mary of Scots. Bacon may have wondered once or twice whether Elizabeth were preparing another victim for the responsibility of another execution. In the later *Apology* he wrote of the rumours that blamed him: "These speeches, I cannot tell, nor I will not think, that they grew any way from her Majesty's own speeches, whose memory I will ever honour; if they did, she is with God, and *miserum est ab illis loedi, de quibus non possis queri.*" It is not likely that she did such things deliberately; she only manœuvred herself emotionally into a position where she could be shocked and horrified at the result of somebody else's action. She had been taught that course for her own protection when she was very young. She had had to pretend to be astonished to save herself from her own knowledge of herself. One day in his house at the Savoy, Cecil cooed to Bacon; and what Cecil cooed to Bacon he was probably cooing to others about Bacon. " I must give this testimony to my Lord Cecil," wrote Francis later, " that one time, he dealt with me directly." (The " one time " refers to the Essex affair, but how much of all the others did the singularity reveal in Cecil's cousin's mind?) He had heard, but did not believe, that Francis was doing some ill office to the Earl. He wished, as on a former occasion, that Francis would follow his own example—" I am merely passive and not active "—" I follow the Queen and that heavily "—" I lead her not "—" My Lord of Essex is one that in nature I could consent with as well as with any one living; the Queen indeed is my Sovereign, and I am her creature, I may not leese her." Francis " satisfied him." But when Cecil began publicly to deprecate, and when to follow his advice might mean precisely (if the Queen raged) doing some ill office to the Earl, and when the Queen went on consulting, and rumours spread . . . There would anyhow be some one to be blamed, whether the Queen made it up with Essex, as half her nature suggested, or the other half of her nature, her distrust of that which fascinated her, her knowledge of the axe that lay to her hand, an awful instrument of freedom, had its violent way. Essex in the one case and the world in the other might be left to suppose that it was all Bacon's fault. And Cecil—well, Cecil could not believe that Bacon was, or had been, behaving like that, but of course if the Queen implied it he could only follow, " and that heavily."

A little before the Cecil interview (which makes it the more curious) the Queen had proposed to dine at Twickenham. Bacon was driven into verse " though I profess not to be a poet " and " this was (as I said) but a toy "; he wrote a sonnet recommending reconciliation. At other times he went farther; he urged her, whatever she did in the main affair, to throw it upon others, but for herself let her send some grace to the Earl, so that the populace who favoured him might not be alienated. And let her, for such messages of goodness, use none of her great people who might be thought to have moved her to it, but some one who was " a mere conduct " of her goodness, some one like himself, in short himself. He was very wise; if the Queen had once begun to send messages and graces, if some word had fluttered towards the Lord Keeper's house, it would have been substantial towards peace and unity. He was very wise; he would not interfere in high matters; let the Queen do as she thought best, only let her increase her fame among the people by at least showing herself benevolent through some minor conduit. In short, if Bacon were to be used, let him be used in exactly the opposite manner to that about which Cecil was talking. Let her pretend to be gracious, and she would (he thought) inevitably lean more to grace. But she would not do it; she discerned in him " inward and deep respects unto my Lord." She did not know what she wanted, but she knew she wanted Bacon to be entirely at her will and pleasure. She was jealous of Essex in his thought, yet—partly perhaps because of the presence of Essex in his thought—she went on consulting him.

She showed him a book dedicated to Essex, and asked him whether there were no cause for treason in it. He made a deferential joke about its plagiarisms—

7

"not for treason but for felony," so much being stolen from Tacitus. She threatened to rack the supposed author, to discover whether some mischievous person were not responsible for it. He risked another joke—"rack his stile"; let him be compelled to continue it, and Bacon would soon know if he had written the original. She asked him of the legal position of Essex's case. He said that Essex might technically have committed contempts, but there were such high defences—great interest in her favour, greatness of place, ampleness of commission, nature of business (men cannot be tied to strictness), distance of place, the Irish Council avowing him, good intention on his part (held sometimes "a dispensation even for God's commands, much more for princes")—it was unwise to make public question of the business. He warned her that Essex had great eloquence and might entirely overpass whoever should speak against him. Better wrap it up privily, and restore my lord with some addition of honour. She spoke of nominating Mountjoy to Ireland. He answered that if her Majesty did not mean to employ Essex again—she broke in, "Essex? whensoever I send Essex back into Ireland I will marry you; claim it of me." He turned the phrase: "Well, Madam, I will release that contract if it be for the good of the State." But about the good of the State nobody was seriously consulting Bacon. She determined to have the Earl's offences declared in the Star Chamber, so as to explain to every one, "but my lord of Essex not to be called to it." He protested it would be against her credit; people would say the Earl was stabbed in the back; justice would have her balance taken from her; let the Queen wrap it up privately. She began to be offended. The Star Chamber meeting was held—on 29th November—with no good result. Bacon was not there; the Queen accused him of absence; he alleged ill-health. She clouded herself towards him for six months, and all that time there was at last " a high silence " between them on my lord of Essex's concerns.

He had perhaps done Essex no particular good, nor himself. But he had saved himself from doing actually what the growing rumours, in the Court and among the people, whispered that he did—incensing the Queen, and that must have been no easy thing. He had treated both the Queen and the Favourite as high and great natures, needing a difficult and delicate composition. But the rumours continued. A letter to Sir Robert Sydney from a friend shows what was being said. " Her Majesty is greatly troubled with the last number of knights made by the Earl of Essex in Ireland, and purposes, by public proclamation, to command them from the place due to their dignity, and that no ancient gentleman of the kingdom give them any place. The warrant was signed, as I heard, but by Mr. Secretary's great care and credit, it is stayed till Sunday the Lords meet in court. Mr. Bacon is thought to be the man that moves her Majesty unto it, affirming that by the law the Earl had no authority to make them, being by her Majesty's own letter, of her own hand written, commanded the contrary." He added that the Queen had sent to the Earl for this letter, but he submissively answered that he had lost or mislaid it for he could not find it, " which somewhat displeases her Majesty. As yet his liberty stands upon those terms ; but Mr. Secretary continues to do good offices, and in time will prevail, no doubt."

Bacon wrote to the Queen, to the Lord Henry Howard, and to Sir Robert Cecil about these rumours. It was being reported that he had declared that Essex was guilty of treason, in opposition to the opinion of the Chief Justice and the Attorney-General. Considering that the Attorney-General was Coke, such a report sounds silly. Coke never minimised treason when there was a great person in question, never at all till he had quarrelled with the King. Francis repeated to Howard precisely what he had always said. "For my Lord of Essex, I am not servile to him, having regard to my superior duty. I have been much bound to him. And on the other side, I have spent more time and more thoughts about his well-doing than ever I did about mine own." But the real question at bottom was of the Queen's mind ? Was Essex in favour or not ? was it or was it not in the nature of treason to support him ? Until the sacred Majesty had declared itself, the moral question could not begin to be decided.

By May the Queen was speaking to Bacon again. The Star Chamber declaration had gone all wrong, had raised more "factious bruits" than it had settled. People said (as Bacon had warned her they would) that the Earl had been condemned unheard. But something else Elizabeth was determined to do. She would have a regular proceeding in the Star Chamber ; not to destroy Essex, only to chastise him. Bacon warned her that the whole business had gone too far for that ; the matter had taken too much wind. She was offended again. It would perhaps be wrong to assert that she had found it impossible to use Bacon as a catspaw, that something in him refused her complete control and yet offered no complete control to the Earl. But she was certainly much more easily angry with him than she had been up to then ; she remained aloof for weeks, and then close on the beginning of June she repeated her intention. He said, in effect, that if she must have her way, she had better keep it as quiet as possible, keep it to the counsel-table, " and there an end." Between them all there was arranged a Court at York House —but not of high treason, only of high contempts and notorious errors. The real high treason was yet unknown; the consultations with Mountjoy and Southampton, the correspondence with James of Scotland, the proposed use of the armies, the talk of seizing the person of the Queen.

It was in this proceeding that Bacon first took a definite and open part against the Earl. He was given—not any part of the Irish affair, but the slightly ridiculous item of the book which Essex had countenanced and which had offended the Queen. It was a long, disagreeable proceeding. The Earl was kept kneeling, first on the floor, then on a cushion, then allowed to stand, then to lean. The intolerably lengthy speeches went on. It was understood what the end of the whole day's business was to be: the Earl would say he threw himself on the Queen's mercy, and the Commissioners would solemnly leave him there. Sir Edward Coke was so offensive that he nearly spoilt the whole pompous and irritating farce, because Essex began to justify himself, which would have ruined everything. But quiet and orderliness were restored; the rhetoric was ended; an ostentation of judgment was delivered, "until it should please her Majesty to release both this and all the rest."

On the next day Bacon reported to the Queen. He suggested to her that she had now shown her victory, that the Earl was in a proper humble frame of mind towards her and had shown it, and that now was the time for tenderness. She gave him the general idea that she agreed with him, and dismissed him to give her a written account of all that had passed, which on two afternoons he read to her. She told him, in reference to the way in which he had written of the Earl, that she saw "old love would not easily be forgotten"; "whereunto I answered suddenly, that I hoped she meant that by herself." By the end of July, the Earl was set at liberty to go where he would, only not to Court.

But Bacon was not satisfied, nor certainly was Essex, nor probably was the Queen. Elizabeth went on giving her learned counsel opportunities of talking to her. On the last day of July he wrote to Essex, and the Earl answered coldly, as was to be expected from any one, but especially from Essex, whose idea of support was that his friends should rally to his house.

There is no sign of Anthony all this time, except that he was ordered to leave Essex House before the Earl was allowed to return. " By her Majesty's express commandment, my lady Leicester [Essex's mother], Lord and Lady Southampton, Mr. Grevell, Mr. Bacon, are all removed from Essex House." The secret intelligence was still being used but for more limited and more personal ends. Of the two brothers, however, it was now Francis who was in evidence. Nothing could be more exquisitely subtle than to picture the two working together, plotting restoration one way or another, seeking it by peaceful means, aware of the possibility of seeking it by others ; the chambers at Gray's Inn to be the centre of that complex conspiracy, and the Queen and Essex, James of Scotland and Robert Cecil, to be its tools, its purpose the establishment of Anthony in control of foreign and Francis of home affairs. Anthony was still thought by Essex's friends to be the agent of communication with Scotland. Francis certainly was drafting letters for the Earl to send to the Queen. Anthony had suggested and Francis prepared two letters, one from Anthony to the Earl, one from the Earl to Anthony, the idea being that if they were actually written and then privately shown by Francis to the Queen it would have a very good effect upon " that deep and inscrutable centre of the Court, which is her Majesty's mind." They are extremely Elizabethan letters. Anthony is to encourage the Earl to hope ; the Earl is to despair, yet with a last thrilling touch of " if I recover the Queen, I will never lose her again." Both of them say nice things about each other ; both of them allude, as would be perfectly natural, to Francis. But it may be believed that was chiefly because it would be perfectly natural ; nothing was to be gained at the moment by causing Essex to recommend him to the Queen.

But all planned letters, all conversation, all recommendation, went awry. Elizabeth was sick at heart, and Essex was clumsy. He wrote adoring letters, and tacked on a request for a renewal of his monopoly of sweet wines. She told Bacon of this, and he answered, in sentences that go deep into his own nature :

"Oh Madam, how doth your Majesty conster of these things, as if these two could not stand well together, which indeed nature hath planted in all creatures. For there are but two sympathies, the one towards *perfection*, the other towards *preservation*. That to perfection, as the iron contendeth to the loadstone ; that to preservation, as the vine will creep towards a stake or prop that stands by it ; not for any love to the stake, but to uphold itself. And therefore, Madam, you must distinguish : my Lord's desire to do you service is as to his perfection, that which he thinks himself to be born for ; whereas his desire to obtain this thing of you, is but for a sustentation."

By the New Year Bacon himself had despaired, and (it is perhaps not without significance) Anthony was approaching his end. The gout and the stone were increasing on him. His brother knew he was ill; the Queen was again angry ; Essex did everything wrong. Francis had one more interview in which he told Elizabeth that she had put him " into matters of envy without place or without strength." He was an *enfant perdu*, one that served " on foot in front of the horsemen,"

suspected and disliked by many because they thought
he had done Essex harm; disliked and suspected by
the Queen because she thought he loved him. He
knew what would happen. His overthrow was at hand,
he knew it, and he would let her know he knew it. He
spoke "with some passion"; she was moved and
gracious; she said "*Gratia mea sufficit*"; but of Essex
not a word. He went out resolved to do no more, since
he only succeeded in procuring no good to the Earl and
possible harm to himself. "I made mine own peace with
mine own confidence at that time." Determined things
to destiny should hold their way.

Quicker than he thought, it came. Robert Cecil and
the Council by the 7th of February heard of great gather-
ings in and round Essex House. They sent to summon
the Earl to come before them. He refused to go; he
said he was ill. On the next day, a Sunday, Francis
heard that four lords had gone to Essex House, that
they were imprisoned, that the Earl was raising the
City, that forces had been sent against him, that he was
fighting, had broken through, had been driven back,
had come by water to his house again, that the lords
were free, that the house was besieged, that the Earl
with fifty or so followers had surrendered and was in
the prison.

Within the next day or two an odd soldier had been
seized, accused, and convicted of an intention actually
to murder the Queen, and promptly executed. Under
so immediately thrilling and bloody a prelude the work
of investigation began. On the 11th the learned counsel
were sent for, divided into companies of three, and set
to help examine some of the prisoners. The Council
itself, also divided into companies, examined the chief.

Francis, with two companions, Mr. Wilbraham and
Sir Jerome Bowes, formed one of these companies. In
the next eleven days the range and scope of the proposed

effort became clear: the intrigues of the wider conspiracy—the proposals to Mountjoy to bring over forces from Ireland, the proposals to the King of Scots to support Essex on the understanding that Essex declared for his succession; and the plan of the closer revolt—how Sir Christopher Blount was to have seized the outer gate of the Court, Sir Charles Davers the Presence Chamber (and the halberds of the Guard), Sir John Davies the Hall, and how then the Earl himself would enter and seize the Person of Majesty, some of them being even prepared, at a pinch, " to have drawn blood from herself." In the name and by the authority of that captive Majesty they would summon a Parliament, and all the Earl's enemies would be brought to honourable trial.

How far the thing had progressed or been meant to progress, whether it was more than talk put into all but final action, whether Essex was still sane enough to know what he was doing, whether even (had it been possible) the Queen might have accepted that as a magnificent and fantastic devotion of her servant to her person, whether she would willingly have lost Cecil to keep Devereux—Cecil gave her no opportunity to decide. On the 19th the conspirators were brought to trial, and for the first and only time he broke his habit and brought his cousin into prominence. He fixed on him to assist Coke at the trial.

By now the whole thing had become to Francis a mere insanity, utterly opposed to clear intelligence. If Essex was a madman he must be treated like a madman. Francis himself was not a young provincial, a country lawyer patronized by a great lord; he had never been overawed by Robert Devereux. He had been born and brought up among those who were most intimate with the Queen, hoping and expecting—half as a right, half as a grace—to be himself intimate with the Queen.

Robert Devereux might be a great man, but Francis Bacon was used to great men. He believed himself to be (in another sense) a great man, and was the less likely to be overawed. He had admired and liked the Earl, but could the small child whom Elizabeth had noticed turn on or desert Elizabeth for the sake of one who had certainly meant—whatever else he meant—to seize the person of the Queen into his custody and compel her to issue warrants and commands as he chose ? The thing was impossible to him. He accepted his duty, and his main concern was to bring the whole detestable business quickly to an end.

One other point is of interest. Anthony Bacon was never put on trial. His name occurs twice in the examinations of the conspirators, as being concerned with the Scottish correspondence. The Government were not anxious to press this side of things more than could be helped. It may have been statecraft that left him scathless. But in the conclusion of the whole ten years' communion of those three it is not quite impossible that the ostentation of Francis's loyalty contrived an additional reason for leaving in obscurity the fallen Favourite's chief Secretary of State, nor that the part which Francis was given to play in the trial was a public testimony of the fact that the Bacons were loyal. In the concealed figure of Anthony more truth of the whole business may lie hidden than has been allowed. There is no need to turn Francis into a sentimental brother, or even to declare that he would never at a pinch have sacrificed his brother to himself. All we know is that Anthony must have been in many minds and that he remained untouched, left to die in a remote obscurity.

The ardent romanticism of our zeal for the self-sacrifice of others has sorrowed over Bacon from then to now. Certainly tares grew in his wheat ; it is likely that he realized how to refuse now would be to ruin his

career for ever. But wheat grew with the tares; the
salvation of the Queen's Majesty depended on the prevention of such wild insanities. He decided; he acted;
he pledged himself to Monarchy for ever; he made haste
to strike. At the trial of Essex he hastened the prosecution. His old antagonist Coke, the Attorney, led
for the Crown, and raged and raved. Arguments grew
between him and the prisoners; the trial—formal and
prejudged as of course it was—went wandering off
down byways. Cecil came out from behind his hangings
(literally, but not metaphorically); Sir Walter Raleigh
was brought in to swear on a folio Testament (the Earl
objected to the "decimo-sexto" size provided—so
fantastic had everything become) that no mischief had
been intended to Essex; Lord Grey and the Earl of
Southampton quarrelled with each other; Coke and
Essex forgave each other. Francis in a short speech
brought back the proceedings to the question whether
the Earl had committed treason instead of whether the
Earl had enemies; he involved Cain and Pisistratus.
The Earl referred to the letters Francis had drafted for
himself and Anthony; they showed that Francis
believed him to have enemies. Francis answered that if
the letters could be produced they would justify themselves. The trial roared on. The Judges were appealed
to: was it treason to go to Court in that manner without
the purpose of violence? The Judges held that it was.
Coke said that in law intentions could only be judged
by acts; the Earl said that in truth intentions could only
be judged by conscience. Francis struck in again, a short
speech, interrupted once by the Earl. He said he had
never known in any trial such favour shown to the
prisoner; the treasons were great and notorious. The
Earl had hoped to raise the City, as the Duke of
Guise had done; he had failed. Now, when the Queen
had taken arms, he pretended it was a private quarrel.

The iron that was in Francis, that had not broken under Burleigh's rebukes and the anger of Majesty, that would remain unbroken to the end of his life, struck—this once in all his life—with the more force for all that had been. "The end was treason." It was so judged.

The trial ended; the execution was determined. Essex made larger and wilder confessions; he blamed others; he accused his sister of inciting him; he died. Francis was ordered to write an account of the conspiracy which the Government might publish; he obeyed and wrote it. The Council took it, considered it, "made it almost a new writing," submitted it to the Queen. She read it; she read everywhere the phrase used by its first author, "my lord of Essex." She struck it out; "Write 'Essex.'" It was done.

The first draft of that necessary document provided, Bacon's usefulness to Cecil ceased. He was dropped again into his obscurity. The Great Instauration had once more failed to find a patron on earth.

## CHAPTER IV

### THE TURNING-POINT: THE HOUSE OF COMMONS

THE clamour and clash of that February concluded at last around one voice—that of Essex monologizing on Tower Hill. It spoke in the stillness and to the stillness, especially to the stillness of the palace where the old woman who was still the Majesty of England was entering in secret upon her own short path to the grave. The Fortune of Cecil had destroyed Cecil's only rival. Raleigh watched from the Tower over the death of the same rival; he said that he withdrew to weep. So high had been the storm, and so thrilling the single distant farewell which concluded it, that there seems to fall upon the whole world of palace and city and courts of law a silence, as if time waited for some new movement of music to begin its process once more. It is the more marked for us because we know the new movement is at hand. There is now no escape from that ordained inevitability; it is part of our enjoyment of the art of history. This art consists in our present knowledge of what must happen counterpointed with our past understanding of the many things that may happen. We are contemporary and everlasting at once. James of Scotland waiting in Edinburgh is a future at once certain and yet undetermined.

Essex was dead; Southampton was in the Tower. The fines of the other conspirators amounted to more than £74,000. They were, as was usual, distributed among the servants of the Crown. Bacon received £1200—about one-sixty-fifth. At the beginning of

August he wrote to his creditor and friend Michael Hickes, "The Queen hath done somewhat for me, though not in the proportion I hoped"; it was impossible, in his financial stress, not to be anxious about such things. By then Anthony was dead; his work cut short, his body in torture, himself suspect, he had come to his end at the close of May. Lady Bacon at Gorhambury was nearing that condition of semi-frenzy into which she fell for the last years of her life. Burleigh was dead; the Queen was approaching death. The universe withdrew the apparition of itself under one complex form and emerged again in another. Francis Bacon was forty years old, and still nobody. Of the Great Instauration nothing had been done; only the small book of *Essays* had lain for a little, more than four years earlier, in the booksellers' shops of London.

In the same shops unreliable texts of *Hamlet* and *Henry V* were being sold, the *Henry V* having the choric matter omitted. But the text being so bad, it cannot be argued that Shakespeare, who had been so publicly devoted to Southampton in 1594, had himself taken care to remove the allusion to Southampton's friend. The Lord Chamberlain's men had come off scot-free from that performance of *Richard II* for which Essex's client, Sir Gilly Merrick, had offered them a double fee. Their manager had been haled up on 18th February, the day before the opening of the trial, and examined, but they had been pressed no further. The play after all was not new, and had been performed at other times. Sir Edward Hoby had invited Robert Cecil himself to a performance in 1595. But the deposition scene, though acted, was not printed in any edition of the play before the death of Elizabeth.

Whatever Shakespeare had thought about Southampton in 1594 (only a year before Essex had presented Francis with that centuries-overrated land, the substitution of what was not wanted for what was; and Southampton is said to have given Shakespeare one hundred pounds), whatever he thought of him in 1601, his company was at Court on 24th February. The contrast between those two great spirits is in both their lives and their writings. Shakespeare's career was one steady rise; Bacon's was a long level of lowness and then a rise. But the power of Shakespeare's style underwent a profound change; Bacon's style became more easy and flexible, but it underwent no serious alteration. If Shakespeare had, *per impossibile*, been in Bacon's place, he would have been Chancellor a dozen years earlier than Bacon was—if he had decided to be. He had the advantage of being able to please ordinary minds while providing for extraordinary. But he would certainly not have refused his services to the Queen because of Southampton's £100 or Essex's land. If Bacon had been in Shakespeare's place there would have been many fewer jokes in the plays. Bacon made jokes certainly; he had a sharp wit; he is said to have " razored " men with the keenness of his tongue; the victims probably thought that the only point was the insult, and we might think so too. He was easy and pleasant with men; at his own table he took care that every one joined in the conversation; he was a good listener. But his ordinary jests were nothing to brag of. The plays, as he would have produced them, would have been more like the solemn oratorical dialogues which his friend Fulke Greville called plays, and the Chamberlain's men would certainly not have been so often at Court.

But the real difference is metaphysical; it is between a man possessed of a particular vision of the universe and a man possessed of no vision but of the universe. It would be almost easier to believe that Bacon wrote Milton; the serious mind aspiring to schematize the universe is in both. But the only scheme in Shakespeare is that of things happening. The College of the Six Days' Work of God in the *New Atlantis* contained all materials necessary for *lucifera experimenta*—" light-bearing experiments." But the instrument in Shakespeare is single. He measures all happenings by the terrific mystery of the decasyllabic line; no other yardstick will serve, and except by that he does not judge. Bacon, working or desiring to work on the universe at the instigation of his spirit, did not perhaps realize how much his own spirit had to do with it. He did not and could not externalize his own desire into that marvellous five-foot knowledge of it. This is the greatness of poetry—such poetry as Shakespeare's—over even Shakespeare's or Bacon's prose; it contains not only experience but man's creation of that experience harmonized into a pattern which he knows to be his own pattern. It escapes the last illusion of reason, that because man must desire and must even know the universe to be reasonable, therefore it is reasonable. It may be true, as Bacon wrote wisely, that poetry " was ever thought to have some participation of divineness, because it doth raise and erect the mind, by submitting the shows of things to the desires of the mind; whereas reason doth buckle and bow the mind unto the nature of things." But what is reason itself but a desire of the mind? Prose may persuade man that he has discovered truth; poetry in its mere metres assures him that he has discovered it as it were by chance, and that even truth must become harmonious to his own nature before he can understand it. If it can—that is what we do not know.

" Perfection and preservation," Bacon had pronounced to Elizabeth, had been what the Queen's Favourite sought of his mistress; " perfection, as the iron contendeth to the loadstone; preservation, as the vine will creep towards a stake . . . to uphold itself."

There are but these two sympathies, he had told her; these two nature had planted in all creatures. These two nature had planted in himself; and with him in his exterior life, as with Essex, the loadstone and the stake were one, the Throne royal of England. Nor were they separate within. Perfection, again he had told the Queen, is "that which he thinks himself born for." Francis Bacon knew very well what he thought himself born for. That perfection involved his preservation; the two went together in his efforts for advancement. But preservation in that great thing involved also perfection in lesser things. His desire for great place involved a personal devotion to the Crown, and devotion to the Crown was the perfection of his political thought. That perfection involved, as he saw it, the harmonious loyalty of the Parliament in which grievances might be dutifully exposed and counsel wisely and humbly tendered; and this again involved his own preservation in the favour of the Commons that he might play as full a part as possible in their service, and help to unite the Commons and the Crown. Perfection and preservation were the angels of his journey; on either side of him, pointing along the same road, they directed him. They were now his only angels; from the moment of Anthony's death, whatever he had done before, he never leaned on any man. His letters, those decorated pats of rhetorical "buttering" (the word is so necessary), suggest a man attempting to lean on everybody. They never quite cringe or crawl, but there are, it must be admitted, moments when one expects them to. Yet that softness and complacency is but the velvet glove on the iron hand. The strong vitality which ruled in his centre flung them from him as a storm flings innumerable raindrops over the earth. Nothing broke him; nothing turned him. "The secret causes of things" summoned him, and instinctively he would use himself or any other, by all but any means, to help to carry the world of men with him in the pursuit of those inestimable riches. He used the most outrageous language with a careless carefulness, and forgot it until he wanted to use it to some one else. He talked of loving this man and the other till one grows ashamed of the word, and he is almost the only English statesman who in all seriousness proposed love as a political scheme. One can laugh at him as long as his back is turned, but when his back is no longer turned one becomes awkward. We are more at our ease with Shakespeare; if he is as intensely aware of his own business, he is too kind to show it.

The two years after the death of Essex went by. Cecil, Essex finally removed, ruled unquestioned, with Coke as his Attorney-General. Public life, for Bacon, resolved itself into those two unsympathetic figures. He did not wish to make enemies, but the archangels would have had to make an enemy of Coke some time or other. Coke despised the younger lawyer; so did Cecil. Most probably they also secretly despised each other. Both of them were careful men, " provident to choose good pennyworths in purchases," as some one said of Coke. Cecil also chose good pennyworths in purchases of manners. But the nicest manners cannot eventually conceal the fact that you have done nothing whatever for your cousin. Coke did not worry over manners. In the April of 1601 there was a scene. Bacon was moving in the Exchequer to have a reseizure of the lands of a relapsed recusant. He said something, " in as gentle and reasonable terms as might be," which annoyed the Attorney, who may also have remembered Bacon's comment at the trial of Essex three months before. He called out angrily, " Mr. Bacon, if you have any tooth against me, pluck it out, for it will do you more hurt than all the teeth in your head will do you good." Francis, freezing as the Attorney fired, answered,

" Mr. Attorney, I respect you ; I fear you not ; and the less you speak of your own greatness, the more I will think of it." To which Coke, in a general torrent of abuse, " I think scorn to stand upon terms of greatness with you, who are less than little, less than the least." Francis threw back, " Mr. Attorney, do not depress me too far ; I have been your better, and may be again when it please the Queen." After which, it appears to have become a mere slanging match, so far as Francis is likely to have let himself go in open court ; Coke never hesitated over such things. He answered " as if he had been born Attorney-General " (which he probably felt he had ; law was his own Great Instauration), told Francis to keep out of the Queen's business and look after his own, declared he was " unsworn," etc. (If only we had the " etc." !) Francis retaliated by saying that he at least always set his service first and himself second, and he wished to God Coke would do the same. Coke taunted him with the arrest for debt. Francis taunted *him* with dragging up old troubles, " being at fault by hunting upon an old scent," and then in face of a final storm from Coke retired into what is called, and so rarely is, " a dignified silence." Once away, however, he sent an account to Cecil and wrote a letter to Coke.

" MR. ATTORNEY,
" I thought best, once for all, to let you know in plainness what I find of you, and what you shall find of me. You take to yourself a liberty to disgrace and disable my law, my experience, my discretion. What it pleaseth you, I pray, think of me : I am one that knows both mine own wants and other men's ; and it may be, perchance, that mine mend, and others stand at a stay. And surely I may not endure in public place to be wronged, without repelling the same to my best advantage to right myself. You are great, and therefore have

the more enviers, which would be glad to have you paid at another's cost. Since the time I missed the Solicitor's place (the rather I think by your means) I cannot expect that you and I shall ever serve as Attorney and Solicitor together: but either to serve with another upon your remove, or to step into some other course; so as I am more free than ever I was from any occasion of unworthy conforming myself to you, more than general good manners or your particular good usage shall provoke. And if you had not been shortsighted in your own fortune (as I think) you might have had more use of me. But that tide is passed. I write not this to show my friends what a brave letter I have written to Mr. Attorney; I have none of those humours. But that I have written is to a good end, that is to the more decent carriage of my mistress's service, and to our particular better understanding one of another. This letter, if it shall be answered by you in deed, and not in word, I suppose it will not be worse for us both. Else it is but a few lines lost, which for a much smaller matter I would have adventured. So this being but to yourself, I for myself rest."

There was not, certainly, a great deal of subservience there. To Cecil there was always more, if indeed it were subservience. It must be considered, however, that it is not the easiest thing for any one to write to a cousin from whose polished amicability all words continually slide off. Bacon sometimes, if Cecil was being useful, as he occasionally was, with money or letters or such pleasant trifles (but never with much money or many letters, and never with anything else), wrote in the full strain of Elizabethan devotion. At other times he would hint that he was not taken in. He sent him in 1602 a letter on Irish affairs, proposing certain courses of action. In the preliminary he remarked that he was not sure whether Cecil understood the full importance of settling the Irish question. If you take this advice, he went on, " you shall show yourself as good a patriot as you are thought a politic, and make the world perceive you have no less generous ends than dexterous delivery of yourself towards your ends ; and that you have as well true arts and grounds of government as the facility and felicity of practice and negotiation ; and that you are as well seen in the periods and tides of estate as in your own circle and way : than the which, I suppose, nothing can be a better addition and accumulation of honour unto you." If Cecil did not like this advice, he was to attribute it to the fact that " I ever loved her Majesty and the State, and now love yourself ; and there is never any vehement love without some absurdity ; as the Spaniard well says : *desuario con la calentura.*"

The Spaniard might have doubted whether the preliminary were quite so artless as it suggested. Cecil, it seems, was thought by the world politic, dextrous towards his own ends, clever and fortunate in negotiations, and well on in his own affairs. But a good patriot, with generous aims, with wisdom of government, and greatness in public life—that presumably he was *not* thought. Vehement love was fairly clear on those points. But perhaps the vehemence was only for her Majesty and the State. Cecil in the course of the next few months had his own vehement love for another Majesty to occupy him.

For in March 1603, after a passion which, if more spectacular, is not much unlike the pain and distress that often attend the preliminaries of that last exodus in less exalted sufferers, Elizabeth died. The mystery of regality was offered, at the decision of her ministers, of Cecil, to James of Scotland. There were others who might have succeeded—Lady Arabella Stuart or the Infanta of Spain. But Cecil had determined, like Essex, on the Scottish King ; unlike Essex, he had the power

to carry out his promises, and his promises still promised
best for himself and (as he saw it) for the country. He
had James proclaimed, sent messages and representatives
northwards, and at last himself set out to meet the
approaching Elect of his mind. James came slowly
and magnificently south; Cecil entertained him with
splendour at Theobalds. James entered London and
was anointed and crowned. He entered into the awful
estate of kingship, no less awful that it was his by the
will of those who were now his servants, as he most
firmly believed, and they almost as firmly. The chief
of them entered into nobility; he became Robert,
Lord Cecil, and remained Secretary. In 1604, the very
next year, he became Viscount Cranbourne and Baron
Essendon; in 1605 Earl of Salisbury; in 1608 Lord
Treasurer. He died in 1612, having, with a remarkable
freedom from nepotism, still refrained from doing anything that could be avoided for his poorer and less
noticeable cousin.

Bacon, unlike Essex and Cecil and other great ones,
had had no opportunity of being in touch with James
before the Queen died. He had to do his best when the
succession was a declared fact. Five days before the
Majesty of Elizabeth departed he had written to his
friend Michael Hickes, who was secretary to Cecil as he
had been to Burleigh, asking him whenever convenient
to let the Secretary know " he is the personage in this
state which I love most." He wrote to the Earl of
Northumberland saying that it had just occurred to him
to mention how much he loved him; the letter confined
itself to the positive, and may be held consistent with
the superlative in the letter to Cecil. But both letters
contained the assurance that they came not out of any
straits of his occasions but merely out of the fullness
of his heart. That the Queen was on the point of death
was a dreadful but general, not particular, coincidence.

He wrote to two Scottish acquaintances urging them to recommend him to the King, and promising to do as much for them as soon as opportunity arose. He wrote to the King himself, with an allusion to his father's high position and to the King's benevolence towards Anthony; he even went so far—it is farther than he usually allowed himself—as to say that Anthony's endeavours and duties had been mostly common to both of them, "though by design (as between brethren) dissembled." If it had been so it seems as if it must have been ten years earlier. He may have known of later plans, but hardly taken part in them. The letter is a superb effort; it has seven sentences but contains five hundred words, of which one sentence alone accounts for one hundred and forty. It begins with one Latin quotation (from the Song of Solomon) and concludes with another. And it finally ends with Francis "thirsting after the happiness of kissing your royal hand." He wrote to two or three old secret-service friends, and to John Davies the poet, ending " So desiring you to be good to concealed poets, I continue, Your very assured, Fr. Bacon." Which may be set against the " though indeed no poet " of the *Apology*. But it is a curious phrase, only something small with which to discredit the by-no-means concealed poet who, with his fellows of the Chamberlain's men, soon to be the King's men, was to have four yards of crimson cloth for his sacred Majesty's procession.

He sent Northumberland the draft of a suggested proclamation which was not used. But he was at last sent north with a dispatch, and came into the King's presence. He wrote of it :

" It may please your good Lordship,
" I would not have lost this journey, and yet I have not that for which I went. For I have had no private conference to any purpose with the King ; and no more

hath almost any other English. For the speech his Majesty admitteth with some noblemen is rather matter of grace than of business. With the Attorney he spake, being urged by the Treasurer of Scotland, but yet no more than needs must. After I had received his Majesty's first welcome, I was promised private access; but yet, not knowing what matter of service your Lordship's letter might carry (for I saw it not) and well knowing that primeness in advertisement is much, I chose rather to deliver it to Sir Thomas Erskine, than to cool it in my hands, upon expectation of access. Your Lordship shall find a prince the farthest from the appearance of vain-glory that may be, and rather like a prince of the ancient form than of the latter time. His speech is swift and cursory, and in the full dialect of his country; and in point of business, short; in point of discourse large. He affecteth popularity by gracing such as he hath heard to be popular, and not by any fashions of his own. He is thought somewhat general in his favours, and his virtue of access is rather because he is much abroad and in press, than that he giveth easy audience about serious things. He hasteneth to a mixture of both kingdoms and nations, faster perhaps than policy will conveniently bear. I told your Lordship once before, that (methought) his Majesty rather asked counsel of the time past than of the time to come. But it is early yet to ground any settled opinion."

Before he left London he had sent one other letter. It was known that Southampton would soon be released from the Tower, since James had a gracious memory of Essex. Southampton's friends and acquaintances began to throng to him. Bacon wrote. How far a letter was really necessary we cannot judge, but Bacon was not the man to leave an unreconciled enemy behind him if reconciliation were possible. If Southampton were to be friendly with Cecil and Coke, as he certainly was, there seemed no reason why he should hold a peculiar grudge against Bacon. Bacon might have left it to him to make the first move, except that Southampton was a peer of England, and peers expected service offered, not service sought. The letter itself was the formal, courteous, and slightly rhetorical letter of those times.

" It may please your Lordship,
  " I would have been very glad to have presented my humble service to your Lordship by my attendance, if I could have foreseen that it should not have been unpleasing to you. And therefore, because I would commit no error, I choose to write ; assuring your Lordship (how credible soever it may seem to you at first), yet it is as true as a thing that God knoweth, that this great change hath wrought in me no other change towards your Lordship than this, that I may safely be now that which I was truly before. And so craving no other pardon than for troubling you with this letter, I do not now begin, but continue to be
  " Your Lordship's humble and much devoted."

The " safely " is a comment upon the whole age. Bacon was not fool enough to write to a man in so many words : " I should like to be friendly now because it won't hurt me," unless something very much more were implied. What of course was implied was the necessity, even the moral duty, of accepting the displeasure of the Crown when and where that displeasure was shown. It was an axiom which Southampton accepted as clearly as Bacon did, and Bacon accepted it not only for Southampton but, years afterwards, for himself, and Southampton accepted it not only for himself but, years afterwards, for Bacon—perhaps more eagerly. The next time they came publicly and dramatically into touch was when Southampton moved in the Lords to send as a verbal answer to the Lord Chancellor's letter of submission that "the Lords . . . intend to proceed according to the right rule of justice ; and they shall be glad if his Lordship shall clear his honour therein."

In spite of all efforts, however, when the new reign was well begun it became distressingly clear that if James graced, as he said, those whom he had heard to be popular, then he had not heard any great things about Bacon's popularity. Francis received, in the usual course of things, a warrant for a position among the Learned Counsel which was, as a matter of fact, convenient, since it seems he had never been formally confirmed as such before. He was no longer Extraordinary but ordinary. He was knighted in July, "gregarious in a troop," which was exactly what he had wished to avoid. And then he was left to himself, which, with Coke leading in law and Cecil in politics, was to be expected. For the second time in his life he seriously considered retiring. He hoped, by selling land, to be out of debt, and have an income of £300 "with a fair house, and the ground well-timbered," and he had proposed to marry, "with some convenient advancement, an alderman's daughter, an handsome maiden, to my liking." If indeed Bacon wrote the Plays, he contained himself marvellously well over this in his letters. He says no more.[1] The King abounded in councillors ; it was very different to the old days, when the quorum was small. Francis felt for the moment incapable of contending with the new time. The cause, or one of the causes, was no doubt simple : while the Queen lived, she was older, much older, than he, and he

[1] He married her magnificently on 11th May 1606. "Sir Francis Bacon was married yesterday to his young wench in Maribone Chapel. He was clad from top to toe in purple, and hath made himself and his wife such store of fine raiments of cloth of silver and gold that it draws deep into her portion." So the gossip of the time. It is a shame to put it in a footnote, but where else can it go ?

could still feel young, pressing forward in the world. But James was only thirty-seven, and Bacon himself was forty-two. At such a moment a man sees all the offices occupied, and a mass of younger men waiting for them. He held no office and he saw no hope. He began seriously to contemplate devoting himself altogether to posterity.

The King was crowned. During the next few months Bacon, not yet quite used to the idea of posterity alone, sent him a paper on the Union of the kingdoms and another on the pacification of the Church. The discourse on the Union began with Persian magic, and laid down principles of natural history, by which means discovering the congruity of Nature and Policy, it arrived at the grounds of " union and commixture of bodies," spread itself over Virgil, the Sabines, St. Paul, Julius Cæsar, Claudius and Machiavelli, touched on the union of Arragon and Castile, quadruply divided the form of union into Name, Language, Laws, and Employment, defined them, insisted that Time and Nature must make that *continuum* which was now *contiguum*, animadverted on the kingdoms of Judah and Israel, and ended with a humble offering of these simple fruits of his devotion and studies. James was polite about it, but then he liked that kind of State document. About the Church, Bacon, not being really interested, was merely political. He only wanted the Churches to be quiet, so that men could hear the news of the Great Instauration. Yet his intellectual concern involved religion. He had, some time before 1603, drawn up a paper, of which our copy, in the hand of a secretary, is headed *A Confession of Faith*. It was his own statement, for his own lucidity, since he never published it, of the Christian Religion, and its interest is in its stresses, and of these the chief has to do with the profoundly fascinating speculation of Christendom : would Christ have become incarnate if man had not sinned ? Bacon had formed the opinion which might be expected ; redemption might be the concern of his soul, but creation preoccupied his mind. "The Lamb of God was slain before all worlds " ; without that counsel, creation could not have been, and God could have enjoyed only Himself for ever. But the Lamb so slain is the Mediator, united to one nature among all created natures, by which union they exist in blessedness or in dereliction ; this is " the perfect centre and mystery of God's ways with His creatures " ; " to this all His other works and wonders do but serve and refer." In this creation, which was entirely good, " He removed from Himself the beginning of all evil and vanity into the liberty of the creature." He noted the three heavenly unities, which exceed all natural unities—of the Trinity ; of the Natures in the Incarnation ; of Christ and the Church : the Mediator being perfected, " so one, as the blessed Virgin may be truly and catholicly called *Deipara*, the Mother of God." For indeed unity was always in his mind. He had wrestled, even earlier in the *Sacred Meditations* which were published with the first edition of the *Essays*, with the problem of evil. Heresies (he said) are of two kinds, against the will of God and against the power of God, the first superstitious, the second atheistical and theomachical, and the latter are the worst, having all the same mystery—" to discharge the will of God from all imputation of evil." It seems an innocent enough desire, but Bacon declared that to do this they either set up a contrary principle of evil, or else, rejecting any such active and affirmative principle, yet proclaimed that the creature, in itself, had a natural operation towards confusion and nothingness. But this was impossible ; no created thing could have any operation merely of itself. Some also declared that man's inward choice, without any chain of causes, produced sin ; as if God only beheld, and did not predestine and preordain. But anything that does not depend on God as author and principle, " the same will be instead of God, and a new principle and kind of usurping God."

There, certainly, he gave it up, adding only that God was, of course, not the author of evil. He was author—but not of evil.

Theological metaphysics were not for Francis. But the force of that meditation is in its desire. The knowledge and power control everything. There is unity; and for unity the Mediator in creation for all things, as the King, " a mortal god," is the unity for the State, as the law of nature is the unity of nature. The prime unity is everywhere reflected ; so he believed and wrote and acted. At a remote and extreme distance the letters to the King, with their flowers, their tropes, and their rhetoric, do but acknowledge, as with a superfluous devotion, the single basis upon which the universe is reared.

One other—two other writings came from him in those months ; significantly contrasted. The one was an act of preservation, the other of perfection ; and yet both partook of both. The one was his *Apologie in certain Imputations concerning the late Earle of Essex* ; the other was his *Advancement of Learning*. That both had some reference to the temper of James is clear. There were still slander and scandal abroad ; he was still called false and ungrateful. He determined not so much to defend his action as to challenge any other action. He did not merely say he had tried not to do wrong ; he said he had done right. He said it in a manner which he could use when he chose, quite different from that stately address to James. The sentences may be as long, but the words are no longer beautifully convoluted into magniloquence ; they drive straight to their end. They assert, they dare contradiction, they defy misinterpretation. It is possible to think that Bacon mistook his duty. But that he saw his duty in this way it would seem impossible to doubt. It ends almost abruptly—" And had I been as well believed either by the Queen or by my Lord, as I was well heard by them both, both my Lord had been fortunate, and so had myself in his fortune." Hardly anywhere else does Bacon come nearer to saying : " So there ! "

Perhaps at this time also he drafted one of those preliminary efforts which he had begun now to plan and produce, a paper which might be a preface to the proclamation of the Great Work, an Apology for himself. It is supposed to be written when his life has " reached the turning-point," when he believes himself to be giving himself wholly up to this sacred industry, to be becoming that other man of whom he dreams, " the propagator of man's empire over the universe, the champion of liberty, the conqueror and subduer of necessities." It is here that he asserts how he believed his nature to possess familiarity and relationship with Truth, how with this nature and for that great end he yet thought a man's country had special claims on him, and applied himself to learn civil arts and to use his friends' favour as far as he modestly and honestly could, that, by such means reaching a place of honour, he might command greater opportunity for the work. It is here also that the fantastic distance into which the eyes of his mind stare is most completely opened in two superb phrases : Whoever wishes works and results from him, " I would have him know that the knowledge which we now possess will not teach a man even what to *wish*." . . . " there is no thought to be taken about precedents, for the thing is without precedent."

He thought he was at a turning-point. He was, but he was turning the other way. In the very commencement, in the first year of James's rule [1] and his with-

[1] " The spring-time of all happiness." The phrase is not Bacon's ; it is (delightfully) Coke's.

drawal, the mere process of things raised him again to
the beginnings of eminence. He had written letters
enough in the past; he now wrote no more—at any rate,
for some time. There was no sign that any one wanted
to employ him; very well, he would reconcile himself
to being unemployed. He knew Coke would not help
him, and he certainly had not much belief in Cecil. The
King showed no signs of grace. His health was breaking
up. He had neglected the thing he could do by himself
for things in which he had to depend on others. He
would do so no more. But his Fortune did not propose
to allow Bacon to escape so easily. He had asked for
legal and political advancement; legal and political
advancement he should have, and see what he made of
it. He had stood from Essex in obedience to the Crown;
he should now serve the Crown. Advancement should
come, not with a rush, slowly—oh very slowly, so that
he should savour it and still desire it, and begin urging
it again, and it should come to his urging, and then it
should come without his urging, until the great climax
of his public career reached him, and he should see what
he made of it. And one thing, the least little thing of
what he did make of it, should softly tread after him
and catch him up and trip him, and its claws should
tear the Chancellor's robes from his back and the Great
Seal from his hand, and fling him into a cell in the Tower
and then out again to his own house, and leave him there
neglected and spurned, and see what he made of *that*.
We have seen it ever since; it is a part of his glory.

He was, in fact, still a member of Parliament, and that
—uselessly enough, one would think—that and one of the
King's Learned Counsel was all he was, and was what
apparently his Fortune proposed he should remain. He
still had no official income. He had been knighted with
three hundred others. In that state of resigned defeat he
came to the Parliament which met on March 19, 1603/4.

He was known and admired in the House of Commons; we do not know if he was liked. But he was found a useful man; he was put on all the Committees. What was more important, he was nearly always the Reporter of the House. His mind, acting with its usual exactitude, had a way of making the business of committees and conferences clear, and committees and conferences were frequent. The Lords and Commons were not the separate august bodies which they now are; one or the other was always requesting conference with the other, which generally meant in effect the conferring of representatives of each. In such conferences a stately distinction was maintained: the Commons conferred standing and bareheaded in the presence of nobility, thus putting an additional strain on the inevitable strain which the attention necessary to follow explanation and argument involved; argument and explanation expressed in solemn rhetoric and florescent verbiage. It was not every one who could hear and understand and remember and lucidly repeat the Lord Treasurer's or the Archbishop's discourse. But Sir Francis Bacon always could. He would on the next morning make clear to the assembled House what the other House had been getting at, with those elucidating divisions of his—first, second, and so on. He was a hard worker; he could always be counted on to serve. He could draft a preamble or a clause; he could put into direct words what a number of country gentlemen might not be able to phrase so well. He did not push his own ideas; he was always willing to take the sense of the House, yet he could give them a lead in a difficulty. He had a high sense of the privileges of the House, and if he was equally sensitive to the greatness and prerogatives of Majesty, that was nothing against him so far with the Commons, who would —most of them—at this time have believed that they were equally pulsating with devotion to the Monarch.

The last Parliament in 1602 had closed in a proud ostentation of loyalty. Elizabeth had declared her love for her people and received the passionate assurance of her people's love. She had bestowed graces and received gratitude. Magnificence had robed magnanimity, and the arch of a kingdom had closed in the adorned and jewelled figure of that terrible Princess. The bright occidental star had faded; but the appearance of his Majesty, as of the sun shining in his strength, had allayed fears and composed anxieties. Nobody yet knew what strange humours the shining of that sun was to breed in the air of Westminster. Cecil foresaw it least of all; Bacon probably a little more than most— he realized it soon enough and grew nervous of Cecil's methods. But at present all was clear.

A small wrangle, in so far as the sun could wrangle with the earth it warmed or the earth with the sun to whom it offered the first fruits of its fertility, began rather sooner than had been expected; began, in fact, as soon as the House met. Sir Francis Goodwin had been elected for Buckinghamshire. Cecil did not want Sir Francis Goodwin, and when the return reached the Chancery which recorded the writs, it was fortunately discovered that he had been at some time or other officially outlawed. The return was therefore by a clause in the Proclamation for the Parliament illegal, and Coke, as Attorney, was instrumental in making arrangements to have it refused and a new writ issued. Sir John Fortescue, a member of the Privy Council, who had been very much on the scene in London when the Sheriff was conferring about the second writ, was chosen. The House, however, having been moved to examine the case, did so, and declared that Goodwin was elected. Coke brought a message from the Lords asking for a conference; the Commons declared it was against their honour to give account of their proceedings. On this the King was brought in ; Coke came back with another message that his Majesty conceived *his* honour engaged that there might be a conference.

It was this jarring of honour with honour, of " his Majesty " and " this House "—a phrase which was to become ominous and fearful—which Bacon desired to avoid. His own experience in 1593 had shown him how easily antagonism might arise. He never went back on his principles, but his language almost disguised his principles. The King fell back on the Judges. The Judges under Henry VI had declared that an outlaw could not sit ; they now declared that Goodwin was legally outlawed. The King desired the Commons to confer with the Judges. Bacon, first on the Committee, reported this charge to the House. He proceeded to urge the conference : the privilege would not be touched ; undoubtedly the House determined its members, but some power of decision before the House met there must be ; let this particular case be left to the King : let the material questions involved be considered ; let them pray to have it explained by a law what their privileges were. But this proposal did not succeed. The House stuck to Goodwin, refused to confer, drew up a long and detailed answer to the King, and sent it to the Lords by a committee with Bacon—despite his disagreement—for spokesman. There were then no formal Government and opposition parties. A man might move, speak, and vote in a particular way, but if the House determined on another way, yet, if he were a suitable member, he might be called on to express the purpose of the House. It is certain that Bacon, whatever views he might hold, never angered his fellow-members by tactless exposition of them, yet he exposed himself. It is certain that he did not refuse to be used as the House wished ; exactly how he allowed himself to be used this incident shows.

The King sent another message, saying that between the House and the Judges he was " distracted in judgment "; for his satisfaction he absolutely commanded a conference. At this the House gave way and submitted, as said Sir Henry Yelverton, to the roaring of a lion, but they warned their representatives not to budge from, but to fortify and explain, the answer sent to the Lords; whatever was said, they were not to go beyond that. Sir Francis Bacon reported on the conference, held in the presence and under the presidency of Majesty. He began by a fine distinction. The King's voice was the voice of God in man. " I do not say the voice of God, and not of man. I am not one of Herod's flatterers." The King, if he heard of it, would have recognized and approved the distinction; it chimed with his views of what a Prince should be, with his piety, with his argumentative mind, and with his folly. But, though the opening was, to our taste, a little crude, the rest of the speech walked delicately. Bacon himself had assured the King that no attack on the honour or prerogative was intended, that the House, in giving to him an account of its judgment, had done more than ever was done before since the Conquest. The King (he now reported) had eloquently, inimitably, magnanimously, royally, sweetly, and kindly answered. There was no question of privilege; all just privileges would be ratified. Parliament was, in this case, everything it claimed to be. Only so was the Court of Chancery. The Majesty proposed the setting aside of both elections, and the holding of a new.

It was apparently Bacon's first public and official meeting with James. They got on admirably. Between the Judges and the Commons accentuating their separate rightful decisions, the sweet reasonableness of the two flowed exquisitely together. The voice of God in man (" in the full dialect of his country ") proposed and the voice of man acceded, also eloquently, sweetly, and kindly. After a slight hesitation the Commons agreed. But they got Sir Francis Goodwin formally to assent first. Sir John Fortescue was probably merely told.

There was another small matter, of no importance save that again Bacon was in favour of bringing his Majesty and this House together. The jeweller Sympson who had caused Bacon to be arrested six years before had now caused the arrest of a member, Sir Thomas Shirley, at the King's entry into London. The House resolved that this was a breach of privilege and committed Sympson to the Tower. Sir Thomas, however, was in the Fleet, and it was easier to get Sympson into prison than Sir Thomas out. If the released Sir Thomas bolted, the Warden of the Fleet might be answerable for his debt. The Warden, not unnaturally, refused therefore to release his prisoner without a full indemnity. The House passed a Bill to free him from any claim, but were prevented from seeking the King's assent by some one pointing out that even to ask the King's agreement would be a blot on the Privileges. They summoned the Warden, by a writ of *Habeas Corpus*, to bring Sir Thomas to them. The Warden refused till the Bill was passed. He was sent for and given over to the Serjeant-at-Arms. Still refusing, he also was committed to the Tower. The Serjeant was sent to his substitute to demand Sir Thomas. His substitute was his wife, who refused to act except at her husband's command. The King sent a message to the House, of his own motion, thus relieving them from the awkwardness of approaching him to defend their Privilege, promising to consent to the Bill. The Serjeant was sent off again to the Fleet; the Warden's wife, in spite of secret assurances, public threats, and an offer of violence, remained obstinate—she must have her husband's command. The Warden was brought from the Tower to the Bar, but the King's

promise, of which he was told, was only a promise; he
insisted on his Bill. He was sent back to the Tower,
with orders that he was to be put in the cell called " Little
Ease." The Lieutenant disobeyed. The House, almost
in hysterics, proposed to fine the Lieutenant, fine the
Warden, throw the Warden out of his offices, send six
members to free Sir Thomas by force, sit no more till
Privilege was secured. Bacon rose: let them petition
the King not to assent to their Privilege, but to give
them the necessary force to carry it out in action. It
was a delicate but effectual distinction, " between
execution and assistance in execution." The House in
essence accepted it. The King was privately asked to
command the Warden to give way. He agreed. The
Serjeant, the Warden, and a new writ, all went back to
the Fleet. The Warden was publicly commanded to
obey the House and privately commanded to obey the
King. He did. Sir Thomas Shirley came out. Sympson
remained in the Tower; "and Sympson," as Bacon's
greatest biographer has said, " had to pay all the costs."

Such small things are but footnotes to history. But
they are footnotes at the beginning of a chapter, and
they are notes on all the persons and bodies engaged, on
Bacon not least. The mind which was secretly employed
on a thing without precedent was here employed on
things which largely turned on precedents. The union
of the whole world in the great work was here paralleled
by the union of powers in the lesser work. The mighty
argument of the age was to turn the weapons of the
Majesty and of the Commons into fell incensed points.
But Bacon did his best not only to turn the swords into
ploughshares but also—a not unimportant point—to
give the ploughshares something to do. Honour too
often jarred with honour; he desired to accord them
into a music fitting " the greatest Monarchy of the West."

There were, however, other and greater matters in

which the confrontation of the twin celsitudes of monarch and subject might rise from a confrontation to a combination, might (in Bacon's phrase) from a *contiguum* become a *continuum*. There was, inevitably, the Union of the Kingdoms, a matter dear to the King's heart and agreeable to Bacon's political vision. There were the grievances of Wardship and Purveyance, bitter to the Commons' hearts and indifferent to Bacon's political sense. He spoke in favour of Union, against which arguments were raised. Should the title of both kingdoms be changed ? If it were, would everything legally done under the old style be still legal under the new style ? Had the Union better be achieved first before the style was altered ? Did any one, except the King, really want the Union ? Arguments were interchanged ; committees sat ; conferences were held. Sir Francis Bacon toiled continually.

Something—only something—of his activity, and of the way in which that activity came before the King, can be seen by a brief table of dates :

28th March : He presents to the King the Commons' reasons against a conference with the Judges on the Goodwin election.
11th April : He meets and speaks with the King at the conference under the royal presidency.
16th April : First speech in the House on Union.
19th April : Second speech in the House on Union.
20th April : He is present as spokesman and reporter at the King's propositions on Union.
26th April : He, alone, deprecates the objections to Union raised in the House.
27th April : Speech to the King on Purveyors.
27th April : Reports on the objections to change of name in the Union.

## THE TURNING-POINT

29th April : Speaks against change of name at a Conference, protesting he does so merely for argument.
1st–9th May : Reports conferences on the Commission for Union.
11th May : He moves to request the King's help in the Shirley case.
12th May : Voted first on to the Commission.
15th June : He speaks against presenting the Commons' insistent and lengthy explanation of themselves to the King.
7th July : Parliament prorogued.
18th August : Patent as Learned Counsel and pension for life of £60.

There is no reason to believe that the King ever particularly noticed Bacon before this session, nor that Bacon in following out his line of action during the session in any way erred from his real opinion in order to please the King. His normal operation as a member of the House had thrust him under the King's notice, and his normal habit of expressing his normal beliefs had done the rest. He was the first-named of the Commissioners from the Commons ; he had at last a definite grant from the Monarch. What was more, he had now before him a business in which he thoroughly believed and to which the King attached importance. His Fortune had at last showed him good fortune. He sent to the King a marvellous summary of the whole question of Union ; on 29th October the full Commission met, and by 6th December the articles of union, as then found possible, were signed and sealed by the Commissioners. The final drawing up of the instrument was entrusted to the Lord Advocate of Scotland on the Scottish side and to Sir Francis Bacon on the English. It was ready for action, and to a large extent Bacon was responsible for having brought it into readiness for action. But Parliament was not to meet again until the next November, and the King did not find anything in which to use him. Nor, it is hardly necessary to add, did Cecil. Nor did Coke. Bacon was left for a while to his own work.

He produced the *Advancement of Learning*, pausing for a moment in his attention to it to write to the Lord Chancellor Ellesmere urging that it was time that a proper and adequate History of Great Britain should be prepared. The King and the Chancellor were the persons to encourage it; he himself had neither capacity nor time nor wish to make a start. But there were workers enough if only somebody would encourage them. Nobody did.

The *Advancement* came out at the end of October. Presentation copies were sent to the great. Bacon wrote letters to the King, to Salisbury, to Buckhurst (the Treasurer), to Ellesmere. Before they had an opportunity of reading it, however, they were distracted by a more urgent summons, or what (to their minds) appeared so, the discovery of the Gunpowder Plot. Historians now tell us that the Plot, if not actually begun by Cecil, who was now Salisbury, was at any rate permitted and encouraged by him. The question whether he began it is perhaps of some importance, since it might be argued that if he found it already in being he delayed public action in order to strike more certainly. It was believed at the time to be a real plot, even by Roman Catholics—Ben Jonson, for instance, who was employed by Salisbury to bring before the Council on a warrant of safe conduct a certain priest " that offered to do good service to the State." Jonson went to the Venetian Ambassador's chaplain, but though he received fair promises at first was afterwards met " with doubts and difficulties," and was obliged to report failure. " I would have put on wings on such an occasion and have thought it no adventure, where I might have done, besides his Majesty and my country, all Christianity so good service. And so I have told some of them." The priest, however, if ever there were a priest, took a different view.

The Catholic Jonson obtruded on the Ambassador's chaplain on 7th November. The previous morning Bacon had been disturbed in his house by a number of Protestant loyalists—the Principal and Ancients of Staple's Inn. They brought with them Thomas Reynolls, a shoemaker, of Holborn near Gray's Inn Gate, and his man John Drake. Reynolls, it seemed, early that morning had sent Drake to a customer living in Fetter Lane, a Mr. Beard, to take measurements for a new pair of boots. It was seven in the morning, and Mr. Beard was still in bed, but sufficiently awake to ask Drake whether there was much watching and warding abroad. Drake told him that Papists and Recusants were being looked for, and added that it was the most heinous treason ever intended. To which Mr. Beard, quite in the approved conspiratorial way, and like a character in Harrison Ainsworth's novels, muttered to himself, only just loud enough to be heard, "It had been fine sport if it had gone forward," and was not laughing or jesting when he said so. It is true he afterwards "spoke against the fact very much," presumably the plot, but that did not satisfy the suspicious Drake, who, after measuring Mr. Beard's foot, went back to the shop in Holborn, near Gray's Inn Gate, and reported to his master this extremely sinister mutter. Mr. Reynolls had been supplying Beard with boots for two years and remembered that he used to lodge, not in Fetter Lane but in St. John's Street, with a Mrs. Mayne. And Mrs. Mayne was rumoured to be herself a Recusant and to bring up and teach the children of Recusants. It was all very suspicious. Mr. Reynolls and Drake communicated with the nearest authorities, the Principal and Ancients of Staple Inn. The Principal and Ancients, carrying Reynolls and Drake with them, all went off to Bacon's lodgings to lodge information. Bacon, not much struck with their tale, nevertheless, examined Drake, took his testimony, and sent it on to Cecil, " not thinking it good to neglect anything at such a time."

It was all he was allowed to do. The Government did not employ him further. Cecil and Coke seized, examined, imprisoned, tortured, re-examined, and executed. The King, Lords, and Commons voted thanks and gratitude and congratulations to Almighty God and to one another, and Parliament was adjourned till January.

It is tempting, if we adopt the view that Cecil knew all about the Plot and encouraged it, to believe that he did so in order to bring the King and his Parliament together in a common emotion of horror, relief, and gratitude; achieving by this rather extreme measure the result which his cousin wished to bring about by more philosophical means. He certainly succeeded— for a little while. Bacon did not succeed, but then nobody ever seriously tried his way. When the Commons met again they were still full of righteous anger against the Roman party, of strong sympathy with themselves, and of considerable benevolence towards the King. They toyed with grievances, discussed purveyance, voted subsidies, wrangled over the Church, imposed penalties on Recusants, and though once or twice they came near disputing with the King they never actually did so. They sat for three months and were adjourned again till the next November, when the really serious question of the Union was raised.

The Union theoretically was desired by every one. But one element of union was naturalization. The gentlemen, merchants, and lawyers of England found themselves confronted with the King's desire to naturalize gentlemen, merchants, and lawyers of Scotland, who would pour south, of course, and occupy and possess lands, monies, and offices. There were two kinds of Scotsmen—those born before the death of Elizabeth (the Ante-Nati) and those born since (the Post-Nati). The Commissioners of Union had agreed to recommend two acts, each naturalizing one of these classes. But when the House, after a good deal of sharp talk on other points of the Union, came to these acts, opposition broke bounds. England was full and overfull of her own people, cramped and crowded with thrusting, hungry and meritorious shoots of her own race. An invasion of thrusting and hungry Scotch would be intolerable. Why, there were multiplying families of Scotch in Poland, and if they multiplied in Poland, what would they be like in England ? And so on and so on.

Bacon rose to take arms against this sea. He succeeded as well as Canute. He insisted that the Post-Nati were already naturalized by birth : to deny this was " contrary to reason of law, contrary to form of pleading in law, contrary to authority and experience of law." But he desired general naturalization of that nation ; he pleaded and argued for it. The Scotch were " *alteri nos*, other ourselves, a people ingenious, in labour industrious, in courage valiant, in body hard, active, and comely." Here was a most fortunate time and place for the union of two great peoples. " I think a man may speak it soberly and without bravery, that this kingdom of England, having Scotland united, Ireland reduced, the sea provinces of the Low Countries contracted, and shipping maintained, is one of the greatest monarchies, in forces truly esteemed, that hath been in the world." Spain dreamt of a monarchy in the West—Spain, who had so often been servant to empire !—because it had ravished stores of gold from unarmed peoples ; and should this island of Brittany, so seated and manned, with store of the best iron, that is, the best soldiers in the world, " think of nothing but reckonings and audits and *meum* and *tuum* and I cannot tell what ! "

The House, however, stuck to *meum* and *tuum* ; it refused to think imperially ; it longed, in the most literal sense, for a Little England. It was not at all clear that even the Post-Nati were naturalized or ought to be, let alone the Ante-Nati. It decided to hold a conference with the Lords and argue that they were *not* ; nobody was naturalized, and there was no violent hurry about naturalizing any one. Bacon was not asked to argue this, but he was appointed to introduce the subject and to report to the House.

It is an admirable example of his work. He had just declared in the House that he thought the whole refusal of naturalization wrong, and the denial of the Post-Nati illegal. He was not asked to modify it. He proceeded to explain to the Lords that the Commons were not opposing the King's wishes but only laying open the inducements that led them to their opinion. They were not rejecting Union but inquiring into it. They were, in fact, behaving modestly and properly, and they had come to talk it over. He left it to other members to give the arguments.

They talked it over that day, and on the next the judges were called in to pronounce whether the Post-Nati were, *ipso facto*, legally naturalized. The Judges pronounced that they were. The defeated and gloomy Commons retired to their own chamber, still convinced that the Nati, Post and Ante, were *not*, because (there was no other reason) the gentlemen, merchants, and lawyers of England did not wish them to be. And after all was not—nobody phrased it quite like that—but still was not the wish of the Commons of England the law ? The Judges said it was not ; they must be wrong. But it was a little difficult to prove it.

This was on 2nd March ; the debates wandered on

for twenty-six days. By 28th March they (Sir Edwin Sandys was the means) had had an illumination. Of course, the *laws* of England and Scotland were different; how could one naturalize ? What was wanted was a union of the laws, a *perfect* union, then—well, that would take a long while, and then they would see. Bacon rose to object. Union of laws would be a splendid thing, and would give opportunity for a recompilement of our own laws, "a work heroical." But to postpone the naturalization would be absurd. There was no ground for it in law or convenience. Distinction between the Post-Nati and the Ante-Nati was untenable. He made a short speech, but he stressed the immediate importance of union. "I will not much labour where I suppose there is no greater opposition." He sat down.

In the end no decision was come to. The King addressed the Houses explaining himself—twice; the Commons argued. By 8th May they had dropped naturalization and a perfect union, and took up merely the question of the removal of hostile laws, for which a Bill was prepared. Sir Francis Bacon was moved to the Chair, objected to, but "with some doubt" installed. He had a heavy afternoon's work. All objections that could be raised were raised. They would not have the word "Union" mentioned; then they would have "furtherance of the Union" instead of "establishment of the Union." They compiled a new title and a new preamble, "which Sir Francis Bacon had much ado to get consented unto." However, by the end of the afternoon they had reached the first clause, and by 30th June they passed the Bill. It received assent. On 4th July the session was closed. The King's desire had received a small fulfilment, and even what he had got was largely due to Sir Francis. Sir Francis, amid all his devotion to the Crown and his concern for the Commons, knew it. Cecil, never very good with the Commons, was now out of their House altogether, and in the Lords. The conditions of 1593 had been entirely reversed.

During those months there had been two shiftings among the holders of eminent legal office, both of which left Coke as Attorney-General. In the first case the Solicitorship was vacant; in the second it was not, though it might have been, had Coke been promoted. On neither occasion is there any sign that Bacon made any effort, or even wrote any letter, to secure advancement. But in March 1605/6 it was rumoured that Coke was to become Chief Justice of the Common Pleas. Bacon had quite definitely told Coke in his letter of 1601 that it would be impossible for the two of them to work as Attorney and Solicitor. But if Coke were to be advanced there might be a place open. He wrote to Salisbury, and the most hostile judgment could not say that he wrote with any kind of flattery or emotional appeal.

" It may please your Lordship,
" I am not privy to myself of any such ill-deserving towards your Lordship, as that I should think it an impudent thing to be suitor for your favour in a reasonable matter, your Lordship being to me as (with your good favour) you cannot cease to be,—but rather it were a simple and arrogant part in me to forbear it. It is thought Mr. Attorney shall be Chief Justice of the Common Pleas. In case Mr. Solicitor rise, I would be glad now at last to be Solicitor, chiefly because I think it will increase my practice, wherein God blessing me a few years, I may amend my state, and so after fall to my studies and ease, whereof one is requisite for my body, and the other sorteth with my mind. Herein if I may find your Lordship's favour, I shall be more happy than I have been, which may make me also more wise. I have small store of means about the King, and to sue myself is not so fit. And therefore I shall leave it to God,

his Majesty, and your Lordship. For if I must still be next the door, I thank God in these transitory things I am well resolved. So beseeching your Lordship not to think this letter the less humble, because it is plain, I remain
at your Lp's. service very humbly,
Fr. Bacon."

No alterations were then made. But in July Coke actually was advanced—and Sir Henry Hobart was made Attorney-General, leaving the then Solicitor where he was. Bacon, modestly and probably with deliberation, lost his temper. He wrote to the King, pointing out that he had been promised the Solicitorship, by the King himself, by Salisbury, by the Chancellor. The continual loss of preferment was a disgrace and a discouragement. He made humble suit that what had been promised should be performed, craving pardon for his boldness. He wrote to the Chancellor, saying that he was " a common gaze and a speech." Every new man came above him ; the little reputation his industry gathered was taken away by these continual disgraces. He wrote to Salisbury, reminding him of all the promises —the assurances—the speeches—he had received, which he had known his duty too well to—to—in fact, to believe. Of course every one knew that Salisbury was an honourable man, and he hoped Salisbury would do something, and do it quickly. Nothing happened at once, but in the course of the next six or seven months he was definitely promised the Solicitorship, and on 25th June 1607 he actually received it. When he knew it there fell on him a melancholy—the darkness that overcame him at times of good fortune ; he went sadly for a while. Almost twenty-eight years after he had returned from France and begun his public career he had at last reached a minor post in the Government. He was then forty-six years old. He had nineteen years more to live, and to live for ever.

## CHAPTER V

### "The Advancement of Learning"

THE King's Majesty had illumined the Throne for two years when Bacon addressed to it one of the most remarkable of his works; learning offering to learning the praise of learning. The knowledge in James was not of the same quality as the knowledge in his future Solicitor, but it was not so different that this new solicitation appeared alien to it. It was static and harsh rather than dynamic and tender, and static learning is a kind of self-contradiction. One purpose of picking up pebbles on the seashore is to be encouraged to pick up more pebbles because of the size, shape, and colour of those curious stones of so-called fact which we collect. James had a tendency to lock the glass of his cabinet and lecture any visitors on the treasures he had collected. Bacon looked forward not merely to walking by the seashore, but to swimming and diving in the waters; "still, leagues beyond those leagues, there is more sea." He had written, in his own defence, that it was not possible even to know what to *wish,* so ignorant was man; but the phrase, though profoundly valuable, has its other side. It might not be possible to know what great works were yet to be, but it was at least possible to see where the pattern in man's mind had so far failed in contemplation, and by what fresh discoveries that pattern might be adjusted more accurately to the simulacrum of fact. And as for tenderness, though tenderness is not the most immediate quality of his prose, yet there abides in it a certain shyness, almost a humility. The sentences are statements, dynamic statements, but there will appear suddenly in them at times a lovely deprecation or doubt, almost unnoticeable unless one is sensitive to it, but very attractive once noticed. " This I think I have gained, that I ought to be the better believed," " the admiration of whom hath carried me too far," " this I am induced to speak," " if my judgment be of any weight," " I am zealous and affectionate to recede a little from antiquity . . . as may stand with truth and the proficience of knowledge," " let those which are skilful in them judge if I bring them in only for appearance," " I could not be true and constant in the argument I handle if I were not willing to go beyond others ; but yet not more willing than to have others go beyond me again," " the errors I claim and challenge to myself as mine own." Bacon was proud of his great argument as he saw it—" this thing is without precedent "—but he was not vain : " I have put my service first and myself second "—all the clamour for place leaves that sentence, a false commonplace of the quarrels of all men, in him fundamentally true.

The opening of the *Advancement* is touched here and there, as it were with unconscious accuracy, by the experience of the writer. There is, of course, the dedication to the King. The " of course " is the only criticism that can be offered, and its ambiguity is a real ambiguity. For " of course " Bacon, needing advancement, a master of the trick of words, turned his mastery to serve his need, and hoped that the King might advance learning in a more local and personal sense than the book itself recommended. Of course he dedicated it to the King—and hoped for the best. But no less of course he, catching at every chance to advance the hope on which his heart was set, endeavoured to draw the attention of a monarch, admitted to have a real interest in knowledge, and desired that the royal mind should begin to look to the Great Instauration. Of course he dedicated it to the King—and hoped for the best. " Preservation and perfection " still ran before him.

There is, of course, the address to the King. It is followed by a defence of, a panegyric upon, learned men, with some allowance for their faults and frailties. Learning, in this sense, is " the pure knowledge of nature and universality, a knowledge by the light whereof man did give names unto other creatures in Paradise . . . according to their proprieties." The mind of man joyously receives " the image of the universal world . . . as the eye joyeth to receive light." Dear light, how Bacon loved it ! Yet even so great knowledge needs something else, without which it becomes venomous and malign ; to become truly sovereign it needs charity. It is an unexpected word to find just there, especially with that insistence upon it, but so it is. Wonder is the seed of knowledge, but neither wonder nor knowledge will serve, unless all things be applied to charity and not, as in the lack of charity, to a proud swelling.

This is fundamental. But other objections are raised by the enemies of learning. " Politiques " say that it makes men useless for purposes of government, because it makes them too irresolute or too positive or too overweening or too incompatible with the times ; it makes them love leisure and privateness ; it relaxes discipline. " Politiques "—did some past lesson of Burleigh's reverberate through his nephew's mind, the nephew who had taken all knowledge to be his province, and had (somehow) never much been helped by an uncle who had taken politics only for his ? Such objections have rather " a countenance of gravity than any ground of justice " ; that was what the young Francis had never been able to say to the countenance of gravity that had rebuked or counselled him. The world now is ransacked for examples of triumphant learning in great place. Dispose the mind to privateness? why, only learned men love business truly; others love it for profit, or worldly honour, or remembrance of their fortune, or for the exercise of some faculty wherein they take pride and so please their own conceits, or for any other their ends. But learned men love business "as an action according to nature . . . of all men they are the most indefatigable." (The records of the Chancery later were to show how true that axiom was.) And with a torrent of other examples he drives away the politiques who "in their humourous severity or their feigned gravity have presumed to throw imputations" on holy learning.

Certainly, learned men may have their faults—assuredly. For example, they too often esteem their masters' or country's good before their own. The corrupter sort of politiques—Burleigh was not that, in his nephew's eyes at least; but there had been one . . . one who had never looked abroad into universality, who had referred all things to himself, and "thrust himself into the centre of the world as if all lines should meet in him and his fortunes, who had never cared what became of the ship of State so long as he saved himself in the cockboat of his own fortunes." In the original the pronouns are not single but plural as the denouncing sentence uncoils itself. But when had Essex looked abroad into universality?

Yet directly after, so intense was Bacon's genius, he struck at what perhaps was his own chief lack. It might have applied to his relations to Essex, had not Essex overthrown those relations; there Bacon had never been subject to the trial. But indeed learned men do sometimes fail "in applying themselves to a particular person." The speech of lovers (he says as much) is not for them. If it is so, " he that cannot contract the sight of his mind as well as disperse and dilate it, wanteth a great faculty." He hastens on to other reasons why that contraction may be unwise. But the thing is said. " The exquisite examination of the nature and customs of one person " was not for him. It was a profound truth, but how exquisitely the thing he never knew was defined in all its beauty and its power !

There is one more separate and personal point, in the whole noble argument, which may be noted with a smile. Sometimes, it seems, learned men have flattered. Innocent, one might think, of the fault ; innocent, one is almost driven to suppose, of any knowledge of the fault, Bacon notes that the modern dedication of books to patrons is not to be commended ; " books ought to have no patrons but truth and reason." In ancient days it was not so ; books were only dedicated to private friends ; or if to kings, then " to some such as the argument of the book was fit and proper for "—as to one who might be in himself truth and reason, as to the Majesty who aroused such wonder in Bacon at " largeness of capacity, faithfulness of memory, swiftness of apprehension, penetration of judgment, facility and ardour of elocution "—but even such courses are to be reprehended.

It is impossible—is it ?—that he should not have realized what he was doing. He knew—did he not ?—or he was less intelligent than has been supposed. Only, knowing, what was he to do—destroy the dedication, lose the chance, the personal and the universal chance ? Perhaps, after all, he did not know ; perhaps his imagination wrote down the high austere doctrine, and his personal belief the expanding admiration. Or perhaps he knew, and excused it to himself as " stooping to points of necessity and convenience," and—how far ? oh exactly how far ?—truth.

He himself marked the limit of truth a little farther on, pausing in the midst of a procession of learned princes to say (a little proudly) that he is willing " to flatter (if they will so call it) " the dead as the living. For it is not any man's praise but the glory of learning in sovereignty with which he is concerned. There seems no reason to believe that this was not literally true. It was literally true that Elizabeth and James were learned princes—our less instructed generation calls James pedantic, and if it knew more about Elizabeth than it does might wonder if she were not also rather over-informed. A Queen who could make an impromptu speech—and a very angry impromptu speech—in Latin ? But Bacon admired such expansions in Majesty, and the pages on Alexander and Cæsar are as whole-hearted as the pages on James. It is not always mere flattery that salutes a living prince as Cæsar ; is not the very word familiar and titular at once ? Perhaps Bacon should have pruned his phrases ; let us leave the moralists to tell him so, and return to the advancement of learning.

After dealing with its opponents, he notes the various defects of learned men, and then the First Book opens on its great business—" to weigh the dignity of knowledge." He begins magnificently with God, "the Father " (he calls him elsewhere) " of illuminations or lights " ; then down he sweeps through the angels of knowledge and illumination, through light, the first created form, through that happy state of man where was no " reluctation of the creature," and enters at last upon two great pageants of learned men, the one religious, as Moses, Solomon, Saint Paul, bishops and fathers of the Church, and the contemporary Jesuits ; the other civil—Theseus, Nerva, Adrian and other emperors, Queen Elizabeth, Alexander, Cæsar, Xenophon. When these have passed, with other their peers, he contemplates the moral virtue and intellectual dignity of knowledge, its most exquisite delight, its immortal and incorruptible nature, whose monuments are more durable than all others, and whose images are ever generative of infinite action. Popular judgments go against it ; Æsop's cock prefers the barley-corn to the gem, and Midas judges for rich flocks rather than the Muses, and Paris for Beauty rather than wisdom or power—" these things must continue as they have been ; but so will that also continue whereupon learning hath ever relied, and which faileth not. *Justificata est sapientia a filiis suis.*"

The Second Part is a map of the contemporary state of learning, or would be a map were not the movement of its style that rather of exploration than of cartography. The words do not merely record facts ; they discover them. They go about time and place ; they do not say " these things are known " but rather " Man knows these things." And man in Bacon is a living, growing, active, and intellectual power ; man is his audience and his subject, his disciple and his discovery. For man to know so much is indeed a great conquest ; but it is a kind of equal if secondary triumph that, in Bacon's style, he should know that he knows it.

Merely to stand at a distance and behold has a value : let us briefly hear the summoning up of all spirits of knowledge to give their account.

Of history—four kinds : natural, civil, ecclesiastical, literary. Of natural history—three kinds : nature in course, nature varying, nature wrought upon. Of civil history—three kinds : memorials, perfect histories, antiquities.[1] (Of perfect histories—three kinds : of a

---

[1] But epitomes—" the corruptions and moths of history "—deserve to be banished, " as all men of sound judgment have confessed." What a difference three extra centuries and universal education makes !

time, of a person, of an action. And some others—as the history of cosmography.) Of ecclesiastical history—three kinds : of the Church, of prophecy, of providence. Of literary history—a deficiency.

Appendices to history—orations, letters, apophthegms. Letters " such as are written from wise men are of all the words of men in my judgment the best." As for collections of apophthegms, we have not Cæsar's, which would certainly have been the best, and for others, " either I have no taste in such matters, or else their choice hath not been happy."

Poesy—" in measure of words for the most part restrained, but in all other points extremely licensed "—is either a character of style or feigned history. As the second, it is one of the principal portions of learning ; its use is to give " some shadow of satisfaction to the mind of man in those points wherein the nature of things doth deny it." This is the equivalent of the modern doctrine of " escape " ; it is not true, but those who hold it untrue must have weighed the accusation and decided against it by judgment. Poesy is of three kinds : narrative, representative, and allusive or parabolical. In poesy, no deficience, but rather more than of any other kind. " But it is not good to stay too long in the theatre. Let us now pass on to the judicial place or palace of the mind "—knowledge.

Knowledge is of two kinds : divinity or philosophy. Philosophy of three : divine, natural, human. But beyond these there is one original, one universal science, *philosophia prima*, to which belong the great primal axioms found in different kinds in separate sciences. Nature treads her prints upon several subjects, and her footsteps are not similitudes but identities. So the principles of nature correspond to the rules of government ; the practice of music to the habit of affection ; the delight of quavering music with the playing of light upon water ; commutative and distributive justice with arithmetical and geometrical proportion. Yet they are not correspondences but truths, and this great springhead of all science, this common parent, this Berecynthia of knowledge, is yet unvisited. " This I may justly report as deficient." Shakespeare—away in the City—was perhaps discovering more of it than the Solicitor-General knew.

Divine philosophy concerns that rudiment of knowledge concerning God obtainable by the contemplation of his creatures ; and is otherwise an inquiry into the nature of angels and spirits. In neither of these any deficiency.

Natural philosophy—two kinds : inquisition of causes and inquisition of effects ; speculative and operative ; natural science and natural prudence.

Natural science, in two parts : physic, metaphysic ; that which is transitory in matter, that which is fixed ; material and efficient, formal and final causes.

Physic, in three parts : the configuration of things, the principles or seeds of things, the variety and particularity of things. None of these deficient.

Metaphysic :[1] the first part — the discovery of " formal causes " ; and here is one of the most excellent inquiries possible to man, the inquiry into essential forms. Man has supposed this discovery to be impossible, yet if possible it is of all the worthiest, and it is, it is possible. Plato knew it—" forms were the true object of knowledge "—but he erred because he supposed those forms " to be abstracted from matter, and not confined and determined by matter." The forms, not of substances but of natures and qualities—of

[1] The word, he says, is here used in a new sense. Physic has to do with " variable and respective causes " ; metaphysic with " fixed and constant causes." It is a branch of natural science, dealing with the everlasting laws.

voluntary motion, of colours, of density and tenuity, and heat and cold, and such like—not examined as in physic for their material causes—this is the great work. " It is the duty and virtue of all knowledge to abridge the infinity of individual experience as much as the conception of truth will permit." This indeed is deficient.

The second part of metaphysic : the inquiry into " final causes," not so much deficient as misplaced. " Final causes " have been mixed with physical inquiries and delayed them, so that the search of science has been neglected. From what cause is the firmness of hides ? Men have given as a final cause that it is " for the armour of the body against extremities of heat and cold," but this does not impugn the other physical cause, that " contraction of pores is incident to the outwardest parts, in regard to their adjacence to foreign or unlike bodies." Plato by his theology and Aristotle by his logic have erred here, intermingling these " final causes " with excursions into physical causes. Back then to discovery, to the fulfilment of all deficiency in the great inquiry !

The third part of metaphysics—mathematic. Mathematics, proportionable quantity, is one of the essential Forms, as Pythagoras supposed " numbers to be the principles and originals of things." More inquired into than any of the other Forms because the mind of man delights in the general rather than in the particular, and mathematics have satisfied that nature. The lofty harmonies of mathematics—he implies—are not to be bowed to " things in themselves," unless they be mixed mathematics, which are auxiliary unto natural philosophy.

Natural prudence. . . .

But it cannot be done ; or, more exactly, it has been done. The angels of man's knowledge have been called up to give account of themselves once in that little book; how can later readers epitomize the already epitomized speech of seraphs? It is not quite the voice of God in man: that description must be left to King James. It is no doubt sometimes mistaken. But the energy and the vision move and expand in page after page, and yet will not allow us to be deceived even by themselves. Universal philosophy—yes, but no rash generalizing. Excited by the grand phrases we begin to lose ourselves, as Sir Thomas Browne delighted to do, in an *O altitudo*! only to be sharply called back to our work-benches. " High and vaporous imaginations " are to be forsworn; back to " laborious and sober inquiry of truth ! " But we are to work in order to solve doubts, not to prolong them; there is no virtue in doubt. Uncertainties are to be ended; irresolutions decided; errors to be corrected; and so at last the kingdom of man achieved.

In the high discussion of the fore-ordained king of that kingdom, the *Advancement* itself advances by the same double method. The phrases of the style alternately expand and contract. Neither the great thing far off nor the little thing close at hand is forgotten. The single word " man " lies at the opening, and then the mere word seems to ramify into all kinds of branches and twigs. Above us the highest leaves flicker in the wide winds of hope; close by us the markings of single leaves distract attention, and the branches seem to invite us to climb. It would be easy to sneer; the alternative title of the *Advancement* is *Jack and the Beanstalk*, for the dream of such a survey of mortal knowledge is to us at times but of a fairy-tale country. But the beanstalk, up which the reader climbs, swaying in the wind at times when the more fanciful and more temporary clauses are touched, is at other times not so much a beanstalk as Igdrasil itself. The First Book is the contemplation of that mighty trunk of universality;

the Second Book is the vision of the climb. The great natural sciences are nearer the bottom; passing these, we reach the middle part, which is called Human Philosophy. In the old tale of Igdrasil this was the place of the worlds, above which the topmost boughs entangled the heavens, and so here this is the place of mankind. Man individual, and man conjugate or civil; man physical and intellectual, seeking fortune or deprived of fortune; man in his invention, judgment, and memory, his magical dreams and his right discoveries; man seeking his different degrees of good; man in his governments. And among all these is the hope of the present age, " in which learning hath made her third visitation or circuit," with the excellency and vivacity of its wits, the noble helps and lights of ancient writers, the art of printing, the openness of the world by navigation, the leisure of the times, their disposition to peace, the consumption of all that ever can be said in controversies of religion, the perfection of your Majesty's learning, and " the inseparable propriety of time, which is ever more and more to disclose truth." So that the night which yet lingers in places round the great divine tree may be dispelled, and men discover all learning, if only " men will know their own strength and weakness both; and take, one from the other, light of invention and not fire of contradiction; and esteem of the inquisition of truth as of an enterprise, and not as of a quality or ornament; and employ wit and magnificence to things of worth and excellency, and not to things vulgar and of popular estimation."

Finally there are at the very top of the tree the heavens themselves, " sacred and inspired divinity, the Sabbath and port of all men's labours and peregrinations." Here are the great mysteries, and the great moralities too—" Love your enemies, do good to them that hate you "—" a voice beyond the light of nature."

Here also is darkness, partly the darkness of the divine counsels, but partly the darkness of man's controversies, false desires, and misinterpretation of the Scriptures. " For the inditer of them did know four things which no man attains to know ; which are, the mysteries of the kingdom of glory, the perfection of the laws of nature, the secrets of the heart of man, and the future succession of all ages." Still looking up towards those hidden things, Francis stayed : there was the operation of the power and knowledge of God, as below is the operation of the power and knowledge of man. He had searched Igdrasil ; he had " made as it were a small globe of the intellectual world, as truly and faithfully as I could discover. . . . The errors I claim and challenge to myself as mine own. The good, if any be, is due *tamquam adeps sacrificii*, to be incensed to the honour, first of the Divine Majesty, and next of your Majesty, to whom on earth I am most bounden."

So much of learning then had been found ; so much had been mistaken ; so much was yet to find. He looked about him over it all ; he lifted his eyes and looked forward.

## CHAPTER VI

### THE APPROACH TO GREAT PLACE

#### i. THE FAVOURITES

ON 25th June 1607 Bacon was made Solicitor. It was just over fourteen years since first the possibility of his appointment to one of the great Law Offices of the Crown had been raised between himself and Anthony and Essex; and since, the Attorneyship given to Coke, the more likely office of Solicitor had been displayed equally unattainably before him. Anthony was dead, and Essex, and Burleigh, and Elizabeth. Robert Cecil, still diplomatic and amiable, remained. Coke remained. The Majesty of James had in it a cold northern gleam, and the rising Favourite now was a meaner man than the violent young patron of the early dreams. The Commons were louder and more combative than they had been; the Judges more obstinate. New faces and other minds were round him. Francis himself was older, more experienced, carrying himself with a greater ease in the world. Only one thing, more defined but not more urgent, glowed unchanged in his heart—the reorganization of the whole of human thought.

The history of his life from that June 1607 till February 1621, all but another fourteen years, can be summed up in one word—work. He was to undergo no such dangerous crisis, exterior and perhaps interior, as he had passed through in his youth. No more such perils awaited him nor any such intimate decision. He had but to fulfil the decision already taken, to follow the road he had determined, to carry out his duties.

Those duties, more specialized and more prolonged, were more exciting though less clear to him than they can seem to us: normality directed his life in a curve of activity of which the result is more evident to us than to him. At first, as Solicitor, he argued; later, as Chancellor, he gave judgment. But as his legal activity was habitual and official in both places, so that activity was directed by the influence of an official thing—the Prerogative. When he acceded to the Solicitorship the Prerogative was yet barely invaded. It lay around the Throne like a park round a palace; it was soon to be let out in suitable building lots, as so much of the Crown land had already been; complex families were to dwell there. The Families may have been the champions of freedom of whom we once heard, or the merely rich of whom we now hear; in either case they seized, occupied, and possessed the royal domain. Yet the metaphor is misleading, for the Prerogative was not a passive pleasance but an active power. It was the peculiar right of the Prince. Elizabeth had possessed it; if she had been prevented from using it, that prevention had mostly been subtle and secret. James possessed it, but even when he ascended the Throne it was already beginning to be insecure. By the end of his reign the armoury it provided was deplenished; in his son's time the last sword in it was broken.

In that growing quarrel between the King and the King's rivals men did not at once discern their proper sides, nor indeed were the loyalties quickly divided. Coke began as a Royalist and ended as a Parliamentarian. Wentworth began as a Parliamentarian and ended as a Royalist. The disputes were confused; the arguments changeable; the skirmishes doubtful. There were treaties and truces. But all the treaties and truces were broken, and the muster of the hostile forces grew yearly nearer the Throne.

The Prerogative, at the beginning of the King's reign, was still in theory a tremendous thing. The Judges still respected it as a thing greater than themselves. The Favourite existed in its shadow, and in some sense as its image ; in the sense that he, by the King's mere choice, stood on the steps of the Throne and might overawe ministers and officials. The taxes were still collected by its authority, except such extra necessities as the Lords and Commons might vote. It assisted or threatened the Church ; it raised or depressed the Nobility and Gentry ; it was the Monarch in action. It was the Monarch in action about and against whom men congregated, but not yet in clean-drilled companies. There were at present few political Ironsides.

The Monarch in action, then, was the proper concern of Bacon's political thought, as mankind in action was of his moral, as nature in action was of his contemplative, as the word in action was of his creative, and himself in action of his personal. The five movements march and countermarch through all his affairs. It is no wonder, as his spirit sought to direct their combined energy to elucidate and shape the unknown future, the next moment which, being so immediate upon the present, is yet so utterly and completely hidden, so that all of us in our occupations are but a small, pitiful, and yet living frieze of brightness upon that unchanging wall of darkness—it is no wonder if we fail sometimes to discern what motive drove one or other of them this way or the other. His energy drove them continually ; never did he cease to pursue at once those five separate concerns, and his imagination did not separate them as ours must to recognize them. They were to him a unity. But he knew what proportion they had in him ; he observed them justly ; and in the end it is inconceivable that he mistook, since his words remain heroic.

There remains, written about this period, one of

those documents which present a man at his work, which indeed present him not merely as working but also as living. In July 1608 Bacon took the opportunity of the beginning of the Long Vacation to clear up his old notebooks. He took a new book; he headed it: "Commentarius Solutus sive Pandecta sive Ancilla Memoriæ." He divided it into two parts: the first being comments transferred from an old *commentarius* from diary and schedules; the second a new and current *commentarius*. A great deal of argument has been spent on this notebook; Bacon's hopes, intentions, doubts, desires, anxieties, and dreams have been called as evidence against the imagination from which they sprang. There can be no objection, so long as the nature of the evidence is realized, and so long as we subordinate ourselves to the same court of integrity. A man who liked writing and order wrote down his thoughts; our disordered minds must not escape accusation because we do not like writing. Any wife who has listened patiently to her husband's stories in order to keep him in a good temper; any hopeful nephew who has been tactful with a rich uncle; any inferior who has opportunely smiled at a superior's jests—had they only written down, "To listen to Jack," " to laugh at the master's puns," would be damned as Bacon has been damned. They do not, because (no doubt) they would be ashamed. But whether they are clear about their shame, and how far that shame extends. . . .

Bacon was always clear. His intelligence, exercised on a mental problem, acquitted itself as admirably as it always did. He began, on that Monday morning, with perhaps the most heroic resolution of all, a resolution carried over from his old diary or schedule:

"To make a stock of 2000[l] allwaies in readyness for bargaines and occasions.

"To sett my self in credite for borowing upon any great disbursem$^{ts}$; Swynerton; Sir Rich. Mullineux; my sister Periam; Antropos; Jh. Howell per Champners; Sr. M. Hickes."

Either immediately or at some future time he crossed these notes out: perhaps because he was to transfer them to some other book, perhaps because his intelligence. . . . But there are similar hopes not crossed out. On the Thursday he went into figures much more fully, estimating his property. And his debts. These are not altogether easy pages to make out, and are of no urgent importance. His wife (it may be remarked) had three feathers ("upright, crooked, flowre de luce") valued at a hundred pounds each, and "the pendants my tokens" valued at fifty pounds. But in reckoning the worth of such things, he puts down "100$^l$," so freely as to make the reader doubtful. "My wyves apparell and furnit," "Myne own apparell. Sabells wardrope stuffe," "The hangings, carpets, cusshins at Gorhamb," "The furniture of my chamber at Graies Inn, w$^{th}$ bookes and other impl$^{ts}$," "My gilt plate," all go down at a hundred pounds each. "My Clocke" is ten pounds; "my pointed and Table diam$^d$," sixteen; "my other Rings," ten: but against this three-itemed thirty-six there appears an inclusive bracket, and against it, "100$^l$." If he really summarized value as that entry suggests, a good deal of his financial stringency is explained. His annual revenue he worked out at 4975$^l$, with various hoped accessories, among which was "the keeping of my howse Gor. chargeless by some fitt person, for the use of a lodging there." His debts he reckoned at 4481$^l$; at the end of the notebook, three months later, on 28th October, he made another list of these, but this time they came to 4740$^l$, in spite of the fact, for example, that Mr. Bradshaw, draper, is queried in the first for

£30, and down in the second for £30, 15s. with £20 paid off. Actually this name is crossed out, so perhaps he was paid.

After the financial notes on that first Monday morning Bacon transported another, to which and to its like he also returned during the ensuing days and pages.

" To sett on foote and mainteyn access with his M. D. of the Chapel.   May.   Jh. Murry."

The Dean of the Chapel was also Bishop of Bath and Wells, and was presently to edit the King's Works, which were published in 1616 (when Shakespeare died. Perhaps the ghostly powers amused themselves in that way with an undeserving world). The other gentlemen belonged respectively to the Privy Chamber and the Bedchamber. They were suitable persons to be channels between Bacon and the King, and such channels he both wished and needed. He noted that he must be privily known to be affectionate to the Scotch—as indeed, politically, he had been. He noted that he ought to have in readiness matter to talk on to any of the great councillors; both "to induce familiarity and for countenance in publike place"; to this in another place he returned, " To have particular occasions, fitt and gratefull and continuall, to mainteyn pryvate speach w$^{th}$ every y$^e$ great persons. . . . This specially in publike places and w$^{th}$ out care or affectation." To this he made a little addition : " qu. for cred$^t$ ; but as to save time ; and to this end not many things at once but to drawe in length." One sees Bacon catching a " great person " in some public place on some particular fit piece of business, almost, as it were, accidentally and to the content of the personage involved who would go on feeling gratefully what a wise, quick, industrious, and tactful worker Bacon was. As indeed he was.

He noted that at the Council table he was chiefly to support Salisbury, " and for the rest sometymes one, sometymes another; chiefly his y$^t$ that is most earnest and in affection." On any unimportant matter he was ready to be defeated, or argued down; not, certainly, on important. Salisbury was a difficult matter altogether; Francis had always been uncertain of his cousin, and that not merely personally. He was doubtful of their personal relations; he was doubtful of Salisbury's political intelligence. He made several notes—he was to "insinuate" himself into Salisbury's estate; he was to correspond with him in a natural "but nowayes perilous" boldness. Vivacity, invention, care to cast and enterprise—but all with due caution. This would, "I judge," please him best and promise most use of Bacon. But also Salisbury was to be reminded of what great things were expected of him; he was to make the King's payments certain, deal modestly with recusants, remedy unlawful transportation, moderate new impositions. It was the first and the last that were the difficulty; in another note Bacon remarks that in corresponding with Sa. concerning levies and such things he must have regard to empty coffers and the alienation of the people. Something more than alienation was on its way; the access of the Commons to the King's Majesty was presently to be by rougher means than by the good offices of bishops and grooms of the chamber. Bacon was already anxious; on the Wednesday he jotted down obscure sentences concerning high politics.

Empty coffers; poverty bringing the King low; the revolt first in Scotland; till then no danger of English discontent; in doubt of a war from thence.

Greatness of some particular subjects; popularity of Salisbury; was he acceptable to the Lower House?

The greatness of the Privy Council.

The greatness of the Lower House.

Query of the office of Lieutenant Constable:

The absence of the Prince if he come to the Crown by wars.

They run on, those curious notes—they leap into personal decision—" Succeed Salsb. and amuz. the K and P with pastime and glory." They dream of a great monarchy in the west—" an apt seat, state, people "—civilize Ireland, colonize the wilds of Scotland, annex the Low Countries. Confederacy or straight amity with the Low Countries. Amplify a monarch in the Royalty. Restore the Church to proper order since Henry the Eighth's confusion. New laws—the lawgiver *perpetuus princeps*. Finish my treatise of the greatness of Britain. " It is likely Salisbury hath some further intent upward." Books in commendation of mixed monarchy or aristocracy. Persuade the King in glory, *Aurea condet secula*.

They were " transported " ; they were jottings taken from old jottings ; they do not declare themselves as new and considered judgments. But are they dreaming of greatness as a danger ? " The greatness of the Lower House." Was he thinking of gathering an aristocracy round the King, glorious in his monarchy, as a show or as a defence ? In what wars was the Prince to come to his own ?

The greatness of Britain was not his sole concern ; the greatness of Francis Bacon counterpointed it. His immediate superior, the distinguished Attorney-General, Sir Henry Hobart, was noted down. " Solemn goose," wrote Bacon brutally, " least wise no crafty. They have made him believe he is wondrous wy." and drew up a list of his disadvantages, with another note elsewhere, " to have in mynd and use ye Att. weaknes$^s$." " The coldest exam. . . . Nibbling solemnly he distinguisheth but apprehendeth not. . . . No gift with his penne in proclamations and y$^e$ like. . . . He will alter a thing but not mend." But that no mortal mind can rightly judge another, one might conclude that Bacon had some grounds for being contemptuous of Sir Henry Hobart—" he never beats down unfitt sutes with law."

But there were also his own present purposes. The sentence on insinuating himself into Salisbury's estate ends : " Noting it to Hickes and $y^t$ my L. hath been once or twice about it," and then, as if the name Hickes reminded him of other things, he is away at Gorhambury ; " Causing the waulkes about $y^e$ wall to be sanded and made handso, against Hickes comyng. So the old waulkes $w^{th}$ rayles and swept : Plott to be made of my poole : and the waulk through Pray wood and $y^e$ stand thear on the hill for prospect." Or, " under that waulke some 4 foote to have a fyne littell stream rune upon gravell and fyne peppell to be putt into ye bottome of a yard and a half over, $w^{ch}$ shall make the whole residue of the ground an Island." There was to be another walk within it, the border with flags " of all sortes of flower de Luces and Lylyes." There was to be a lake with a fair rail, with gilt images round about it and some low flowers, especially violets and strawberries.

In the middle of the lake was to be an island " of 100 broad," and in the middle of that a house with an upper gallery open on the water, a terrace above it, a supping-room open under it ; a dining-room, a bed-chamber, a cabinet, a room for music, a garden ; in the garden a walk between trees ; nothing planted here " but of choyse." There were to be other islands, one with a rock, one with a grotto, one with flowers in ascents, one paved and with pictures ; and each to have a separate fair image to keep it, triton or nymph ; and one with an arbour of muskroses and double violets for scent in autumn, some "gilovers $w^{ch}$ likewise dispers scent."

That the master of these pleasant places might enjoy them more he jotted down his observations on his health, what medicine he had recently taken, its results.

Once, after it, he had found no lightness and cooling but "a symptom of melancholy such as long since w$^{th}$ strangeness in beholding and darksomness, offer to groan and sigh, whereupon fynding a malign humor stirred," he took some more. Also later on : " I tooke a littell of my Troc of Amon. after supper and I tooke broth ymediately after my pill."

"When I was last at Gorhambury I was taken much w$^{th}$ my symptome of melancholy and dout of present perill." But he put that down to "soppe w$^{th}$ sacke taken midde meale." He found that sleeping in the afternoon was a bad thing, but, somehow, could not conquer his inclination to it.

But before all this he had gathered the notes which lay even nearer to his own heart. On Tuesday he set down those with whom he must become intimate for that purpose, so secret and so open, which had driven him since Cambridge. He would make much of Russell, who would draw on Sir David Murray and by him the Prince might. . . . My lord of Northumberland and Raleigh and Haryott the mathematician—all these were themselves inclined to experiments—the physician Poe and his experiments of physic ; other physicians to be gained, Paddy (the King's physician) the likeliest ; learned men beyond the seas—who are they that are so inclined ? the Archbishop is single and glorious—might he be tried ? the Archbishop to be approached on Sutton's will (could Sutton's legacy be used for founding colleges ? It was used for the Charterhouse). Bishop Andrewes—single, rich, sickly, a professor to some experiments ; Sir Josias Bodley ; young scholars in the Universities. And to be *done*—finish the Tables of Motion, the Aphorisms, translate into Latin the *Advancement of Learning*, query an oration *ad filios*, for the young, the young—procure a History of Marvels with popular errors detected, procure a History Mechanique, observations of all mechanical arts, with inquiries of necessary materials, instruments, use of every instrument, the work itself, and all the process, times, and seasons, all observations, all things collateral, incidental, or intervenient ; to plan a place to command wits and pens—speak of this to the King, to my lord Archbishop, to my lord Treasurer, get pensions for four searchers to compile the histories, found a college for inventors, with rules, allowances for travelling and experiment, vaults, furnaces, terraces, galleries, an enginry, workhouses of all sorts, intelligence and correspondence with the universities abroad ; endeavour to abase the price of professory sciences. And always and in every way " to bring in æstimation Philosophy or Universality—name and thing."

So he gazed and brooded and planned and wrote, when the fourteen years of work were but beginning. Into all the details of the work it is possible for specialists only—how many specialists ! how many kinds !—to enter. A man nowadays, who had heard of Bacon, wandering through a library, and taking down the histories, first one kind, then another, the accounts of man's activities through the centuries, would find himself, if he glanced at each index, continually and astonishingly confronted with one name. There it is— in histories of biology and music, of constitutional law and industrial developments, of economics and literature, of philosophy and architecture, of man's creeds and man's knowledge, ponderable and imponderable things —" Bacon, Francis, pp. . . ." Here a paragraph, there an allusion, deprecating comment, judicial summary, exquisite homage, pages and pages of him. There he is, exact, prophetic, mistaken, fantastic, august, intimate—there everywhere he is, imposed on us by the energy, curiosity, and fanaticism of lucidity that filled him, till we grow tired of so much genius and try to forget.

But all that energy, directed into those five move-

ments of his mind, is concerned with things and with
things in detail, holy detail, the test of genius. The
genius of the creative mind concerns itself with detail ;
it may mistake in its judgment, but it is not vague in
its recognition of facts ; it sees them as Shakespeare
saw the eyelashes when he was busy with the young
simplicity of Miranda's spirit—" the fringéd curtains
of thine eyes." So Bacon, dividing and redividing his
speeches and his papers till the clauses seem to out-
number even the fringes of those eyelids, so numerous
are they, ripples on the five great rivers of his being.
In the first of those rivers, flowing securely on through
fourteen years, the Monarch in action, are reflected the
images of the Favourites, the Parliaments, and the Laws.
In the second, men in action, are first the faces of his
friends and enemies, and later more universal figures, the
men of whom he writes in the *Essays*, classes and types
of universal mankind. The third is himself in action,
and this (so far as it was his personal concern) is now
for long almost indistinguishable—its murmur is heard
but its course is hidden till it breaks suddenly into
hurrying and surging life for a little and then disappears,
swallowed up by earth. The fourth, which is nature in
action, at first wanders farther off, and then flows nearer,
shining under the full glory of his sun of great place—
Baron, Viscount, Chancellor, but shining no less with
its own glory when that sun is obscured. But the
fifth—the fifth is rather the name given to the river
into which all those others run than to any separate
stream ; it is the mighty movement which receives them
and is grander than all ; it swells into its fullest breadth
and its noblest course after Francis Bacon has been
buried by its side, as his body lies buried under the tower
of St. Michael near the actual stream from which his
title had its remotest origin ; it is the lordly current
which flows into that well-watered land where holy

Imagination dwells for ever and blesses the consciousness of mankind—the word in action.

The Monarch in action meant the Prerogative among principles and the Favourite among men. The Majesty of James distinguished two Favourites, Robert Carr, Earl of Somerset, and George Villiers, Duke of Buckingham. Villiers was, almost formally, invested with the royal favour in March 1616, Carr having fallen in 1615. James had ascended in 1603, and Carr had come southward with him. He had afterwards been elevated to the steps of the Throne. It would, of course, be widely known what adulatory, what fawning, what time-serving letters the King's officer wrote to the Favourite, what monies, what advancements, what advantages he implored. It would, were there any. The surprising fact is that there are none. There is one letter from Bacon to Somerset; there are none from Somerset to Bacon. It is a fact almost ridiculous. There is a complete blank in such intercourse for thirteen years. Essex—yes; Buckingham—yes; but Somerset—no. After making all allowances for destruction of documents one is still compelled to believe that Bacon wrote very little to Somerset. Entirely at his own expense he presented a magnificent Masque on the Earl's marriage. He took part in the prosecution that destroyed him. He alluded to him twice in later letters. And there intercourse ends. It is surprising on any theory; it is bewildering if Bacon was the time-server and opportunist he is often thought and sometimes seems to be. But it is perhaps comprehensible.

Two of those rare allusions may help to explain. One occurred in February 1615 in the letter Bacon wrote to the King explaining that he was the right person to be made Chancellor. It was after Somerset's committal on a charge of murder, and after Bacon had begun to grow acquainted with Villiers, and Villiers to be marked

for advancement. It is therefore in a sense suspect.
But as it is almost the only piece of personal evidence
we have we must do our best with it. His Majesty,
Bacon says, made him Attorney of his own motion, save
that " my Lord of Somerset, when he knew your Majesty
had resolved it, thrust himself into the business for a
fee." The second reference is in a letter to Villiers,
9th April 1616, also, for the same reasons, suspect.
Bacon thought " no man was liker to be a pensioner (of
Spain) than Somerset, considering his mercenary nature."
Assuming the worst, Bacon chose, for every kind of
selfish reason, to blame Somerset, but he still chose to
blame him for being mercenary. Assuming the best,
he thought Somerset was mercenary. It is our only
reason; that it seems hardly enough is merely due to
the fact that we have not troubled to understand what
Bacon was or what he did. The one thing that he
certainly was not was mercenary. He was magnificent,
but he was never mercenary. He hated a clutching
hand always and everywhere. And if Somerset wanted
to bargain for his favours it supplies an entirely adequate
explanation of why no petitionary letters ever went to
him. Absurd and contradictory, false and hypocritical
as it may seem, Bacon believed in doing things for love.
That remarkable blank has lain for three centuries in
mute testimony to the singular honesty of his mind.
He was always consistent in faults and visions. He
disapproved of bargaining; he approved of gracious and
willing interchange. He was not ashamed of money;
money was one of the methods by which men conversed
with each other and were related. He held it no more
undignified to give the King money than to give him
any other service, and as worthy of note. The separation of money into a solitary, secret, and shameful
thing seems to be modern. But bargaining about it—
that he did dislike. His hatred of it even blasted itself

a place, years afterwards, from the Lord Keeper's chair. In the year 1617 there was brought before him a cause of the sort, which had previously been before the Lord Chancellor Ellesmere, and been by him dismissed. An appeal to the King by the plaintiff had brought the cause before Bacon for re-hearing.

There was in Berkshire a gentleman named Anthony Blagrave, with a son John Blagrave, who in August 1613 had a desire to be knighted. He was acquainted with a certain John Freeman of London, who had served in the wars, and had—or pretended to have—many friends about the King's person. John Blagrave talked the matter over with him, saying that his friends were urging him to achieve a knighthood. It was understood between them that by means of his friends Freeman should move the King to bestow the honour, and in return the new Sir John would show Freeman some small consideration —Freeman claimed that this was £300; John and his father, who probably was to pay, claimed that it was " far under " that sum, and was in any case only to be paid if the knighthood should be bestowed within a fixed time. After much labour and expense (according to his own statement) Freeman succeeded; with no use of Freeman at all (according to John's) the dignity was offered. John stated that he postponed accepting till the fixed time was over, and then went to James and received it. The parties differed in their account of the method, but they both agreed that neither the £300 nor any lesser sum had been paid. Freeman brought an action against son and father. The son swore he had never promised except under conditions which had not been fulfilled; the father swore that he had always dissuaded John from speaking to Freeman about his wishes, and had certainly never mentioned the matter himself. And that talk of expense was absurd—he and John both swore that. The evidence before Bacon showed that they were right; Freeman had been trying to cheat them. The cause was dismissed—with the additional intimation from the Lord Keeper that he entirely disapproved and disliked the suit "because it tended to the making of matters of knighthood venal and mercenary."

It was not mercenary and venal to give money to the King and to be knighted; but to commune about it, to make it the subject of contract, to touch this high bestowal of grace with private purchase and secret bargaining—this was what offended Bacon, gazing from his Chancery seat as from his place in the Privy Council on holy and generous interchange. To give freely and take freely—that was the secret of statesmanship, as of learning, as of life itself. One might ask or plead, but not wrangle; that dimmed the fine execution of a fine intention. He had in himself always some such fine intention. He would not accept the "assurance of the Chancellorship" because he would not endure the relation between himself and Lord Ellesmere which would arise from such an assurance. It is true he also wanted to be Privy Councillor (he was offered the choice between the two). But it would be a good thing for the Realm for him to have a seat at the Table. It is true it would also be a good thing for him. But the good thing for him would help him to draw attention to the Great Instauration. It is true the Great Instauration was more himself than himself. But whether this is folly or wisdom, conceit or devotion, egotism or altruism, is for moralists to decide. Such a vision is as much not oneself as it is oneself, and that double fulfilment is only reconcilable or separable by God. It pleased God to separate it in Bacon. Meanwhile the mercenary bargain was a thing wholly opposed to glory, the glory of which he had learned and poets had sung in those old days of his youth. Elizabeth, who had understood that dream and so acted in it that we when we remember her have for three hundred years lived and thought in it also, was dead. The person of James was neither by appearance fitted nor by choice determined to pursue and possess so rich a dream. The art of Elizabeth was to make herself one with Majesty; James rather appropriated Majesty to himself. In a somewhat similar way Elizabeth had worn her learning as a cloud of golden splendour, while James contracted it into a coronet, golden no doubt but worn as a personal adornment. It was perhaps but a trick of the Queen's behaviour, effective because of the strength of her determination to remain Queen of England. But at least she imagined herself as Queen of England, so that it is not absurd to think of Spenser and Shakespeare also imagining her in their lines. James knew he was King and tried to enter into that imagination, but he failed, not entirely through his own fault. His comments on Majesty and the Prerogative read rather like critical explanations of Shakespeare, while Elizabeth is the play itself—*Hamlet* and *Henry V* and *Antony* with Cleopatra —Enobarbus's Cleopatra—and all, not excluding *Titus Andronicus*.

Bacon, however, did not see the change. Majesty was always Majesty. He discerned and to the best of his ability devised a great future for that Majesty; he saw in his vision a long line of kings " that twofold balls and treble sceptres carry." The almost divine decisions of those sacred and anointed persons were to be carried into effect at home by their Favourites, their Ministers, their officers, their lawyers, their servants. Abroad they were to be, if less obeyed, hardly less respected; they were to stand on the extreme of Europe, the Monarchy in the West, a Monarchy amplified in royalty. He had touched on this at the conclusion of his speech in the House for the Union of the Kingdoms; he had noted it in his private *commentarius*; he meant to dwell on it in his treatise on *The True Greatness of Britain*.

That he looked no farther than to Nationalism, to the firm establishment of the Monarchy of the West, is certainly true. He was not unwilling to look through foreign wars to the advancement of its glory, and nowhere proposed to subordinate it to some sovereign Emperor or League. The schism in Europe forbade. The universality of thought was separated from the particularities of government, and the bell that was to call learned men together was also at odd times to ring alarum for the English against the foreigner. That disposition is comparable to the division of his mind between politics and philosophy. His imagination was uneasy at the contrast between immediate political causes and the fundamental unity which underlay politics and all other knowledge, and was sometimes stirred to regret. But such regret was inevitable.

Towards the end of his occupation of the Attorneyship, when the Lord Keeper was already ill and the Attorney inevitably saw his chair vacant, and as inevitably hoped to fill it, Somerset fell. He was accused, with the Countess, of the murder of Sir Thomas Overbury in the Tower by means of poisoned tarts. Our natural desire to read of wickedness in high places, the desire that has nourished itself on Tiberius and the Borgias, has taken pleasure in imagining even darker intrigues within that dark plot. There are indeed the most thrilling properties; it is a wonder no poet has yet made a neo-Elizabethan drama out of them. Thomas Overbury, politician and author, imprisoned in the Tower by the machinations of the unscrupulous Favourite; his death; the rumour two years later that reaches the Secretary Winwood; Winwood's conversation with Sir Gervase Hellweyse who had at the time been Lieutenant of the Tower; the hinting at "great persons"; the appointment of

Commissioners by the King; the arrest of Weston (once under-keeper at the Tower), of Mrs. Turner (procuress and ruffmaker), of Franklin (apothecary and venom-merchant); their execution; the occult sorceries in the background; the committal of the Earl and Countess of Somerset; the strange contradictory parting of the King from the Favourite; the appalled and pious rhetoric of Coke from the judgment seat, the public reading of the evidence against the great prisoners before they were put on trial; the wild and growing rumours—that the Earl had declared he would reveal something which he had kept secret, that the King durst not bring him to trial, that midnight messages had gone to the King at Greenwich by the mouth of Sir George More, that the King, weeping with distress, had begged help of Sir George, that a secret promise had been given to Somerset of entire freedom if he would confess his guilt—all this has suggested the painting of a picture of James like King John whispering in the ear of his own physician "Death . . . a grave," of the need of murder to destroy a witness to appalling vice, of James plotting to destroy Somerset, his cast-off love, of James trembling and fear-stricken, of miserable iniquity and indescribable subtlety of hate and terror. It may be so, and it may be that the King's Attorney, like the King's Chief Justice, was working at the King's will. Evidence in those high fantasies of death hardly counts; we believe what we will. The exquisite figure of George Villiers is appearing in the background—" full of delicacy and handsome features," " hands and face especially effeminate and curious," " affable and gentle." Between the royal vices to which he was about to minister and the royal powers which were to minister to him, he advances towards glory, with the Attorney helping to clear the way before him. A double corruption has tainted the heart of the herald of man's lucidity of knowledge and empire of power; the worms that coil in his heart strike their poison through the tongue of Sir Francis Bacon.

It is more likely to be but a Borgia dream; more probably Bacon took his part in the prosecution of Somerset as in any other of the inevitable troubles of his office. It was a police affair, but also a political. He wrote, among other things, in an ignorant prophecy, that "the downfall of so great persons carrieth in itself a heavy punishment, and a kind of civil death." Bacon had to take a good deal of trouble over the matter. The King was certainly not anxious to bring Somerset to trial, as Elizabeth had not been anxious to bring Essex to trial. They had been lovers. But Coke's oration of horrified credulity had given expectation wings. He had raved of death and destruction, of plots worse than the Gunpowder, of the mystery of the death of "that sweet babe, Prince Henry."

Bacon, examining the evidence, found it "of a good strong thread" but needing to be well spun together. Opinion had been so excited with talk of plots and deliverances "as great as ever happened to any of the children of Israel" that the mere facts would be disappointing. A public trial which found Somerset innocent would have the worst results both ways; he would be free and would hate the King ever after, and public opinion would believe there had been trickery and suppression. If Somerset would confess, this could be avoided. Efforts were made to get Somerset to confess; mercy was practically promised, whereas if he refused to confess and were found guilty, his danger was clear and imminent. The Countess at her trial confessed; the Earl refused to confess, and the King was determined that no mercy should be shown except upon confession. The trial took place; Bacon acted as prosecutor, and the accused Earl was found guilty. He said nothing about the King, and he and the Countess disappeared into the Tower for six years. George Villiers, already uniquely illumined among all the courtiers by the special favour of the King's person acting from his Majesty, mounted the steps of the Throne. By a fortunate conjunction of circumstances, a conjunction so fortunate that the possibility of a royal treachery whispers rumours in the ear, James was enabled to be off with the old love in the most definite manner before he was on with the new. He proceeded to encourage the new. Honours and estates were waved on to the charming figure of the beautiful young man now elect of Majesty. Bacon had never been on with the old love ; that difficulty of mercenary bargains had lain between. But Villiers was not mercenary ; he was so far hardly proud. He was generous—not in Bacon's sense but in his own ; however, at present the difference was hardly noticeable. The Attorney-General's letters were agreeably deferential, but deferential with an air. In the new air of power Villiers was stepping delicately, and the Attorney impressed him.

He seems to have recognized, as Essex had recognized, something great and preservative in Bacon ; he asked him for advice. Bacon gave it him—perhaps, as Essex had found, rather more than he expected, and perhaps in a more serious style. He warned him in the most solemn manner, as became " a hermit rather than a courtier." " You are now the King's Favourite. . . . Remember then what your true condition is . . . remember well the great trust you have undertaken. You are as a continual sentinel, always to stand upon your watch, to give him true intelligence. If you flatter him, you betray him. . . . Kings must be answerable to God Almighty (to whom they are but vassals) for their actions, and their negligent omissions. But the Ministers to Kings, whose eyes, ears, and hands they are, must be answerable to God and man for the breach of their duties, in violation of their trusts, whereby they betray them."

The whole kingdom looked on the new Favourite as the rising star; no man thought his business would prosper unless Villiers supported it or at least did not oppose it. This, Bacon warned him, could not be avoided, " unless you will adventure a precipice." It is not likely that Villiers had the smallest wish to adventure the precipice; he was quite willing to be the master of all suits. Bacon went on to give him rules. He was to have all suits of importance set down in writing, and let his secretary underline in each petition the real matter, " which always lies in a narrow room "; let copies be made, since neither Villiers himself nor a few private friends could " comprehend the true reason of all things," and let those copies be sent to suitable advisers—a copy to each, not revealing the one to the other; and so let an answer be determined and swiftly, reasonably, and fairly delivered.

Suits would fall into several classes. In religion let the Favourite remain faithful to the Church of England and its doctrine as in the Thirty-Nine Articles; to question that is to endanger the stability of our Religion " which hath been sealed with the blood of so many martyrs and confessors as are famous through the Christian world." So in law let him take care of the Common Laws of England; let great advice and intelligence be had from the Judges, both on the laws and (after circuit) on the state of England; let none be advanced to the Bench but " only with an eye upon the public good "—for " in the laws we have a native interest; it is our birthright and our inheritance." Let men of great experience be used for matters of State. For matters of peace and war, the King was settled for peace—" *beati pacifici.*" But security is an ill guard; let all be prepared, commanders, arms, ammunition, ports and forts. Civil war is terrible ; let prince and people pray and work against it. For a foreign war to enlarge empire " I have not much opinion either of the justness or fitness of it." Foreign Plantation and Colonies are honourable and profitable ; but no man is to be compelled to it ; if any schismatic or criminal settles there he is to be sent back ; " no extirpation of the natives under pretence of planting Religion ; God surely will no way be pleased with such sacrifices " ; in the establishment of trade, let care be taken that the export of home commodities " be more in value than the importation of foreign," and let foreign commodities be for necessity and pleasure, but not for luxury. Let native commodities be advanced, and our countrymen employed before strangers. Above all, " I would recommend to your care the encouragement to be given to husbandry, and the improving of lands for tillage : there is no such usury as this." In matters of Court, let the Favourite not much interpose, except in his general trust not to suffer the King to be abused. But there, not to draw envy upon himself, let him tell the King and then let the King pretend to find it out by accident.

Finally, let the Favourite bear himself discreetly between the King and the Prince, neither making the father jealous or the son suspicious.

At some later moment—hardly of leisure but of change of labour—Bacon revised this letter, either for Villiers himself or as a general *Letter of Advice to a King's Favourite*. He enlarged it, but did not greatly alter it. A few additions are perhaps worth noting.

The Favourite will often be solicited to prefer scholars to church livings ; let him remember " that these are places not merely of favour ; the charge of souls lies upon them." Let him see that the patrimony of the Church be not sacrilegiously diverted to lay uses. (Bacon, after all, had not inherited *much* of his father's land.) Colleges to be cherished. " This kingdom hath in this later age been famous for good literature ; and if preferment shall attend deservers, these will not want supplies." (It was about the end of August ; but probably Bacon had not heard that Shakespeare was dead at Stratford. Unless of course he had to find another *imago* for his plays.)

" By no means be you persuaded to interpose yourself, by word or letter, in any cause depending, or like to be depending, in any court of justice, nor suffer any man to do it where you can hinder it ; and by all means dissuade the King himself from it, upon the importunity of any either for their friends or themselves." If any " should indirectly or directly bargain for it, let him be rejected with shame." The practice of allowing fit men who were picked for sheriffs to avoid serving, and others to be nominated, " and both for money " is to be utterly condemned. Parliament is " more properly a Council to the King . . . to advise his Majesty . . . than a court " ; its true use is very excellent. But if privilege and rights should be unjustly enlarged, " they might lessen the just power of the Crown, it borders so near popularity."

" For the true art of building of ships, for burthen and service both, no nation in the world excels us." The planting of wood both for shipping and building is commendable ; so also of orchards, kitchen-gardens, hop-yards ; so is draining of drowned lands, settling of dairies, making navigable rivers, planting hemp and flax, breeding cattle, especially horses ; minerals—lead, copper, iron, tin—are to be worked. Fishing is to be encouraged in itself and as a support to the navy. Monopolies are to be by no means admitted under the colour of public goods ; they are the canker of trade.

The mind of the reader plays with the alternatives of history, devising futures. If Bacon had been obeyed ; if Villiers had been sympathetic ; if James had been gracious—if the Royalty had enlarged itself upon such maxims—what would that century have shown? Could the power of the Monarch in action have repelled the Families? would the Prerogative have succeeded, recovered Crown-lands, defeated enclosures, raised funds, renewed itself in a triumphant Stuart line? And would the common people of England have been more fortunate so? That at least is not very likely; the luck of the poor would probably not have been much better, as assuredly it could not have been any worse. For it was not merely that Bacon's advice was not taken; his imagination also was out of date. He was almost the last man in England to believe in philosophical kingship; the principle of Majesty had eluded its possessors nearly as soon as it was defeated by its opponents. Like the secret of many another sacrament, it seems to fade from the world at the moment of manifestation.

In fact, therefore, his imagination being alien to the King and the Favourite, his counsel was, on the whole, neglected. His mind was passed over during the reign of James, as under Elizabeth he himself had been passed over. Few men, setting their heart upon great place in order to achieve the high purpose of their heart, have, both before and after achieving it, at the same time been so consistently ignored. His master did not follow his political counsel; the new Favourite grew away from him as the Elizabethan Favourite had done; the Commons admired, used, refused, and overthrew him; his friends were polite but not much more than polite about the Great Instauration. He was honoured lethargically. The King was gracious and touchy, and the Favourite both followed and set the same example. His spiritual energy was ignored; his loyal energy was accepted as duty—which it was, but it might have been a dynamic duty, had there been any machine for that dynamo to set in action. He succeeded to high office

almost by the mere exhaustion of opposition, and at
the precise moment when he began to use that office for
the purpose to aid which he had always sought it, it was
taken from him. Thus his concern for himself in action
failed by his fault, as his concern with the Monarch in
action failed partly by that Monarch's fault. During
his lifetime he could not create the great concern with
nature in action which he desired, and his judgments of
men in action were strangely incorrect. Nevertheless,
those two concerns are prolonged for us, partly because
of their own strength, partly because they were caught
up into the power of the last, the sovereign greatness of
the word.

### ii. THE PARLIAMENT

Francis Bacon was a man who did not like making
enemies: it was unwise and futile, against both preservation and perfection. He made them, of course;
every one does. But he had not the soul of a saint or
the mind of a bigot or the temper of a fool, and somewhere in or between those three capacities the resulting
capacity of making enemies, beyond those created by
accident, lies. His father is reported to have preferred
checking a jest to annoying a friend—almost the best
thing we know about Sir Nicholas. Bacon is reported
to have had a sharp tongue. But he had also had a
training in caution during the years of subserviency,
and a tenderness of nature existed in him which is
sometimes indistinguishable from a tenderness for
himself. He hated quarrels; his terrific energy was
devoted not so much to putting people right as to putting
things right. Religious quarrels were resounding all
about him, and they were futile and mischievous enough.
In a general way he could be rude to professors of old
habits of knowledge, but even there he kept to a general
way. He denounced the enemies of Majesty, but he was

said (not, certainly, by one of them) to have done even that with tenderness for the criminal. It is a little difficult to believe that, while reading the speeches, except that one remembers the ostentation of the age. Rhetoric was a necessity ; rant almost a duty. Quiet, moderate exposition would have been thought ineffective and probably treasonable. Disliking then the creation of enmity, he preferred always, if he discovered enmity, to lift it into a world of intellectual pattern. A benign fate allowed him, for a large part of his life, to do so ; it was a benignity not without its perils. Opposition between principles is sharpened when those principles are incarnated ; but so is opposition between incarnations when principles can be discovered in them, as they so generally can. The whole objection to his behaviour to Essex is the fact, if it is a fact, that he too rapidly allowed his personal gratitude to be defined by his duty to the State, and lost in the definition. There he had had a personal devotion to the Queen to assist the change, if it were a change. In the case of his two later antagonisms there was no change. He had never been Cecil's friend—Cecil had seen to that, and he was never Cecil's enemy—Cecil died before any opportunity arose. He had never been Coke's friend, but he did become Coke's antagonist. Two of those great activities came together in his mind ; his concern with the Monarch in action and with himself in action. Coke had stood in his own way, and presently Coke came to stand in the Monarch's way. Preservation and perfection united themselves once more, as they did so often in Bacon's life. He acted, and no one—certainly not himself—could be absolutely certain how far the two motives intermingled. It is perhaps why his last years were unpreserved and the perfection of his vision was passed on to us freed from the troublesome success of its dangerous twin.

There were between the appointment to the Solicitorship and the fall, three Parliaments : that of 1610, that of 1614, and that of 1621. The first was distinguished by Salisbury's effort to pass the Great Contract ; the second by the effort of the Undertakers ; the third by the attack on monopolies and referees. All of them involved a continual attempt of the Crown to persuade the Commons to provide it with the necessary finances for the government of the country, and of the developing refusal of the Commons to do any such thing unless control and direction of control were in their power. The irresponsibility of the landowners—except to themselves—was to be substituted for the irresponsibility of the Crown—except to itself. No doubt, on the royalist theory, the Crown was responsible to God ; but on the Commons' theory, so was each member of the House. The clash was as much religious as political ; but it was primarily economic. It would not be quite true to say that both sides were anxious to serve two masters, but both were certainly anxious to follow " preservation and perfection."

In all things Bacon desired concord ; in religion, not so much (though partly) because he thought it " the will of God," but rather because he thought that will of God with which he was anxious to busy himself could only be carried out when things were quiet. When in 1609 the King and the Pope had been, directly and by episcopal and cardinalitial champions, exchanging defences and defiances, Bacon sent Lancelot Andrewes an MS. copy of his *Cogitata et Visa* with a letter, beginning : " Now your Lordship hath been so long in the church and the palace, disputing between kings and popes, methinks you should take pleasure to look into the field, and refresh your mind with some matter of philosophy." He had no wish to be harsh on the Recusants if only they would give assurances that they would keep quiet ;

the contemporary Jesuits were learned men, and many another wise Papist might be interested in some "just and perfect volume of philosophy." As for Spain—Bacon did not believe in the terrible ogreish figure which sent the neurasthenics of Puritanism into the last ditch of their emotional defences. He thought Spain was collapsing. And even the "greatest inquisitor in Spain" might allow his works. He could not believe, he wrote to his Roman friend Toby Mathew, that the world should be grown to such an ecstasy as to reject truth in philosophy because the author dissenteth in religion. He was wrong. The greater ecstasies no doubt emerge into the highest lucidity where the principles of existence can be beheld, but the lesser ecstasies have by no means the same power. The reputed saying of the Khalif Omar's of all books but the Koran is still their cry: "if they disagree, blasphemous; if they agree, superfluous." When the *Novum Organum* was published, there were some found to call Bacon atheist.

With the letter he sent to Toby Mathew a copy of his book *De Sapientia Veterum—Concerning the Wisdom of Antiquity*. It was a pretty invention, a small volume retelling some of the old myths, Orpheus, Cadmus, Dædalus, and so on, and providing each of them with a scientific, civil, or philosophical meaning. He had once proposed to disparage the knowledge of the Greeks, and to pretend—or at least to adopt the not unfamiliar tale—that long before the Greeks a noble intellectual civilization had existed, of which these fables only had come down to us. "Where's your Aristotle now?" The meaning of these fables was not, he admitted, certainly intended by those lofty forgotten poets who composed them, but it might have been. For, as he wrote, "Who can hear that the *Giant Typhon* cut off and carried away *Jupiter's* sinews, and that *Mercury* stole them from Typhon and gave them back to Jupiter; without at once perceiving that it relates to successful rebellions, by which kings have their sinews both of money and authority cut off; yet not so but that by fair words and wise edicts the minds of the subjects may be presently reconciled, and as it were stolen back, and so kings recover their strength ? "

This meaning would not perhaps have immediately occurred to a modern mind. But the management of symbolism in this way is familiar to us; it is the method by which amusements are turned into gospels, and sometimes into persecutions. What of the number three or the beast in the Apocalypse? But we are not politically minded, so we imagine and symbolize other things—the ecstasies of love or the doctrines of religion. Deucalion casting stones behind his back signified to Bacon that the restoration of things can only be achieved by a return to general principles. The tale of Love signified the attraction of the atom. Antiquity had looked forward to Francis Bacon and intelligently invented fables to suit the need of the Great Instauration.

He finished his letter, concluding: " My great work goeth forward; and after my manner I alter ever when I add. So that nothing is finished till all is finished. This I have written in the midst of a term and Parliament; thinking no time so precious, but that I should talk of these matters with so good and dear a friend. And so with my wonted wishes I leave you to God's goodness." The next day he rose in the Commons to report to them contemporary wisdom, a great work of his own day, of which nothing was finished since it was never finished. It was Salisbury's effort to extract as much money as possible without giving away more of the Prerogative than he could help, and the Commons' effort to do away with as much of the Prerogative as possible while giving as little money as they could help.

The reasons alleged on both sides for demanding and retaining were justice, freedom, ancient rights, and the will of God. The results of that dispute to-day must (presumably) be the will of God; justice and freedom are more difficult to discern.

There had been in the last Parliament a discussion concerning Purveyance. It was generally regarded, or its accidents were, as a grievance to the subject. There had been some discussion on other rights of the Crown, feudal claims of Wardship and Tenure. The Government, confronted with its lack of ready money and its yearly deficit, was prepared to bargain. But as it did not want to give more than it could help, it did not want to say exactly what it would give. It knew what it wanted to get; it wanted £600,000 down and a yearly revenue of £200,000. In his opening speech, of which Bacon was part reporter to the House, Salisbury was not so definite, nor was he at all definite about the " retribution " he offered for such " contribution." But he was driven to exact proposals in a little while and put forward ten points of the Prerogative which were thought troublesome, and which " on good consideration " the King might be prepared to yield. The ten points were mostly points which had to do with the quiet and convenient possession of land by landowners. They included, among others, the abolition of Purveyance; a promise by the King to be bound by the Statute of Limitations, and to abolish " that part of his Prerogative *Nullum tempus occurit Regi*." " What a jewel were this," Salisbury exclaimed, " if the King should part with it ! " It undoubtedly was. So, though he did not say so, was another: that the legal maxim *Intentio Regis est regula legis* should be changed; and that all the King's grants should be taken in a sense favourable to the subject. And so, though of minor scintillation, were the rest.

But the Commons were covetous of larger jewels:
the names of which were Wardship and Tenure. Sir
Francis, then Solicitor, was sent to make representations
to the Lords, begging them to join in a general petition
to the King that he would give permission for them to
treat of the King's rights on those high subjects. As in
the case of the Union the King's Solicitor coloured his
business with his own mind. He asked certainly, but
he declared he left it all to the King. He thought there
were reasons to discuss those points; but he added that
they did not think themselves competent " to discern
of the honour of his Majesty's crown or the shrine of his
conscience "; they could not know more of them than
" as men use sometimes to see the image of the sun in a
pail of water." The King, moved either by his Treasurer's
policy or his Solicitor's rhetoric, graciously assented.
The Commons, a fortnight later, offered, in return for
abolition of tenure by which the Crown would lose
£40,000 yearly, one hundred thousand pounds yearly;
a net gain of sixty thousand. The Government, by
Salisbury, explained that there seemed to have been
some misunderstanding; it wanted first the £600,000
plus the £200,000 per annum, without compensation.
It would then discuss whether, for further compensation,
wardships and other burdens of tenures (the nominal
honour and title of tenures the King must keep) might
be abandoned.

It was this kind of deliberate or accidental chaffering
which caused Bacon to despair of his cousin. The
Crown and the Commons were engaged in bargaining,
in wrangling rather, of a nature calculated to induce the
worst emotion and produce the worst effect on both sides.
Bacon was far too intelligent not to see that at best a
great innovation was being made. The King had held
Wardships and all other matters of tenure by right.
Whatever compensation he got in exchange for them he

was bound to hold by vote, that is, at the pleasure of the Commons. They might pretend it was a permanent agreement, but it would be their agreement. And Wardship would be gone. It was clear, since the Crown was in such need of money, that something of the sort might have to be done. But need it be done in that way? He delivered a speech on another embroiling question—could the Speaker deliver to the House a message received through the Privy Council or must he receive it immediately from the King? Bacon urged that the King's word was the King's, whether it came directly or indirectly; the channel was no matter. But his central plea was for harmony—concord of Sovereignty and Liberty. Tacitus had said of Nerva . . . Apollonius had said of Nero . . . but they had a prince who was more like Nerva than Nero. Let them be as tender of his authority as he was of their liberty. Let them dismiss this unnecessary doubt. "It is one use of wit to make clear things doubtful. But it is a much better use of wit to make doubtful things clear; and to that I would that men would bend themselves."

It was in fact the continual raising of the troublesome question, "Can the King do this or that?" which caused so much excitement. On the question of Impositions—on goods coming into the kingdom—it arose again. Could the King lay Impositions? The King sent to say that the Judges had decided it was a part of the power of the Prerogative; he warned them not to discuss it; he went on to talk as though he could, if it came to that, impose on all property. But any particular impositions he was prepared to consider as grievances; and he would even promise not to lay any more without first hearing what both Houses could say. The Commons broke into debate and assertions of their right to discuss everything and anything, including every kind of Prerogative. They always could;

they always would. " But Sir Francis Bacon took upon him to answer these reasons." He distinguished. There was the right to discuss any interest of the subject or of the commonwealth, anything that could be called a grievance ; if the King inhibited that, he would have the King informed of the liberties of the House. But there was no corresponding right to discuss an essential point of the Prerogative ; if the King inhibited that, the House had always submitted. As . . . he gave precedents. The solution now was easy ; let the House present Impositions as grievances but not question the royal power. But the Commons would not be so content. They insisted on disputing the actual power, and on that Bacon stood for the Crown. He defended the King's right ; he asserted it was according to the fundamental laws of the kingdom ; he declared that though grants of customs had often been made by consent of Parliament yet they belonged to such things as " had perfection enough without Parliament "; he urged that the law could not provide for all occasions, and for this (as for others) reposed a special confidence in the King. The legal arguments all that day ran high ; precedents, maxims, statutes, were quoted in interchange. But underneath all was the problem of Wardship—if the King had power, he had money by right ; if he had not, he had it by vote and at the pleasure of the Commons.

Eventually, however, on this point the House came round to Bacon's point of view : they would not expressly challenge the Judge's decision ; they would include it in the petition of grievances. They sent Bacon, with twenty others, to present it. At the foot of the Throne he did so, repeating to James the admirable comparison between him and Nerva (to whom he now added Trajan), begging that (excellent Sovereign !) the King would hold the sound of grievances but as *gemitus columbæ*, the mourning of a dove. All was meant in goodness of heart and loving loyalty. He added a peroration of his own experience of the King's continual grace and favour.

In such addresses to the King he coloured the wishes of the House with his own devotion ; when he reported the Conference he coloured that report with his own sense of gracious royalty. Had both powers judged themselves as he judged them they might have agreed ; sometimes, so highly did he impose his own view of them on each other, they almost seemed to be agreeing. But there were difficulties which even Bacon hardly understood. Money is bad enough as a cause of quarrel, but religion is worse. The Commons had religious as well as financial grievances ; they drew up a list which the King said was long enough to serve for a tapestry. The doves were mourning loudly about deprivations, excommunications, the High Commission, proclamations, jurisdictions, impositions. The King fed them slowly and reluctantly. Salisbury could not get them to agree to a bargain, nor Bacon bring them to offer their free generosity to the Majesty.

The conferences and counter-conferences, the debates in the House and the declarations of Majesty, by which the slow, yet not so slow, transmutation of sovereignty took place are for the general histories. In this Parliament Bacon had done what he could to reconcile in action the increasing contention. But after a final effort to buy over the landowners the Great Contract broke down ; in the autumn the Parliament was dissolved, having given small supply. Before the next was called, Salisbury was dead.

On the event Bacon knew that the long rivalry, an interior rivalry, was done. The amiable and breachless wall which for many years Robert Cecil had offered his cousin disappeared, and a wider, more open world lay before him. Salisbury died on 24th May 1612 at Marlborough; on 29th May Bacon began a letter to the King which shows a sudden hope of release—" affection. . . . I could never show it hitherto to the full; having been as a hawk tied to another's fist that mought sometimes bait and proffer but could never fly." In the first sudden release from that dead fist the released hawk poised for a sweeping flight. He dropped the letter he had begun; two days later he wrote another. Still in the flood of release, he spoke of the dead man, not yet quite freely, but impersonally—" a great subject . . . a great servant . . . a fit man to keep things from growing worse, but no very fit man to reduce things to be much better." The secret, courteous face, the quiet, managing voice, the master of all affairs, the man who had stood in his cousin's way, who had been Treasurer and Secretary—" he loved to have the eyes of all Israel a little too much upon himself . . . to have all business still under the hammer, and like clay in the hands of the potter to mould it as he thought good; so that he was more *in operatione* than in *opere*." What had Salisbury ever achieved ? " He had fine passages of action, yet the real conclusions came slowly on." But now, now, there was room for a Parliament: now supply and loyalty might both be fulfilled.

Another thought came to him. Salisbury was dead. Salisbury had hindered Francis Bacon with promises and spoiled the Parliament with contracts. But the man who was a peremptory royalist and yet popular in the House, who had defended the right of imposition yet had been sent to lay the grievances of impositions before the King, might not that man be as it were a reflection in little, in his own action, of the true union of sovereignty and liberty ? So far he had only possessed a power of speech, and not overmuch of that, but now if. . . . He wrote a third letter; he offered himself for the Secretaryship.

" It may please your excellent Majesty,

" My principal end being to do your Majesty service, I crave leave to make at this time to your Majesty this most humble oblation of myself. I may truly say with the psalm, *Multum incola fuit anima mea*; for my life hath been conversant in things wherein I take little pleasure. Your Majesty may have heard somewhat that my father was an honest man, and somewhat you may have seen of myself, though not to make any true judgment by, because I have hitherto had only *potestatem verborum*, nor that neither. I was three of my young years bred with an ambassador in France, and since I have been an old truant in the schoolhouse of your council-chamber, though on the second form; yet longer than any that now sitteth hath been on the head form. If your Majesty find any aptness in me, or if you find any scarcity in others, whereby you may think it fit for your service to remove me to business of State; although I have a fair way before me for profit (and by your Majesty's grace and favour for honour and advancement), and in a course less exposed to the blasts of fortune, yet now that he is gone, *quo vivente virtutibus certissimum exitium*, I will be ready as a chessman to be wherever your Majesty's royal hand shall set me. Your Majesty will bear me witness, I have not suddenly opened myself thus far. I have looked on upon others, I see the exceptions, I see the distractions, and I fear Tacitus will be a prophet, *magis alii homines quam alii mores*. I know mine own heart, and I know not whether God that hath touched my heart with the affection may not touch your royal heart to discern it. Howsoever, I shall at least go on honestly in mine ordinary course, and supply the rest in prayers for you, remaining, etc."

Whether he even sent the letter we do not know, but it is for us in itself a kind of peak. His belief, not

so much in himself as in his vision of political concord,
thrusts upward in it; from that willing height we
discern the sincerity of his belief. He would have taken
responsibility, had the King allowed; he would have
made every effort to put his creed into action, to preserve
and perfect the Monarch in action, to preserve Prerogative, to perfect justice in its employment by the
use of law, by the submissions of Parliament, by advice
and rule. He believed the King had goodwill to his
subjects and the subjects to their King. He that
hindered had been taken out of the way. The light of
that willing oblation of himself falls over all his counsel,
only still at different times a sudden rage when he thinks
of the dead man shakes him. In September he sent
the King a note on the inquiry into the royal finances
which was then proceeding.[1] And there all his anger
blazes out. Yet however thrilled with those long years
of defeat and suppression, however coloured by a personal bitterness, it was still the political mistakes of
Robert Cecil on which he harped. Cecil was gone, and
the King need no longer make himself cheap; he could
dwell in his own Majesty. No more need the wants of
the Crown be scheduled and tabled, to be talked over
for months by Lords and Commons; no more should
courses of revenue which of old were *arcana imperii* be
printed and published to the world; or " worms of
aldermen " be entreated to lend at 10 per cent. to save
the Fortune of Majesty; or contracts—if contracts
must be—made for quick payment not for good bargains;
or projects begun and then blasted, and the King left
with the scandal. No more should there be one " to
pretend even carriage " between your Majesty's rights
" and the ease of the people and to satisfy neither."
All that was done, gone with the deviser. There had

[1] James did not make him Secretary of State; he made him a
sub-commissioner of this economical inquiry.

been a time, when he—Bacon—read the King's book against Vorstius and Arminius, and saw the majesty of God delivered from degenerate philosophy, "*perculsit illico animum* that God would shortly set upon you some visible favour, and let me not live if I thought not of the taking away of that man."

He stopped ; he thought ; he struck the last sentence through. But that was what he felt when he thought of how Robert Cecil had treated the awful Majesty of England, the mortal god on earth that was the King.

Compared with this fervour of reprobation later references are almost polite. Salisbury's death had removed a great deal of discontent and carried it into the other world—he had always had an artificial animating of the Negative—*animalis sapientia*—his bent was to do little with much formality and protestation. He had certainly done precisely that for his cousin ; deliberately or not, the Cecils had artificially animated the Negative with amazing success. There had been, for Francis, no promotion. But undeniably also there had been for the King no supply. The maddening thing for Francis was that he approved of Parliaments ; he thought them a necessity for the proper information of the Crown. He had laboured with all his might to reconcile what his cousin with all his art had managed to divide, and through that division had floated up, neither the glory of Majesty nor the content of the people (these two being indeed one), but the grisly animation of the abominable Negative. Well, he was gone at last.

Unfortunately he left successors. When, in 1614, it was decided to call another Parliament, Bacon once more urged his views on the King. James was to put off the person of a contractor and rest on the person of a King. He was to treat the new Parliament but as a trial, and proportion his expectations. Supply was important, but not so important as to part from the Houses with love and reverence. It was ostensibly to be called for some other business of estate, not directly for money. Let it be given out that the King's revenue could be and was being adjusted so as to do away with the need for money (" which I partly think is true "). And let there—let there be no canvasses, no busy workers on Majesty's behalf. In short, let the King shine like the sun in its strength, and so encourage the fertility of the earth he illumined.

Other advice was given by other advisers. The King was counselled to abandon all hope of helping himself except by Parliament, to forbid all speeches against Parliament, to be very gracious everywhere, to do away with all grievances, to accept (in fact) the terms of Parliament. This done, so those counsellors (chiefly Sir Henry Neville) told him, they would " undertake " that the Commons would vote him the money he needed —and now, despite more sale of Crown lands, needed more than ever. The King and the Government proceeded to neglect both Bacon's advice and Neville's. They interfered with the elections, which Bacon had begged should not be done. The King's opening speech stressed supply, and brought him in the character of a petitioner, and (inevitably) of a royal, obstinate, and eager petitioner. He certainly talked of love, but of love in terms of money. He said he would offer a gift ; he would heal some grievances. Afterwards the Secretary of State urged the need of supply.

The Houses met on 5th April and were dissolved on 7th June. There were a number of new members, and in order to instruct them in the true way the House went over the question of Impositions again. It discussed Church affairs. It heard rumours of Undertakers and investigated them. It set to work to prepare a still longer petition of grievances. It granted no supply.

It closed in a state of dispute and general disapproval without any achievement beyond the reducing of the Bishop of Lincoln to tears because he had made derogatory remarks about the Commons. The Commons, when they heard of it, had been wrought up to such a fine frenzy that they had considered refusing to sit any more until something or other had happened to the Bishop. Even when the Bishop's tears were reported by the Lords a member complained that these were " tears of fear and terror, not of repentance "; another wanted him declared " unfit for the King's ear, house, the place he holdeth, or the society of reasonable men." The Lords had hinted that they ought not to be questioned upon matters spoken in their own House, especially when there was no evidence before the Commons but rumour. The reasonable men in the Commons were distracted by this " slightness of satisfaction." In the midst of the uproar the Houses were dissolved, at the beginning of June.

The Archbishop of Canterbury now appears on the scene. It had occurred to the Archbishop, so he told the Bishop of Norwich, that, in the straits of the Crown, the Bishops might make some kind of freewill offering, such as the best piece of plate each possessed. He went on to say that the King had graciously approved, and the Council and nobility in general had taken it up. Some Bishops (he thoughtfully added), who had only small pieces of plate, had sent them in filled with gold; others, who were unwilling to part with pieces of plate, had redeemed them with gold. " No poor man " was " to be grated on "; only those who were of ability. He entreated the Bishop of Norwich to follow up the suggestion diligently.

The idea, in fact, spread; gifts began to pour in. The Earl of Salisbury sent £300; the Secretary gave £100; the Lord Coke gave £200. (The rest of the

Judges, it was said, came but slowly after ; it is the only example of the Judges dissenting from Coke.) Letters were sent to the shires, and Bacon, by then Attorney, submitted a paper of " Points to be observed."

It was, in itself, an idea which might have come from Bacon's own mind ; the great men and gentry of the kingdom willingly and lovingly offering their riches to supply the King's necessity. But as matters of love so frequently do, except in moments of intuitive passion—and even Francis did not think the country gentlemen were all filled with intuitive passion, especially some of those who had been lately at Westminster—it needed careful handling. He noted, above all general rules, three : (i) no show of compulsion of any sort, no authoritative pressing ; (ii) no touching or dealing with the meaner or poorer sort of people ; (iii) the better sort to be encouraged to an appetite to give cheerfully and plentifully. Between sympathetic passion and prophetic irony the spectator observes the Attorney-General attempting to provide for these three fundamentals of love. Benevolence and Contribution, as illegal or undesirable terms, are to be forbidden ; this is a gift, oblation, or what not. Every one is to give by what means he chooses ; there is to be no precise method dictated. There are to be no official letters ; individuals are to recommend it to other popular persons. There is to be no official collector ; different districts can choose their own. It is to be generally rumoured (Bacon was always quite clear and intelligent about rumour ; it existed—it was bound to exist ; it ought therefore to have its tongues instructed what to say) that schedules of names of those giving would be shown weekly to the King and Prince, and similar copies should be spread abroad to encourage others not to fall too low. No fees are to be taken from it ; the whole is to go to the King's debts, especially the Navy, Ireland, etc. ; no part of the plate is to be given away, and if any of this is passed to the Jewel-House or the goldsmiths they are to answer for it to the King. The City of London is not to rate by companies, "whereby it may reach to the poor," but only deal with the richest men of each company, and so in all counties and towns; no man to be importuned or pressed. It is to be done at once, hotly and closely, otherwise it will be *acribus initiis, fine incurioso*. If any Recusant gives largely, it must be understood that it is not in exchange for secret toleration. Though it is not to be compulsory, any who maliciously deride, scorn, or slander the frank disposition of the King's subjects, or dissuade, defeat, or divert it, are to be punished. The King is to issue a proclamation of thanks.

If it could have been done at all, it might have been done so. Bacon, like Shakespeare, felt in his bones and his blood that Government was natural to man, and Bacon was in close touch with the King's Majesty, and Bacon was not in possession of any lands about which he might ever have to argue with the law officers of the King's Majesty. The men who were, away in Wiltshire or Cumberland, were much more inclined to think that their own government rather than the King's was natural to man, though they had not yet fully worked out the arguments which proved this. The King, with or without advice, departed in an immediate particular from Bacon's points. The oblation was made official; letters were sent from the Council. It may still have been possible to love the King, but few landowners had any passion for the Council. The Council wrote to the sheriffs and judges of assize, deepening the official colour. When moneys delayed, they inquired, examined, summoned persons to London, wrote sharply to a Lord Lieutenant. The whole transaction took on the appearance of shaking contributions out of people's pockets.

It was, literally, a matter of " If you don't love me to a proper extent, I'm determined to know why, and if you possibly can, you shall." Necessity and authority again transformed themselves into apes of passion, and the apes went running about the country with money-bags, while the Council played the patriotic organ in London.

At Marlborough a Wiltshire mayor applied to a gentleman of local standing, Sir Oliver St. John. He sent a letter in answer, to be read to the Justices if the Mayor chose. The Mayor did ; the letter was read. It said—at great length, but no more at Elizabethan length, rather at Puritanic and Biblical, that this kind of Benevolence was against Law, Reason, and Religion. It produced precedents, and argued that what Parliament had refused, the Commons distracted (that is, separated) ought not to grant. It then accused the King of committing the dreadful sin of perjury, violating his Coronation oath, offending the Divine Majesty, and giving advantage to another Henry IV (if such an one should rise up, which God forbid). It remarked that any one who contributed was plunged into a hellish danger, by very irreligiously and uncharitably helping forward the King's Majesty in that grievous sin, and incurring the Curse (51 of H. 3 and 25 Ed. 1) pronounced against such abettors by the then Bishops. So Sir Oliver St. John, leaving others to their own conscience, but having made clear what would probably happen to them if they paid, commended the Mayor to the grace of the Almighty and ceased.

He was prosecuted in the Star Chamber by the King's Attorney, who (he himself modestly said) " meant well," especially in a long panegyric on the King. It was no more than an official business ; by this time St. John had changed his mind. He wrote a submission and was dismissed. The submission was much, much longer than the offence, which (he acknowledged) was wicked, wretched, reproachful, blasphemous, injurious, slanderous, and seditious. He quoted Psalms, Leviticus, Ecclesiastes, Proverbs, James, John, and Kings. His heart groaned and his bowels yearned. He had (beloved) lied. The King was a perfect marvel of goodness. Parliament (Mr. Attorney had made clear) had not refused aid. He acknowledges his great iniquity.

It was but an incident of Bacon's work. But that ridiculous scene, with Sir Francis lauding James heavens-high and the pious prisoner retracting his views of God's will, perjury, and the oblation, is the inevitable comment, the perverse and bitter comment of the world on the proposed exercise of love. Into so mean a close our exalted ideas dwindle; in such a malodorous air the distorting mirrors of our minds show us infinite dreams of beauty. The oblation brought in some £66,000, and the King's necessities were not noticeably relieved.

In the next Parliament, the last in which he sat, and then having removed from his place among the gentlemen to the presidency of the nobles, Bacon was to play a very different part. He was to be a means of a temporary accord between the King and the Families, interweaving and unifying them as he had always desired to do, but at the expense of something other than his time, labour, and oratory. But at least his Fortune spared him the humiliation of being the subject of a bargain. Cecil and those who thought with Cecil had held that contracts were the best method of appeasing the subject and supplying the Crown. Bacon had always denounced them. Yet he, no less than they, thought that the King should bestow graces and the Parliament gifts.

Nothing is more certain than that two persons (and therefore, I suppose, two bodies) can exchange graces and gifts, in such a nature that not only is bargaining absent, but that the exchange itself is a denial of bargaining. But then this nature must be of a free and loving disposition; it must be a state of reciprocal love, definite however mild or however passionate. Exchange is either negligible or commercial or generous with love. Bacon certainly did not think this exchange negligible; he hated it to be commercial. He believed therefore—it is shown by his continual counsel—that it could be in love. He believed that a state of high political affection could exist between the King and his Parliament; not in some ideal world but in seventeenth-century England. He believed it so much that he thought it was the only thing of any practical value. Men who fell back on merchandising were "not well seen in rules of estate and the pulses of people's hearts"; "empirics of Parliament," their "wisdom reached but to that they observed last." Either Bacon was the greatest of practical ironists or he himself felt in himself " the pulse of hearts."

The King was never to admit himself in want; the King was to come princely. "I am of opinion that the King should not for profit diminish one iota of majesty." Ah Gloriana! ah Magnificence! In the mind of the boy whom she had petted and laughed at—" my young Lord Keeper "—the young man she had snubbed and consulted, the Queen he knew before ever he knew Essex, still walked remotely as the Majesty of England. In her time and a little after, " the ancient majesty of the kings of this realm was then preserved," wrote the man of fifty-five, the King's Attorney-General, pleading for love and high confidence between the Throne and the Commons of England. He himself had never bargained —no, not when Elizabeth frowned. He had never made the smallest effort to deny his beliefs for his own profit. He believed that such a state of amity was possible; he conjoined in his thought the fair intentions of the realm.

He pleaded everywhere and continually for an agreement in love. The word "love," we must believe, meant something to that master of words and student of facts. Yet it did not mean what it usually means to us, but something much greater or much less. The essay on Love lacks the whole romantic vision of that glorious illumination of sex. It seems to us cold, and (for a wonder!) rather stupid, and it confirms our sense that "the exquisite examination of the nature and customs of one person" was not for him. Homosexual (as Aubrey said) or heterosexual, his mind had no capacity for that; even in less intimate relations he often misjudged. It is by no means certain that this lack is not a failing incident to great imaginations. We know nothing of Shakespeare, but Milton and Wordsworth have been accused of it, and Dante's personal passion was for a spirit; living people, they say, fared less well with him. The imagination is, despite itself, preoccupied, and even love-poetry is not the same as love. To be an object of love and a subject of poetry is not always the same thing; a cruel experience lies in the division. If Bacon's belief that the use of poetry was to give "some shadow of satisfaction to the mind of man in those points wherein the nature of things doth deny it" were anywhere true, it might be true here. The essay on Love does not, in that sense, yield any shadow of satisfaction, but that is because of its own strong passion for lucidity. He was not aware of our romantic ardours; the reason is simple—he existed before a great part of their cause had been fashioned. He was already about thirty before Marlowe asked on the city stages the prime metaphysical question of all these ardours: "What is beauty? saith my sufferings then." He was forty before Desdemona and Cleopatra, Imogen and Perdita and Miranda, appeared. He probably knew Ben Jonson; he dedicated a book to George Herbert; he may have met Donne. But he is not likely to have read the *Songs and Sonnets*. He never saw the full procession of the Dianemes, the Antheas, the Ianthes, the Julias, the Amorets ; never toyed with Amaryllis or Neæra's hair in poetry, nor (for all the signs) in life ; never read the *Coy Mistress*, the *Elegy to an Unfortunate Lady*, the *Epithalamium*, the *House of Life* or the *Angel in the House* or *One Word More*. He had no illusion—not even disillusion ; he could not even lose our contemporary splendour of romantic love, he could not come after it, for as yet it had not been. Three centuries of association were lacking to him as to all the Elizabethans ; the only begetters of that ensuing poetry were themselves inevitably without its health and happiness or whatever in place of health and happiness it produced. If those adorable poets had only not concentrated so mightily on love-in-blank-verse ! It is Marlowe and Shakespeare—others before them, of course, but still they—who are responsible for our feuilletons, our novels, our headlines, our placards. " What is beauty ? saith my sufferings then ? "

It is to be remembered whenever we read the word *love* in Bacon's letters, or Jonson's, or any. Shelley would have said that Bacon writ of love as Harvey said he writ of science, "like a Lord Chancellor." He knew no more of the circulation of that exalted passion than of the circulation of the blood, except what his own blood taught him, and in neither case did it teach him very much. There is but one striking phrase ; in the *Sylva Sylvarum*—" the aspects that procure love are not gazings, but sudden glances and dartings of the eye." It is in the 944th natural fact which he notes in that book. But what was wanting in him as a physical ardour existed as an intellectual principle of State affairs. A clearer and no less exalted passion possessed him ; if he tried to find laws for it our moralists and monogamists at least can hardly blame him. He composed rules for the Benevolence, meant not only to direct but to excite it, but to him it remained a matter of spirits *bene volentes*. He had written that learning was only justified by charity; without which it was but a proud swelling. He desired charity between the Crown and the Commons, finding it both credible and possible. And if that charity lacks certain exquisite sensations it does not lack, perhaps it intensifies, an energy of goodwill. It was some such energy of goodwill to which, in his letters, his books, his State papers, Francis gave the name of love. We have followed the fire of the poets rather than the clarity of his devotion; perhaps we have been wise. But that is no reason to deny to him his own use of the word, nor any excuse for failing to see how much beyond our own capacity was his dream of the interchange of sweet honour and generous will.

### iii. THE COURTS

In 1535 Henry VIII had issued a commission to Cromwell, for " all and every kind of ecclesiastical jurisdiction, authority, or power " which either belonged to him as Supreme Head or could or ought to belong to him. Cromwell had issued sub-commissions. Edward VI had issued a general commission in the form of Letters Patent in 1549 to a number of bishops and other clergy, ministers of State, and lawyers. Mary issued new Letters Patent in 1557 to twenty-two commissioners. Elizabeth on her accession issued commissions similar to those used by Cromwell, but after the passing of the Act of Supremacy, she issued new Letters Patent in 1559, very like those of 1557. From 1559 to 1641 the High Commission remained in being, but a change came over it. It had begun in effect by being a visitorial body to check and chastise heresies and other ecclesiastical offences. It did this work steadily, although of course the heresies and the offences altered under succeeding monarchs, and chastisement in 1558 under Mary affected quite different people from chastisement in 1560 under Elizabeth. Even a number of the commissioners were changed. But this, constitutionally and legally, was of no importance. The Letters Patent were issued and the commissioners toiled on. Under Elizabeth, however, they gradually became a permanent Court for ecclesiastical affairs; they took on the management and decision of cases; they became, in fact, a law court. With this gradual establishment of a new thing the Judges of the King's Bench and of the Common Pleas were in violent disagreement. From 1580 they occasionally issued " prohibitions " which suspended the case in the High Commission until the common law judge decided whether it contained anything " temporal." If it did not, he withdrew the prohibition; if he thought it did, he let the prohibition stand and left it at that. In 1607, after a difficult argument, the judges, especially Coke, loosed a flood of prohibitions. The situation grew more and more serious. Efforts were made at reconciliation of the two jurisdictions. But the common law judges practically denied that the others had any jurisdiction—except here and there, in " enormous " matters, and they themselves would decide what " enormous " matters were.

There was a meeting before the King, in which Coke and the Majesty came to bitter words. There was a meeting before the Chancellor in which Ellesmere was sarcastic. Coke and the Archbishop quarrelled. By 1610 the Commons were petitioning against the Commission. The King had forbidden Coke to issue prohibitions. The Chief Justice pursued his own devices, issued prohibitions, and took an occasion to mention how two justices had once held that a man who killed one of the pursuivants of the Commission had acted in self-defence, since the Commission had no right to arrest.

There was another grand meeting in which the Archbishop and Coke quarrelled. There was yet another at which the King argued with the Judges, and at last agreed to issue new Letters Patent; which he did. But he did not placate the Judges, who by Coke's mouth protested that the Letters were contrary to law and left the room at Lambeth where the proceedings had taken place. This was in 1611, and Coke was still Chief Justice of the Common Pleas.

In August 1613, however, the Chief Justice of the King's Bench died. The natural successor was that " solemn goose " Sir Henry Hobart, the King's Attorney. But moved perhaps by the fact that in the previous year Providence had shown favour both to the King and himself by calling Robert Cecil out of this world, Sir Francis Bacon determined to be a little Providence on his own in regard to his other enemy. Coke was Chief Justice of the Common Pleas. It was an office of more income but less dignity than the King's Bench; it was also a place from which the Prerogative could be more easily hampered, if not actually attacked. As things then stood the Prerogative needed all the assistance it could receive, and Francis thought of a means by which the King's precious balm might break the obstinate Coke's head. The paper in which he laid his reasons before James illumines more than the mere promotion.

"REASONS FOR THE REMOVE OF COKE

"Reasons why it should be exceeding much for his Majesty's service to remove the Lord Coke from the place he now holdeth to be Chief Justice of England, and the Attorney to succeed him, and the Solicitor the Attorney.

"First, it will strengthen the King's causes greatly amongst the judges. For both my Lord Coke will think himself near a privy counsellor's place, and thereupon turn obsequious, and the attorney-general, a new man and a grave person in a judge's place, will come in well to the other and hold him hard to it, not without emulation between them who shall please the King best.

"Secondly, the attorney sorteth not so well with his present place, being a man timid and scrupulous both in parliament and in other business, and one that in a word was made fit for the late Lord Treasurer's bent, which was to do little with much formality and protestation, whereas the now solicitor going more roundly to work, and being of a quicker and more earnest temper, and more effectual in that he dealeth in, is like to recover that strength to the King's prerogative which it hath had in times past, and which is due unto it. And for that purpose there must be brought in to be solicitor some man of courage and speech and a grounded lawyer; which done, his Majesty will speedily find a marvellous change in his business, for it is not to purpose for the judges to stand well disposed, except the King's counsel, which is the active and moving part, put the judges well to it ; for in a weapon what is a back without an edge ?

"Thirdly, the King shall continue and add reputation to the attorney's and solicitor's place by this orderly advancement of them, which two places are the champion's places for his rights and prerogative, and being stripped of their expectations and successions to great place will wax vile, and then his Majesty's prerogative goeth to the wind. Besides, the remove of my Lord Coke to a place of less profit (though it be with his will) yet will be thought abroad a kind of discipline to him for opposing himself in the King's causes, the example whereof will contain others in more awe.

"Lastly, whereas now it is voiced abroad touching the supply of places, as if it were a matter of labour and canvass and money, and other persons are chiefly spoken to be the men, and the great suitors; this will appear to be the King's own act, and is a course so natural and regular as it is without all suspicion of those by-courses, to the King's infinite honour; for men say now, the King can make good second judges, as he hath done lately; but that is no mastery, because men sue to be kept from these places. But now is the trial in those great places how his Majesty can hold good, where there is such a great suit and means."

It will be seen from the last paragraph that it was not the Prerogative alone which was in Bacon's mind. " Other persons " meant chiefly, but not only, Somerset. Money was offered for great place on all sides. It did not appear to Bacon as improper as it does to us, unless and until it clouded the supreme Majesty. Let the King be seen in action; let there be no question of bribes or canvassing. James assented. Coke was graciously handed upstairs, being made a Privy Councillor at the same time. Bacon became Attorney.

Somerset heard of the proposal and tried to extract money; "he thrust himself into the business for a fee," wrote Bacon later. It is doubtful from whom the fee would come; not, certainly, from Coke, who only wanted to stay where he was. It may have been Hobart; it may have been the new Solicitor, Sir Henry Yelverton.[1] The diplomacy of Francis Bacon seized the opportunity of the Favourite's marriage with the Countess of Essex to present a Masque, entirely at his own expense: the *Masque of Flowers*, acted by the gentlemen of Gray's Inn. The magnificence was preluded by a pathetic scene in the Court of Common Pleas. On his last day there Coke took leave " dolefully." He

[1] Who presented the King, to his intense delight, with £4000 on his appointment.

wept ; the rest of the Bench wept ; most of the officers
of the Court wept. The Common Pleas dissolved into
lamentation. A few days afterwards the new Lord
Chief Justice met the new Attorney. " Mr. Attorney,
this is your doing ; it is you that have made this great
stir." " Ah, my lord," Bacon answered, "your lordship all this while hath grown in breadth ; you must grow
in height or you will prove a monster." But the measure
of breadth which had been used in the Common Pleas
was carried up to the King's Bench ; it was the measure
of a man, that is, of Sir Edward Coke.

Meanwhile, with a world clearer around him than
ever it had been before since he returned from Paris to
begin his career, the King's Attorney settled to work.
Cecil and Coke, one permanently, the other temporarily,
were out of the way. The Chancellor Ellesmere was
sympathetic in ideas and friendly in person. The King
was more than sympathetic in political ideas and gracious
in person. The Favourite, if not friendly, was not
hostile. The Solicitor was harmonious and a man of the
Favourite's party, a dependant of the great house of
Howard who supported Somerset. A second edition of
the *Essays* had been published in the previous year,
in which also two essays of another kind had been
attempted, preludings of the Great Instauration, the
*Descriptio Globi Intellectualis* and the *Thema Cœli*. He
did not publish these ; he laid them by, and went on
reading and writing, drafting and redrafting, preparing
the *Novum Organum* for the time when the bell so long
expected should begin to call wits together. He was
fifty-three, but what was age to so high a calling ? He
found that he needed another nine years before the great
summons could be published.

Meanwhile there was his official work and his civil
work. He delivered in the Star Chamber, and afterwards published, a charge against duelling, which James

was determined to suppress; the principal part of the punishment he recommended was that the offender should be perpetually banished from the royal courts, because this debarring was a kind of darkness to all good spirits and presumably more distressing than the irremissible fine which was to accompany it. The speech had some rich passages, especially when he declares the erroneous imagination of honour which is the cause of duels to be "no better than a sorcery that enchanteth the spirits of young men, that bear great minds, with a false show, *species falsa*, and a kind of satanical illusion and apparition of honour." And though this is by no means all that can be said, for there are conditions of human life which seem to demand no poorer a solution than the introduction of challenge and the point and touch of death, yet to the civil magistrate such individual needs must always be subordinate to the quiet of the Republic, and certainly even death itself can be cheapened into fashion and a rash bravado. James may have disliked duelling from a natural horror born in him from that pre-natal crisis when his mother by the light of the candles caught from the overthrown table saw the daggers flashing over her musician and favourite, and felt her husband's arm holding her away from interference with the savage deed. But Bacon disliked it as sheer waste and insolence.

He took part in several cases of treason. A member of an Irish deputation had been commanded to state his opinion concerning a doctrine of regicide extracted from a book by the Jesuit casuist Suarez. He answered that it concerned matters of faith, in which he was no judge; he submitted his opinion to the judgment of the Roman Church, but for himself he would bear true allegiance to the King. He was prosecuted, sentenced, and allowed to go without payment or detention. It gave Bacon opportunity for an extremely Protestant, historical, and legal speech, in which he committed himself to the view that murder, adultery, rape, Mohammedanism, and Arianism, were apparently all equal breaches of the moral law. It is an accidental sentence, but it shows how "false philosophies" were then regarded. On the other side, a Puritan clergyman named Peacham was found to have prepared an incendiary sermon, threatening the possibility of sudden death to the King and wider massacres *Deo volente. Rege obstante*, Peacham was examined whether any persons of high place were privy to these prophecies, since it was thought probable if so that they might also be privy to their execution. It was not perhaps quite as unlikely as it sounds. That Peacham should be proposing to state publicly that the King might be stricken with death like Ananias or Nabal was prophetic rant. But that he should write that "getting of the crown-land again would cost blood, and bring men to say—This is the heir; come, let us kill him," was rather different. There had been a good deal of trouble over the alienated crown-lands and the efforts of the Government to discover any whose owners held them improperly, in order to extract money. And there is not very much about the crown-lands in the Old Testament and less in the New (except, of course, the crown-lands of the kingdom of heaven). "Do you know, or have you heard," they asked him, before torture, in torture, between torture, and after torture, "of any conspiracy or danger to the Prince, for doubt of calling back the crown-lands?" Some of the landowners and gentry might easily have preferred a Puritan rising to the calling back of the crown-lands. He had denied it—not to the satisfaction of the Council, who had issued a warrant to two of their number together with the Attorney, Solicitor, and other officials, to put him to torture. Where, however, he remained obstinate. The

King was inclined to prosecute him for treason, but first he assented to a proposal of Sir Ralph Winwood's that the " book " should be submitted to the four Judges of the King's Bench with the question, " Is it treason ? " He wrote to order it, and found himself once more up against the determined Chief Justice of the King's Bench.

The taking of the opinions of the Judges in that manner was at that time a common thing. But their opinions were asked as a body. To ask the opinions of a body where Coke presided was to ask Coke's opinion only. The Council, by the Attorney and other lawyers, inquired separately. They went to Coke first, who objected strongly; it was not according to the custom of the realm. He did not think his brethren would do it. Bacon said that it would be a sound idea for him to leave his brethren to look after themselves; the King wished it done in this way, and what they all had to do was to obey. He brought Coke to agree to this, and immediately took aside the Solicitor and the other two lawyers and sent them off to consult with the other Judges before Coke could get at them. Judge Doddridge agreed at once to read the papers and give an opinion; so did Justice Crooke. Justice Houghton (" a soft man ") rather hankered after a conference with his brethren; they had all been in the Crown's service, whereas (he said) he himself was not much acquainted with this kind of thing.

Bacon reserved himself for Coke. He took him the papers and contrived tactful ways to let the Chief Justice remain true in the abstract to the first opinion (" with which he is most commonly in love ") while breaking from it in this case. He " partly understood " that the other Judges had made no difficulty (which was at least two-thirds true). Coke refused to believe it; he was sure they would ask to confer. Bacon suggested that some people might—just might—think that if Coke were so sure of it he might have helped to bring it about. And with that he left him.

Presently he went back for the decision, and indulged in a little legal argument on the case itself. Coke listened more politely than usual, and even made notes. But he still refused to commit himself, even though the King's Attorney hinted that the King was more likely to blame Coke's backwardness than his own negligence for any delay. The Chief Justice, still hoping against hope, said that when the rest were ready he would be.

In the end, however, he gave a decision. Peacham had not, according to him, committed treason because he had not disabled the King's title to reign. The other Judges were reported to disagree with him. Bacon advised the King to cause a general rumour to be spread that all the Judges were only in doubt on the actual publication of the treason. Meanwhile the poor old wretch in the Tower, though he had remained determined under the torture, gave way under the strain. He uttered names of the gentry implicated ; then he denied even that the original writings were his ; he said that his former admissions had been to avoid torture. At last he was sent down to Somerset, tried, and condemned. He was kept in prison at Taunton for seven months, and then he died.

There were other cases ; between these and the Parliament the year 1614 went by. In 1615 and 1616 came the fall of Somerset and the rise of Villiers. In 1616 the warfare with Coke renewed itself. The preliminary dust of legal technicalities arises about the more sinister and picturesque figures carrying the envenomed tarts to the Tower.

The new Chief Justice of the King's Bench had carried into his more dignified office the same conviction that not only he, but he just there, and so was always right, which had filled him as Attorney, exposed itself in the

Common Pleas, and spent itself occasionally against a mind which attempted—with whatever success—to refer all things to universality. Coke did not propose to let the Prerogative escape from its subjection to law, and law tended to mean, not merely law in general, but law in the particular Court over which Coke presided, and even to become concentrated in its president. Both the Crown and the Commons had had difficulties with the Judges, but the difficulties of the Crown were more frequent and more diverse. Coke was contending for power, as were the Prerogative and the Privilege of the House. He saw himself as the august decision that stayed the proud waves of his rivals. Unfortunately the greatness of his office depended rather too much on the willingness of the waves to be stayed; if they took no notice the house of the Lord Chief Justice might be undermined. The sea of the Commons was surging not round the Courts but the Throne. But the sea of Majesty was surging dangerously round Sir Edward Coke.

The Peacham case had swept up and retired. In 1616 there was trouble over a Crown appointment to the Court of Common Pleas: a matter of making of writs. The particular case brought the Attorney-General into court to argue that the Judges could not proceed, since the interests of the Crown were concerned, till the permission of Chancery had been obtained. He spoke for two hours and a half; Coke himself, half impressed and for once generous—as those two violent opponents could be—said " it was a famous argument." Bacon himself thought well of it. " I know the Protho-notaries," he added, " are servants of this court, but I know the court will more remember whom *they* serve than who serves *them*; and therefore I pray, as the King commands, that the proceedings in this assize be stayed, and that the plaintiff be ordered to sue to the King, if he will." And he quoted the sentence he had

used to Essex, so long ago, the formula of devotion:
"*Obedience is better than sacrifice.*"

But why was Chancery so important ? " Your Majesty knoweth your Chancellor is ever a principal counsellor or instrument of monarchy, of immediate dependence upon the King." He had tried to have Coke commanded not to proceed till he had seen the King : the Chief Justice had led the Judges forward to an immediate hearing. Eventually this particular case was compromised and the crisis postponed.

But only postponed. Chancery had been thwarted in its movement to ensure control over all cases touching the King. Coke, a little later, proceeded to try and restrain it still farther in cases touching other courts. Suitors who had lost their cases in the Courts of Common Law sometimes proceeded to Chancery and there obtained a more satisfactory judgment. It was not a custom which Coke (unless indeed he had been Chancellor) could bear. Two cases of the kind had just occurred, in which Chancery had redressed wrongs which had been legally inflicted by the Common Law. The Chief Justice remembered *Præmunire*, that ancient statute fashioned to prevent appeal from the secular English courts to the ecclesiastical court at Rome. Since it had been passed under Edward III *Præmunire* had been used in unexpected cases and to destroy unexpected persons. But it can never have been used more curiously than when Coke encouraged two rascals to set it in action against Chancery, when (as James saw) he set the King's claim in action against the King's court. Indictments were preferred against every one who had taken part in the proceeding. No human being from King to cowherd, if Coke could stop it, should hereafter find any shelter from the decrees of the Common Law.

The Attorney-General rallied himself and other lawyers to the aid of the King. They declared that

Chancery was justified, and they invited the Majesty to uphold its undoubted rights. Meanwhile the Chief Justice went on asserting the perfection and preservation of the Common Law. The King had given a living to the Bishop of Lichfield; it was claimed that the living was not his to give. The King commanded Bacon to tell the Judges they were not to proceed till he had had opportunity to consult them. Bacon immediately sent a letter to Coke, saying that it was the King's pleasure he should let the rest of the Judges know this. The messenger returned with a verbal answer to the effect that Bacon could let the Judges know if he chose. It was against legal etiquette; Bacon left etiquette behind and wrote. The Judges on the same day, however, proceeded with the argument and sent word to the King saying they held the Attorney's letter to be contrary to law; it was a matter of private interests which could not be delayed. The King replied that he was thrilled to hear of such judicial zeal, and he hoped that no cases of an earlier date than this remained yet unsettled.

On 6th June 1616, Coke and the Judges were brought before the Council. High Commission, Peacham, prothonotaries of Common Pleas, *præmunire*, presentations— all came to one thing in the end: was the Monarch in action an active power in the law? was the decision of Prerogative part of the decision of law, and how far, and when? The dispute fashioned itself to one question: were the Judges, if summoned by the Majesty, bound to attend, hear him, counsel him; and stay proceedings in the meantime? The Attorney declared that they were. The Chief Justice answered that it was not the Attorney's place to dispute with the Judges, but only to plead before them. Sir Francis said that he had a right to declare the truth in the King's name against any subject. The King, quite vehemently, agreed with his Attorney. The Judges were asked what they would

do in similar cases in future ; they all agreed to the
King's desire, except Coke, who said that when the case
came on he would do what was fitting for a Judge, but refused to say what he thought was fitting for a Judge. The
Council at last broke up, the Judges giving a general promise
that in future they would observe the Prerogative, and
thus leaving the Chief Justice more or less alone.

But from the King's side the Chief Justice was not
now to be left alone. Providence once more deigned to
unite Bacon's personal emotions with his public duty.
He regarded Coke as one of the most dangerous enemies
of the Throne, and that fact gave vivid life to his own
personal hostility. He admired Coke's legal greatness,
but that very greatness was an added danger. The
Chief Justice was suspended from the Council and from
the exercise of his office, and bidden to review and revise
his published " books of Reports." He did so ; in
thirteen volumes he found five small mistakes, and
declared himself willing to disavow them. The King,
on 15th November, removed him from his office.

The least tamed of the lions who (in Bacon's metaphor)
stood under the Throne was no longer to roar over its
shoulder at the scandalized Monarch. The King's
Attorney-General had put a bit in his mouth and sent him
to wander restlessly in his own cage. It was a great piece
of work for the Monarchy. Within eighteen months the
King, perhaps without realizing it as much as Francis, procured another. The Lord Chancellor, old, ill, exhausted,
died. Bacon was made Lord Keeper. The sun appeared
to have every likelihood of uninterrupted shining in its
strength as soon as it returned from Scotland, to which it
was then on the point of departure, and at last the
occupant of that long since deserted cradle in York House
was to return to York House as its master, the president of
the Council in the King's absence, " Privy Councillor," in
Fuller's phrase, " as to King James, so to Nature herself."

## CHAPTER VII

### The Lord Chancellor

On 7th March 1616/7 Sir Francis Bacon was made Lord Keeper. On 7th May he went to take his seat in the Court of Chancery. He went in all the magnificence he could gather; at long last the exterior triumph of his life had come. He was fifty-six; nine years remained. The Great Instauration was not yet published; the bell was not yet ringing, but the tower was built and all was nearly ready. It was fitting—it is not unfitting even to us—that he should go magnificently, for the knowledge of what went with him. The prophecy of man's empire passed through the London streets; the eyes that sought the secret causes of things looked on the London crowds; the mind that rejoiced in the thoroughfares of light took its pleasure in the colours and sounds of that civil pageant. Unity was for a moment rightly devised. The glory of the Lord Keeper was one with the glory of the Father of Salomon's House; the noise of the crowd mingled with the sound of the waves on the shore of the New Atlantis, and the voices of the lawyers with the echo of the everlasting labour in the College of the Six Days' Work of God.

He went, and with him went his splendour: his own great retinue, a multitude of servants bravely clad; serjeants-at-arms and seal-bearers; clerks and officers of Chancery; the gentlemen of the Inns of Court; the Lords of the Council; the Judges; peers, knights, and gallants, to the number of two hundred horse ("all that could get horses and footcloths"); the followers of the

Queen and the Prince sent specially by those royalties. In the centre the Lord Treasurer and the Keeper of the Privy Seal rode on either side of him, horsed between, in a gown of purple satin. His friends honoured him; the world acclaimed him; amid such manifestations of a magnificence which is meant, and cannot but be meant, as the reflection of and response to a universal magnanimity, he came to the Court; before that great assembly he took his seat. He spoke to them in the voice that Ben Jonson loved, while they, as Ben Jonson has told us of his audiences, did not dare to cough or look aside lest something should be lost, and had but one fear—lest he should make an end. He had a habit of pulling at his bands while he spoke, as it were twisting his argument out of them. His sentences were full " of his own graces." So he had spoken to the Commons, who, sometimes dissenting, always heard him *non sine magno applausu*. So he had spoken in the Courts, reprehending error, yet pitiful to the accused; perhaps after all Oliver St. John had more excuse than we know for his change of heart. So now he exhibited his mind and purpose to that hushed audience, defining before them the duties of his high office in law. He laid down the principles of his intentions and of his rule in Chancery. He had made laws for himself that he might justly administer the law. Strangely quickly for Bacon, on that day he freed himself from speaking of the King's commandment, as if that day were peculiarly his own; once at least he permitted himself to refer to " my father " and once to " a domestical example," as if only now he entered into his birthright. And once, when he was promising to add afternoon to forenoon and a fortnight of the vacation to the term, all for dispatch of business, once the voice that so charmed and held his hearers swept into a confession that covered many greater things: " only the depth of the three long vacations I would reserve in some measure free for business of estate, and for studies, arts, and sciences, to which in my nature I am most inclined." From that high chair the first herald note sounded, soft but portentous, the personal confession—proud and shy—of the universal summons to universality, " to which in my nature I am most inclined." He would be direct and speedy, patient of care, impatient of abuse. Also he knew, he a lawyer by descent and by experience, that young lawyers were never heard, and clients sought to great counsel; therefore on certain days he would hear the bar, after nine, till eleven, or at least half-past ten, so to help the generality of lawyers and ease the clients. " My lords, I have no more to say, but now I will go on to the business of the Court."

It ended. He wrote the next day to Buckingham to say—it is perhaps the greatest lie Bacon ever told—that all " this matter of pomp, which is heaven to some men, is hell to me or purgatory at least. It is true I was glad to see the King's choice was so generally approved, and that——" and so on and so on; service to Buckingham, devotion to the King. It was surely a lie; Francis Bacon loved magnificence. It was surely a fault; he need not have said so; the Lord Keeper should have been above such unnecessary exaggeration. It must be one of those silly remarks which annoy one in him—pointless, superfluous, untrue. It must be in him what exists in every man—the diabolic comment, the gross after-piece to the solemn play. If only he had been as much older than us in all things as he is in all but a few! But the gods give us something to mock in the wisest men, except Shakespeare.

It must have been all that. And yet he was a man who suffered interiorly when good-fortune fell on him. When he knew he was Solicitor a darkness took him. When he ascended before the world (he wrote afterwards

—in a prayer, not to Buckingham or James but to the Divine Father of Lights), " I descended before Thee." Perhaps the letter to Buckingham spoke the truth after all, and a purgatorial night of subtle purification held that great power enchained while the glorious ostentation of his Fortune blazed about him.

In the New Year he was made Lord Chancellor ; and in the July of 1618 he was raised to the nobility under the title of Verulam. It was said in January that he was becoming thrifty ; he had dismissed sixteen of his gentlemen in attendance. A few odd pages of accounts in his secretary's hand from 24th June to 29th September 1618 are left to show us something of his state. He received in that time £4160, 12s. 10d. He spent £3711, 4s. 2d. Certainly he was just to the good. Of the disbursements a good deal goes in small sums to those that bring him presents. Northampton's man, " that brought your Lordship a buck," got £1, 2s. ; Mr. Faldoe's man, bringing ten fat wethers, got £2, 4s. ; the same went to my lord of Ormont's man, bringing a cast of Irish hawks ; and the same to " a poor pilgrim " who brought, apparently, nothing. Mr. John Murray's man bringing a book from the King received £4, 8s. ; whether the increase was due to the King or to the book—it was probably the King, because Sir Arthur Gorge's man had only 10s. also for bringing a book, a shilling less than " a poor man " who brought his Lordship grapes, and than he " that carried the glasses of the Confectionary to Windsor and back again." The Dean of Windsor's servants, when Bacon left, pocketed £1, 14s. in tips, and " at Hampstead " (with whomever Bacon dined on 31st August) they got £2, 11s. " The washwoman for sending after the Crane that flew into the Thames " received five shillings ; so did " one that rode twice to London, by your Lordship's order, for beer " ; so did " a woman " who brought a hare. There are a hundred pounds written down as gifts, but there are a number of other entries "paid by your Lordship's order," which may or may not have been gifts. Goodman Fossey, a poor man, netted a pound by a petition; Goodwife Smith, a poor woman at Gorhambury, beat him by two shillings. Mrs. Spencer had £3, 6s. and her maid £1, 2s.; the hope that we have at last discovered Bacon in a scandal is defeated by a near entry that "Jo: Spencer, your Lordship's late servant," had had £1, 2s.: the maid was probably the daughter. The servants at Gorhambury, when the Lord Keeper left, received £15, 14s.; as gifts or board wages is undeterminable. "Rambridge his child" got £1, 2s.; so did "one Knight's wife," a poor woman; the weeders in the garden only 2s.—perhaps the energy of the Lord Verulam had watched them weeding. All the "gifts and rewards" amounted to £302, 7s.

The next part of the schedule is the bills. Another £70 goes to Humphrey Leigh for money given to the poor, and more—over a hundred pounds—in interest. Mr. Neave the upholsterer got £200 out of a bill of £647; Mr. Parkinson the linen-draper, £50 off £158; Mr. Wade the grocer, £20 out of £26; Mr. Collins the ironmonger got an old bill of £21 in full; Mr. Pemberton the silkman had £50 out of £130; Mr. Glover the tailor, £50 out of £65; Mr. Markham the silkman, £50 out of £326. "A fair ruby set in a ring" cost the Lord Keeper £20; a dozen handkerchiefs cost him eighteen shillings; two dozen socks the same, and a looking-glass for his lordship's case the same. "The Picture drawer for your Lordship's picture" took £33; "a fan for your Lordship," £1, 10s. Thus expenses mount up.

Yet, as in similar cases, it is not definite extravagances, it is the whole style that makes the difference. The Lord Verulam lived, as we do, on the edge of collapse. But in whatever kind of great place one finds oneself, it is one's duty to adorn it ; economy is then immorality. " The doctrine of largesse " is as harsh a doctrine as any, and may easily compel personal austerities. It is easier for some than for others, but so is all economy. We are too inclined to allow the thrifty to believe in their own morals ; thrift certainly, but as a compensatory personal virtue to the doctrine of largesse.

He was building also, at Gorhambury and at York House, where he spent £300 on erecting an aviary. His household about this time consisted of some seventy servants. He had two chaplains, two chief secretaries, a serjeant-at-arms, a steward, a seal-bearer, a gentleman of the horse, a chief gentleman usher, two gentlemen ushers, two yeomen ushers, one auditor, two or three legal subordinates, six gentlemen of the chamber, a server, and a score of gentlemen waiters, four pages, a doorkeeper, a barber, a messenger, two master cooks, three yeomen of the wardrobe and one of the horse, a master of the wine-cellar, two servants " of the ewry and the pantry," four butlers, a bottleman, and a cook. Besides these there must have been scullions and stable-boys, and all the floating population which at York House and Gorhambury reflected glory from and on their lord. On all these his largesse descended, and on those other servants coming with gifts from great persons —with garden seeds, bucks, cherries, sweetmeats, salmon, stags, books, quails, orange-flowers, turkeys, horses, heath pouts, fat wethers, ducks, partridges, apricots, fat bullocks, Irish hawks, sugar cakes, pheasants, cheeses, red deer, strawberries, swans and godwits, fruit, pears, muskmilians : on these and on " Jo Large, your Lordship's old servant that brought your Lordship a letter " (£1, 2s.), and on his coachman (£3, 6s., " as a gift "), his bottleman (10s. " as a gift "), on Mr. Trowshaw, " a poor man and late prisoner in the Compter " (£3, 6s.), and, finally, to boys at Eton, sons of acquaintances, " to

Sergt. Finch his son and Mr. Johnson's son at Eton, by your Lordship's order, £1, 2s."

Less than three years afterwards, the Lord Chancellor, accused and on the verge of destruction, left London for Gorhambury. There went with him so magnificent a company that the Highness of the Prince, meeting him on the way and observing that blaze of glory, that goodly troop of horse gathered to wait on his coach, said smiling, " Well, do what we can this man scorns to go out in snuff." It is pleasant and possible to believe that they went, not as by hire but in love. For he had, they said, a generous mind to his servants. " He was a good master," wrote his chaplain Rawley, and went on to add that, whenever places or offices came into his disposal, he presented his gentlemen to them " gratis," without taking any gifts or fee. Which, adds the chaplain, was the reason that so many young persons of blood and quality attached themselves to his retinue. It was hardly the master then who, in that exchange, can be called mean or avaricious. " If he were abused by any of them it was by the error of the goodness of his nature, and the badge of their indiscretions and intemperances." " He and his servants," wrote Fuller, " had all in common, the men never wanting what their master had." There was a story current, but long after his death, that the Lord Verulam kept a drawer filled with gold for his occasions, from which many of those gentlemen helped themselves as they would, and it is said also that when he was told of it he shrugged and said, " I cannot help myself." Either it was blackmail for those same indescribable orgies, or for some other evil secret of State (perhaps he poisoned the Overbury tarts), or it was the error of the goodness of his nature. He would have learning richly adorned, but (he had said long ago, before he held any office) learning itself needed one quality in its possessor—charity.

15

One of those servants remains to us. His name was Hunt, "a notable thrifty man," and he left an estate of a thousand pounds annual value in Somerset. He was, so it is said, the only servant the Lord Verulam had who would never become bound for him. My lord was wont to say to him, "The world was made for man, Hunt, and not man for the world." If indeed Hunt was thus unique, there must have been a princely spirit abroad in that glory which made St. Albans seem as if the Court was there, when the Chancellor came to Gorhambury, "so nobly did he live." But charity and magnificence and learning went together; he spent money on experiments in natural science, "diving into many of her abstruse mysteries. New conclusions" (it is still Fuller speaking) "he would dig out with mattocks of gold and silver, not caring what his experiments cost him, expending on the trials of Nature all and more than he got by the trials at the Bar, posterity being the better for his, though he the worse for his own dear experiments." And as he spent money, so he spent his leisure; in learning and entertainment and love. "He contemned no man's observations, but would light his torch at every man's candle." After dinner, it was noticed, men would hasten to make notes of the things he had said, but he did not monopolize conversation; he drew men out on their own subjects. But himself afterwards, as after walking or going abroad in his coach, "he would fall to reading again, and so suffer no moment of time to slip from him without some present improvement." So there existed at York House the mind which (to give Macaulay his chance of honour) "moved the intellects that moved the world." Fuller was more daring—"None can character him to the life save himself. He was, in parts, more than a man."

He had music played in the next room while he worked, as Drake did while he dined; his table was strewn at meals with sweet herbs and flowers, "to refresh his spirits and memory." " Sensual impressions of joys," he noted in his paper *Of Life and Death*, " are bad ; ruminations of joys in the memory, or apprehensions of them in hope or imagination, are good." He was speaking of the prolongation of life ; but the sentence reflects the music and the flowers which accompanied him, refreshing by their sensitive delicacy the spirit which still, in its glory, thought of " change rather than continuance." He trusted creation but mistrusted the world ; by that scent and sound the qualities of creation nourished his apprehensions and soothed his mistrust. For something of a similar refreshment, he used in April and the spring to go abroad with his coach open to the rain, because of the wholesomeness of " the nitre in the air and the universal spirit of the world."

On his first appointment there was an expectation abroad in the town that the new Lord Keeper would not be strong enough for his work. Private subjects and the Commonwealth, it was feared, would suffer. The Council would be hampered and Chancery at a stand. Star Chamber days would be put off. But by the close of the Easter term, on 2nd June 1617, he wrote in a reasonable triumph to Buckingham that he had made even with all business ; the lawyers were drawn dry of their motions ; not one cause unheard, nor one petition unanswered. He had heard the rumours about himself, that he would not be able to go on. " But that account is made. The duties of life are more than life. And if I die now I shall die before the world is weary of me, which in our times is somewhat rare." He did not so die, yet also he did. The world of Westminster and Theobalds was to weary of him, but foreign nations and future ages have never wearied of the rest, of the last years, of the very last month and week of his life. His perfection preserved itself to the extreme limits of his mortality.

Meanwhile he gave himself, the term ended, to affairs of State, and somewhat mingled both State and Law in his charges to the Judges, single or corporate. He compared them on their circuits to the planets of the kingdom. They had a great stroke in the affairs of the government. The Judges of Common Pleas were the lions under the throne, both lions and under the throne. The Barons of the Exchequer were warned that the King's prerogative and the law were not two things; the Prerogative was law and a principal part of the law. There was not one law of the head and another of the body, but "all is one entire law." Coke thought the same thing, but the anatomical comparison lacked one point—it did not decide whose was the mouth that pronounced the law and what nervous communication most readily affected the speech of that mouth. It was, however, from Coke not as lawyer but as rich man that a sudden storm shook the Lord Keeper and threatened to sweep him from his lofty seat. There are so few anecdotes of the kind in all that industrious life that the tale may be retold; not least for the conclusion. And one smaller anecdote first. Toby Matthew, who had always been his friend, had, years before, turned Roman and, after a short imprisonment, been allowed to leave the kingdom. Attempts were made to get the King to permit him to return which (under conditions) he did in 1617. Bacon carried him off to Gorhambury where he remained. The Lord Keeper was blamed for it: "it is thought *aliquid nimium* that a man of his place should give so much countenance to one so affected. And some stick not to say that former private familiarity should give place to public respects." It was precisely that for which others had blamed Bacon years before. Whether he seemed to support or seemed to abandon his private familiarities for public respects it was sure to be wrong. But he went his own way, for all his reputed obsequiousness ; at Gorhambury the Recusant remained.

Sir Edward Coke had been removed from office about the middle of November 1616. But by 14th December it was rumoured that he was still in high favour, that he was to be made a Baron, that he was to be employed again in some other place. " Either his friends (whereof the Queen and Prince are two) or else his money, or both together, hath so turned the current." A week later, rumour had gone further : " some interpret this kindness to be but for the compassing of a match for the Lord Villiers' brother with one of his daughters." The King, the Lord Villiers, Sir Edward Coke, and the Court were then at Newmarket, and there the match had been first mooted—between Buckingham's brother, Sir John Villiers, and Coke's youngest daughter. At that time, however, it broke down, owing to Coke's refusal to give as much money as the Villiers family required ; he had said that the King's favour being so variable, he would not buy it too dear. It was not until the next June (1617), after various other difficulties had shown him the inadvisability of being on bad terms with the Favourite, that he renewed overtures, sending apologies, protestations, and proposals through Sir Ralph Winwood, the Secretary.

It was in the next month that the business came officially to the Lord Keeper's knowledge. There had been in June a long dispute before the Council, between Coke and his wife, over their respective property, which at Bacon's suggestion had been referred to arbitration and settled with general assent if not complete satisfaction. But now Lady Compton, Buckingham's mother, came to the Lord Keeper on Sir Edward Coke's behalf. Lady Coke (Lady Hatton she was always called, the lady Francis had once thought of marrying, to whose mother Essex had written that his client would rise in his profession. He seemed to have done so)—Lady Hatton disapproved entirely of the proposed match, and had carried off her daughter to a private place, asserting that she was already engaged to the Earl of Oxford. The Earl of Oxford was then in Italy, and no one else could certainly contradict her. Lady Compton applied to Bacon for a warrant to recover the young lady. Bacon, without much to-do, refused it. He had heard of the marriage as a thing proposed by Winwood, and he thought it an unwise thing. He had no high opinion of Winwood, who had helped Sir Henry Neville to muddle with contracts and bargains the Parliament of 1614, and he thought he was pushing himself forward into affairs. Bacon was naturally opposed to any alliance between the dominant Villiers house and the disgraced Coke. And he thought that general opinion of the possibility of Coke's return to favour would do a good deal of harm to the King's service owing to the inconveniences which attended on Coke's peculiar character and capacities. He wrote to Buckingham, away in Edinburgh, pointing these things out, with a parenthesis saying that though friends adverse to Coke might fall away from the Favourite if the marriage were pursued he himself " out of pure love and thankfulness " would always be faithful. Yet he begged that the affair should either be wholly dropped or at least postponed till the Court returned to London. The mother had stolen the girl for fear the father should ; Winwood had made a complete mess of it. He ended with a sentence which must have annoyed Buckingham intensely : " hoping your Lordship will not only accept well, but believe my faithful advice, who by my great experience in the world must needs see further than your Lordship can."

By now the Favourite had grown out of his first deference. Attributed fatherhood was very well, but attributed fathers who took this tone, especially on matters in which their children were already committed, were tiresome. The Favourite did not for a moment believe that the Lord Keeper, now nearly sixty, could see farther than he could, and it was for himself and the King to decide on such high matters. He was so far right that the morals of that age would have held that, if a match were approved by the head of the house on each side, there was no one else (except the King) who had a right to interfere. In this case the King, Buckingham, Buckingham's mother, and Sir Edward Coke all approved. Only Lady Hatton objected; we know nothing of the young lady's feelings. It was not an affair of State; nobody could see why the Lord Keeper was interfering at all. The reasons he gave in his letter were ridiculous and presumptuous. The Lord Keeper must be put in his subordinate place. The King did not answer; the Favourite did not answer for some days, and then discharged an abrupt note.

Meanwhile in London things were growing wilder. Lady Hatton came violently on the scene. On the day when Bacon had written to Buckingham, the letter being done, and he unwell, he had gone to lie down. There arrived suddenly Lady Hatton and a friend, Lord Holles. The lady demanded to speak to the Lord Keeper; his servants refused to wake him. She begged to be allowed to wait in the next room, so that she might be at hand when he rose; the doorkeeper rashly obeyed, gave her a chair, and left her. Lady Hatton waited a little, heard nothing of the Lord Keeper, got up, and went and banged at the door of the bedchamber. The Lord Keeper, startled out of his sleep by the noise, shouted for his servants. They ran up, opened the door, and in they all went, Lady Hatton among them. She apologized, she soothed, she explained, she entreated. She was "like a cow that had lost her calf"; her husband had behaved scandalously; he had gone to the house where the calf was, smashed the door with a piece of timber, found and carried off the calf to his coach ; and could the ill-used mother have an immediate warrant to bring the daughter to the Lord Keeper or the Council or some one ?

The Lord Keeper, who had at first been annoyed, was pacified, but he did not then give her the warrant. Perhaps he referred her to the Council ; at any rate, next day, she first sent a petition complaining " in somewhat of a passionate and tragical manner " that she had been deprived of her child, and later on came herself to the Council. But by then it was known that Coke, before he had acted, had been wise enough to get a warrant from Winwood. Lady Hatton declared that her daughter, by reason of the shock, was in danger of her life, and needed such " physic and attendance " as could be got in London. The Council therefore wrote to Coke, requesting him to hand over his daughter to their clerk, a Mr. Edmondes, at whose house she was to be kept. Meanwhile Coke was to be heard in his defence on the Tuesday.

When the clerk, however, interviewed Coke, Sir Edward declined to send his daughter that night ; Monday morning would be time enough. The Council, hearing this, supplied the clerk with a warrant to the next morning. On Monday, therefore, the clerk went " with assistance " to take the lady ; but Coke had determined to obey and at the same time brought her in by a different road. To Mr. Edmondes' house friends on both sides thronged at once, and the Council hastily directed that only two visitors should be allowed ; one chosen by Sir Edward, who decided on the bridegroom-elect's mother, Lady Compton, the other by Lady Hatton, who decided on her mother, Lady Burleigh.

Before the Council on the Tuesday Sir Edward accused his wife of plotting to carry his daughter into

France. The Council were rather carefully polite about the marriage, not doubting but that Sir John Villiers "would seek her in a noble and religious fashion, without any forced consent of the maid and with consent of both parents, and the rather because part of her fortune did depend upon her mother's disposing." This delicate reminder having been offered to every one concerned, especially to Sir John, they decided that so great a riot as Sir Edward had made, in the King's absence, without even calling in a constable, was a serious matter, and commanded the Attorney Yelverton to prosecute Sir Edward before the Star Chamber. The Huddler seemed to have huddled his own business rather badly. There were sharp passages between him and Bacon when he offered to justify the riot by law, "which was ever his old song," wrote the Lord Keeper, thinking of what appeared to him to be Coke's habit of discovering that the law was what at the moment Coke might want it to be.

The Lord Keeper and the Council, however, were ignorant of one thing. It was known that the Secretary had been forward—officious, Bacon called it—in pushing the match. But no word had come from Scotland : or rather it was not known what word had come. On some day soon after, before the prosecution had begun, Lady Compton was before the Council, and a great person— probably Bacon—commented on the warrant issued for Coke, saying that it was liable to a *præmunire*, and that while some people served Buckingham out of affection others did it from faction and ambition. Winwood took up the challenge; he defended his actions; he said they were urged on him by the Queen; lastly, he produced a letter from the King approving of everything he had done from first to last. "*Ad quod non fuit responsum*"—the appalled Council stared at Winwood and realized that they were in serious difficulties. Yelverton was told to patch up a reconciliation between

Coke and his wife; the prosecution was dropped: a postscript was added to the official letter to the King recounting the latest proceedings, saying that father and maid were now living in unity at Coke's house, by the endeavours of the Attorney, and the whole business was left to the King's pleasure.

The Lord Keeper, however, was not prepared to leave his position wholly undefended. He suspected that something was wrong in Scotland. He wrote to the King, saying that if Sir Edward Coke now desired the marriage it was because he (Bacon) had helped to humble him, that he was certainly not afraid of Coke, and that he hoped, if the King wished the match to go on, he would send direct commandment:

" That I may conform myself thereunto: imagining with myself (though I will not wager upon women's minds) that I can prevail more with the mother than any other man. For if I should be requested in it from my Lord of Buckingham, the answer of a true friend ought to be, that I had rather go against his mind than against his good: but your Majesty I must obey; and besides I shall conceive that your Majesty out of your great wisdom and depth doth see those things which I see not.

" Now therefore, not to hold your Majesty with many words, which do but drown matter: Let me most humbly desire your Majesty to take into your royal consideration, that your state is at this time not only in good quiet and obedience, but in good affection and disposition. Your Majesty's prerogative and authority having risen some just degrees above the horizon more than heretofore, which hath dispersed vapours. Your Judges are in good temper. Your Justices of Peace, which is the body of the gentlemen of England, grow to be loving and obsequious, and to be weary of the humour of ruffling. All mutinous spirits grow to be a little poor, and to draw in their horns, and not the less for your Majesty's disauthorizing the man I now speak of.

"Now then I reasonably doubt that if there be but an opinion of his coming in with the strength of such an alliance, it will give a turn and relapse in men's minds unto the former state of things, hardly to be holpen; to the great weakening of your Majesty's service.

"Again, your Majesty may have perceived that as far as it was fit for me in modesty to advise, I was ever for a Parliament; which seemeth to me to be *cardo rerum* or *summa summarum* for the present occasions: but this my advice was ever conditional, that your Majesty should go to a Parliament with a council united and not distracted; and that, your Majesty will give me leave never to expect, if that man come in; not for any difference of mine own, for I can be *omnibus omnia* for your Majesty's service, but because he is by nature insociable, and by habit popular, and too old now to take a new ply, and men begin already to collect, yea and to conclude, that he that raiseth such a smoke to get in, will set all on fire when he is in.

"It may please your Majesty, now I have said I have done; and as I think I have done a duty not unworthy the first year of your last high favour. I most humbly pray your Majesty to pardon me if in any thing I have erred; for my errors shall always be supplied by obedience. And so I conclude with my prayers for the happy preservation of your person and state.

"Your Majesty's most humble, bounden, and most devoted servant,            FR. BACON, C.S.

"From Gorhambury, this 25th of July, 1617."

He wrote the same day to Buckingham.

"MY VERY GOOD LORD,

"I do think long to hear from your Lordship touching my last letter, wherein I gave you my opinion touching your brother's match. As then I showed my dislike of the matter, so the carriage of it here in the manner I dislike as much. If your Lordship think it is humour or interest in me that leads me, God judge my sincerity. But I must say, that in your many noble favours towards me, they ever moved and flowed from yourself, and not from any of your friends whatsoever; and therefore in requital give me leave that my counsels to you again be referred to your happiness, and not to the desires of any of your friends. I shall ever give you, as I give my master, safe counsel and such as time will approve."

The King answered in a letter which is lost; the Favourite in one which remains:

" MY LORD,
"If your man had been addressed only to me, I should have been careful to have procured him a more speedy dispatch: but now you have found another way of address, I am excused; and since you are grown weary of employing me, I can be no otherwise in being employed. In this business of my brother's that you over-trouble yourself with, I understand from London by some of my friends that you have carried yourself with much scorn and neglect both toward myself and friends; which if it prove true I blame not you but myself, who was ever
" Your Lordship's assured friend,
" G. BUCKINGHAM."

Certainly when Buckingham lost his temper he did it effectively. There was nothing more to be said. There was no possible doubt in that age that the authority of a father, especially if combined with the authority of the King, was sufficient to enforce a marriage. Bacon had no ground for further objections. What the young lady thought we do not know : whatever she thought it would not have mattered much, and least of all would it have seemed important to Bacon. He had no great opinion of romantic love, and as opposed to the will of the Majesty of England it would have seemed to him foolish and wicked. *Rex locutus est ; causa finita est.* He intimated to every one concerned that he would support the match. He wrote to the King, acknowledging that he had misjudged, apologizing for his error, but pointing out that he had had no word to direct him, that (as he had said before) Sir Edward Coke was all the better for a little firm treatment, that he had supposed he was serving the King and still thought that he had, to the best of his judgment, served the King, but that he accepted the King's decision. It is a submissive letter, but it is not by any kind of means an abject letter. There were considerably fewer flowers in this bouquet than Bacon was in the habit of dispatching. Given that Bacon sincerely believed the King's judgment to be better than his own, it is a perfectly natural letter. "After the King hath resolved," he had written in May concerning Spanish business, " all men ought to co-operate, and to be neither active nor much locutive *in oppositum.*" He was hurt now—probably because Winwood had been told and he had not ; if it had been any one else he would have been offended. But mortal man is not " offended " with Majesty. He submitted.

The correspondence, however, continued. The King was chiefly annoyed at the refusal of a warrant to Lady Compton ; he conceived that Lady Hatton had made the " first violence " by carrying off her daughter. Bacon should have recovered her, and then argued. But also Bacon, professing a " parent-like " affection for Buckingham, had added that " the height of his fortune might make him too secure, and that a looker-on sometimes sees more than the gamester." This, the

King considered, meant that Buckingham might " mis-
know " himself, might, in fact, grow proud and self-
conceited. Whereas actually he was less likely to be
that than any courtier the King had ever known, and
no one but Bacon, " the only phœnix in that jealousy in
all the kingdom," would think so. Had not Bacon once
recommended a certain person to be one of the Barons
in our Exchequer in Ireland, and had done it so badly
and had himself gone so far in the business, that the
King had been indisposed to the grant, and Bacon's
credit would have been a little blasted, if Buckingham
had not intervened; even running " a hazard of the
hindrance of our own service, by preferring a person
to so important a place whom you so slightly recommended." Flowers, it will be observed, were a necessity
in recommendations; it was the disadvantage of their
epistolary style. And so, with something like a threat
that worse was to follow, " we commend you to
God."

Bacon did not answer this extremely long and
unpleasant letter in detail. He wrote that he hoped to
defend himself, but—he must say that all he meant by
Buckingham's being " secure " was that his Lordship
might not foresee " the unfaithfulness of friends and
malignity of enemies and accidents of times," as Guicciardini said of Venice, " their prosperity had made them
secure and underweighers of perils." It was convenient
of Guicciardini, and it would have been an extremely
neat piece of tactics in flattery on Bacon's part, if it
had not happened that he probably meant it.

The Court, returning in this cloud and thunder, had
reached Coventry, where the Attorney-General Yelverton
met it. Buckingham was still furious. He met
Yelverton with promises of what he would do to his
enemies; they should see his favour by his power.
Bacon was forgetful, ungrateful, unfaithful, as unfaithful

as he had been to Essex and Somerset.[1] The Favourite declared that he was ashamed he had been so deceived. The Court was full of the excitement of expecting the Lord Keeper's disgrace; petitions against him were being prepared; "as your tongue hath been as a razor to some, so shall theirs be to you." Sir Edward Coke, also at Coventry, was triumphant; he was very bold with the King; he was again to be made one of the Council; he swore his daughter was passionately in love with Sir John Villiers. The King showed Yelverton a doubtful favour. All kinds of tales, slanders, rumours, and prophecies were abroad. Yelverton begged Bacon to come at once. "The sight of you will fright some. . . . Seem not dismayed but open yourself bravely and confidently, wherein you can excel all subjects, by which means you shall assuage some and daunt others."

Alas for posterity, the Lord Keeper remained in London, and we lost a high historic scene. It is noteworthy that Yelverton thought Bacon's mere appearance would have a good effect. He loved magnificence, but it seems he was a man who could carry magnificence. Into such a centre of hostility, the King threatening, the Favourite raging, Coke triumphing, the Court murmuring, it is not every one who would be invited. But Yelverton had no doubt—" Come, justify us all, retort on Coke, open yourself bravely, excel all, amaze some, daunt others, come." It is not as a master of subtlety, flattery, and obsequiousness that Bacon is begged to appear, but as a lord of presence and capacity. "The sight of you will fright some . . . come."

The Court returned. The Council at that moment had before them a certain Baynton who was accused of having threatened to kill the King under cover of presenting a suit. Bacon took the opportunity to propose

[1] Somerset! The collocation of those names is sufficient to show how lightly, in such a mouth, the first was used.

the revival of an old Commission for Suits, not merely
to prevent the King being killed but to save time and
money. He was aware that the King gave away far
too much money. He had an interview with Buckingham and they parted in satisfaction. The Lord Keeper
offered, if the Favourite wished, to make submission in
writing. The Favourite allowed himself to regard this
as sufficient reparation. He went to the King and (so
he said) persuaded him to promise to blame every one
of the Council in general and no one in particular. All
three of them were in a slightly awkward situation. By
that time also the " boldness " of Sir Edward Coke may
rather have palled on the Majesty. Buckingham disliked feeling a fool, and to have every one round him
blaming the Lord Keeper because he himself blamed
him was enough to make him feel the fool he was not.
The Favourite was neither a fool nor a coward. He was
young, he was spoilt, and when he wanted anything he
raged and sulked till he got it. Bacon gave him all he
could expect in gratitude. His other letters had been
finer ; but perhaps it is not wholly a bad thing to write
nobler letters under the threat of anger than when
things are fair again.

The marriage took place. There was an intention
of bringing Lady Hatton before the Star Chamber for
conspiracy, disobedience, and other misdemeanours,
especially the invention of the engagement to the Earl
of Oxford, who apparently knew nothing of it. But in
that case no one could have expected the newly-married
bridegroom to receive, through the bride, " that part of
her fortune which was at her mother's disposing " ;
Coke had already paid some £30,000 and was unlikely
to pay more. He was back at the Council Table by
28th September. On 30th October the Earl of Buckingham went in pomp to bring Lady Hatton to the King,
to whom she had submitted. She was set at liberty on

2nd November. Winwood had died on 27th October, and this fortunate circumstance allowed him to be blamed for whatever she had done wrong. On 8th November she gave a great banquet at Hatton House. The King, the Prince, and the Court were present. Winwood, let us hope, was present in spirit. The Lord Keeper was present. The King and the Lord Keeper both drank Lady Hatton's health. Sir Edward Coke was not present and did not drink Lady Hatton's health.

The correspondence between the Lord Keeper and the Favourite became thicker if not more intimate than ever. One of the most curious things about it is that it never is intimate ; few of his letters are. Occasionally, to Lancelot Andrewes or Toby Matthew, he can speak freely, but to the King, to Cecil, to Villiers, to that peer or this official, never. We, knowing " what he was born for," " to what in his nature he was most inclined," continually if unconsciously expect his preoccupation to appear ; we wait for a sudden betrayal of his confidence to his correspondent, or at least to us, in some allusive phrase. It never comes. The modern reader begins to feel indignant with him ; why does not the man give himself away ? So much rhetoric and not a word of his most private concern. But Bacon would not have thanked us for our anxiety, since we are interested only in him and not in the Great Instauration ; therefore he would not have cared, had he known, to satisfy us. The letters refuse us the heart of their writer, for all their flagrancy. Their flagrancy, therefore, their phrases of devotion, sound a little hollow ; there is nothing within them. But that is due to others rather than to Bacon ; something would have been there quickly enough had Cecil or Essex or Villiers really cared. " It is a poor centre of a man's actions, himself." Himself seems indeed to be the centre of Bacon's, but that is because no one would attend to that other centre upon which his mind moved. In the Chancery and the Court as in Gray's Inn and Twickenham, it remained a stranger through the days of his pilgrimage.

Some half-dozen times a year, some thirty in all, the Favourite wrote desiring the Lord Keeper's interest in persons who had suits before him " as far as justice will permit." It is certain on Buckingham's own showing that nevertheless sometimes they lost their suits. It is likely that Bacon, " rash with theories " of the Prerogative, would have stretched, without breaking, his rule of law, as it is certain he would not have broken nor even stretched his law of justice.

In the two years that followed, various high matters had place in which the Lord Verulam was, by his office, involved. But they throw no further light on his own imagination nor are they of any personal interest. Sir Walter Raleigh, who had been in the Tower since the beginning of the reign on a conviction of treason, attainted and (so the lawyers held) civilly dead, was allowed to make his last attempt on gold mines in the New World, failed, and returned with a new accusation of having attacked a friendly nation, *i.e.* the Spanish territories, burnt and pillaged a town, and slain its nationals. It was an act which offended James's personal idiosyncrasies and his political schemes. It was an act for which he should be called to account. But Coke and Bacon both agreed that as he was civilly dead already this was impossible. The Commissioners appointed to consider the case, of whom Bacon was one, after examinations and many sittings, offered two proposals. One : let him be executed and let a public narrative of his new offences be issued ; two : let a public hearing before the Council, Judges, and others be held, in which his offences should be declared and the legal reason for the proceeding be explained. Sir Walter was to be heard, but no sentence to be pronounced ; only the Lords and

Judges to give their opinion upon the justice of execution upon the old attainder. After which, a solemn act of council to be made.

Eventually the King did neither. He and the Favourite decided that Raleigh should be heard again before the same Commissioners, but not in public ; that he should be executed on the old sentence, and that afterwards a Declaration should be published. As in the case of the Benevolence, the Majesty almost followed Bacon's advice but not quite. Ostentation of the facts was needed, but the King was afraid of Raleigh's wit and dared not risk it. The Declaration, in which Bacon was said to have had a hand, stated that his new heinous crimes (which it rehearsed) had made him utterly unworthy of the King's further mercy, but since he could not judicially be called in question the King was enforced to have him executed upon his old attainder.

The last of the old Queen's court had vanished ; besides Coke there was now hardly any one with whom Bacon could have spoken familiarly of Elizabeth.

Another great case was the prosecution of the Earl of Suffolk for corruption and maladministration. His wife was joined with him in the accusation, and when her lawyers pleaded that judges (*ergo*, ministers) might accept " gifts," *xenia* (*xenia* had come to mean the usual New Year's gifts), by a refinement of irony the universe encouraged Bacon to say with a smile that New Year's gifts could not be accepted all the year round. Suffolk was fined, imprisoned, and pardoned in the usual way. He kept his seat in the Lords.

These were the two great law cases. In politics the Lord Verulam recommended Commissions for the encouragement of manufactures, for staying money within the realm, for provision of corn and grain, and direction (if needful) of public granaries, for preventing the depopulation of towns and houses of husbandry, for the recovery of drowned lands, etc. He took a definite part in pressing economies on the Court, though not so to reduce the public glory of the Majesty ; and engaged in every effort to procure a proper income for the Crown. "We find additionals still, but the consumption goeth on." He drew up a set of Rules for the Star Chamber. He submitted papers, advising on foreign affairs, advising a great navy, advising the calling of Parliament, preparing Proclamations, planning the King's speech, devising loyalties. He delivered charges to lawyers on their promotion ; among others to Mr. Whitelocke, who was to be put to be Chief Justice of Chester. In that charge there is a hint of how it was that, applauded and admired by the Commons, he seems to have been so easily attacked by the Commons. The Commons, it will be remembered, were largely country gentlemen. "Look," the Lord Keeper charged Whitelocke, "look to suppress the power of such gentlemen in the country that seek to oppress and suppress their poor neighbours ; for it is no great ill thing in a judge (though I have heard it hath been laid to some men's charge) that in causes before them the poor have advantage against the rich. If it be so, it is an error on the best side."

For all his love of magnificence he never really loved the rich, nor those who "engrossed profit." Very early in his career he had moved an Act against Enclosures ; there was nothing much to it. Acts against enclosures might be passed, but they could not be enforced. But that kind of comment appears again and again. In his speech on Purveyance he had told the King that the knights and burgesses who made up the House, though they tried to fulfil the trust put in them, yet perhaps too often "we do speak too much out of our own senses and discourses." But in that matter they were speaking for the poorer men. It was the poorer men whom he wished not to be asked for contributions to the Benevolence ; let the richer men pay. Thomas Sutton, founder of the Charterhouse, had left his money to found an hospital. Bacon commented : " if such an edifice, with six thousand pounds revenue, be erected into one hospital, it will in small time degenerate to be made a preferment of some great person to be master, and he to take all the sweet, and the poor to be stinted, and take all the crumbs ; as it comes to pass in divers hospitals of this realm, which have but the names of hospitals, and are but wealthy benefices in respect of the mastership, but the poor, which is the *propter quid*, little relieved." He therefore wished the money (if it might be done fairly and legally) spread over " some number " of hospitals rather than concentrated in one. In that he only followed out in another sphere a principle he had laid down at an earlier date (1601) : " It stands not with the policy of the State that the wealth of the kingdom should be engrossed into a few pasturers' hands." It is not a maxim one would certainly expect to find in the mouth of a son of Sir Nicholas Bacon and a nephew of Sir William Cecil's, who, if they were not the most notable of the pasturers upon the lands of the convents and abbeys, had done their best with what they in their time could absorb. But the *Essays* continue the same doctrine : " ever a state flourisheth where wealth is more equally spread " ; " money is like muck, not good except it be spread " ; " in countries, if the gentlemen be too many, the commons will be base " ; let farms and houses of husbandry be " maintained with such a proportion of land unto them as may breed a subject to live in convenient plenty, and no servile condition " ; " keep the plough in the hands of owners, and not mere hirelings." In our own day he might have been a Distributist. In general, he thought, the bulk of the population ought to belong to three classes : the farmers and tillers of the ground, owning their own lands and ploughs; free servants—" a thing almost peculiar to England "—belonging to the splendour and magnificence, the great retinues and hospitality of noblemen and gentlemen ("no ways inferior unto the yeomanry for arms"); handicraftsmen of strong and manly arts as smiths, masons, carpenters, etc. Soldiers he added to these, and a nobility, but this not numerous; and ought also to have added the scholars for whom he longed.

It was from this high place and survey of kingdoms that he at last addressed the world. In October 1620 he published the *Novum Organum*.

## CHAPTER VIII

### THE "NOVUM ORGANUM"

"*FRANCISCUS de Verulamio sic cogitavit: talemque apud se rationem instituit, quam Viventibus et Posteris notam fieri ipsorum interesse putavit.*"

" Francis of Verulam thought after this manner ; and held reasoning with himself such as he supposed it might be to the interest of the living and those who come after to know."

It was the great gamble. Many there be that seek the way to the concern of future generations, and few there be that find it ; still fewer whose thought, as distinguished from a chance song or action, deserves it. Each generation, as it grows old, tends to prefer the sayings of the dead ; they are easier and more gracious than the new, plangent, and difficult idioms of the young. But Francis of Verulam did not desire the attention of posterity on such easy terms ; he had not spent twelve years to build a shelter for the middle-aged. He was busy with the perfection of the mind—he desired to try all means "*si quo modo commercium istud Mentis et Rerum restitui posset in integrum.*" And so distracted from such integral commerce had the mind become that it was necessary to teach it again, to reconstruct human knowledge on sure foundations. " Nor was he unaware in what loneliness this experiment must be made, nor how hard and incredible a thing it is to win faith—*quam durum et incredibile sit ad faciendam fidem.*"

As if he saw himself in the far past of antiquity, a scholar long since dead, he recounted how that scholar had found no other man who had applied his mind to like things, how he had therefore determined to publish what had been done, not from ambition but from anxiety for the work, lest if he died there should remain no trace of it. For all other ambition had seemed poor in his eyes—"*aliam quamcunque ambitionem inferiorem*"—compared with the work between his hands, which was a thing either negligible or so great that it sought no reward but its own merit. "*Aut nihil est, aut tantum ut merito ipso contentum*. . . ." And then, recalling himself from that classic distance and becoming again one with the scholar of whom he wrote, he offered the dedication of the work to the King, telling him that it was a thing entirely new and yet very old, being made after the model of the world and the nature of things and the mind. He claimed no credit; there was something of accident in what men thought as well as in what they did or said, and such a chance had brought it into his mind. "*Quiddam quasi fortuitum*"—"a thing fortuitous, as it were"—so he looked back to those Cambridge days, and the inspiration that might so easily not have been. As in that speech when the Lord Keeper had taken his seat in Chancery, there is in this book peculiarly little of James—even less than then. One sentence only compares him in four likenesses to Solomon, and that only as a brief prelude to a request: that he would take order for the collection of a Natural History, "true and severe (unincumbered with literature and book-learning)." "I have provided the machine but the stuff must be gathered from the facts of nature." And so he closed the dedication: "Deus Opt. Max. Majestatem tuam diu servet incolumem.

"Serenissimæ Majestati tuæ
Servus devinctissumus
et devotissimus
FRANCISCUS VERULAM,
CANCELLARIUS."

After so long meditation, so much delay, so many efforts, the thing was at last to be expressed. The last twelve years had determined its arrangement. He went on from the Dedication to explain the complete Plan. The whole great gospel was to be put forward in six parts. The First Part, though it had not been so called, had already appeared, for it was a statement of the knowledge already available, and this the *Advancement of Learning* had given. It was insufficient ; much remained to be done—directions for or examples of the fulfilment of all deficiencies in what had already been done. The Lord Verulam intended, he said, not to enter those unknown regions of knowledge like an augur seeking for omens, but like a general taking possession. However, for the present he postponed any further conquest.

The Second Part was the present work, the *Novum Organum*. Its particular business was to equip the intellect for the exploration, not of what remained undone from the past but of the studies which were yet in the future. The mind was to be furnished with helps, directed by rules, raised and exalted. In the past it had been used " to overcome an opponent in argument," now it was " to command nature in action." The oldest logic had been concerned with syllogisms, words, notions, but of the closeness of those notions to facts it had taken little heed. It had held in reverence the natural motions of the intellect. But the natural motions of the intellect were themselves suspect. It had accepted the information of the well-disposed senses as final. But the senses were themselves deceitful, though doubtless they supplied means of discovering their own deceits, as the intellect provided rules for the correction of its own delusions. By the delusions of the mind, the deceits of the senses, by the desire of the heart for disputation rather than truth, science, and in science all man's true knowledge and man's true power, had been led astray. The fault of each was similar; it lay in the reference of information and judgment to the nature of man and not of the universe. Both sense and intellect confused their own natures with the nature of that which was exposed to their knowledge, and this double confusion issued at last in sterile wrangles. Yet all knowledge in nature must be sought from sense—"unless men mean to go mad"—and all truth in nature must be determined by the mind. There remained then, as man's greatest need and hope, the rectification and purging of those twin capacities: the sense by the method of experiment, the intellect by the method of induction. "The office of the sense shall be only to judge the experiment; the experiment itself shall judge the thing." Induction "shall analyse experience and take it to pieces, and by a due process of exclusion and rejection lead to an inevitable conclusion." Much had to be refuted in which man had put his trust—intrusive Philosophies, perverse Demonstrations, natural Human Reason. But this being done, then there was place for the true relation between the nature of things and the nature of the mind, "the strewing of the bridal chamber of the mind and the Universe," out of which marriage might spring "a line and race of inventions that may in some degree subdue and overcome the necessities and miseries of humanity. This is the Second Part of the work."

And this, in effect, was all that was done. But the Plan proceeded to define and explain the business of the other four Parts, toward which efforts were made at different times; they never found totality. For the race of inventions could not arise to aid mankind unless the high marriage be first consummated. The Third Part, therefore, was to be a Natural and Experimental History. Harvest must be awaited; it was not for the Lord Verulam or his friends and scholars to rush "to reap the green corn." Once let the work be begun, the axioms discovered, the process and nature of things made plain, results would be produced not singly but in clusters. The instrument of the mind being rectified, there was the necessity of providing it with stuff to work upon. Facts, facts, and still facts, were necessary; the world must be searched for them; no argument or thought or genius could supply their place—" this we must have, or the work must for ever be abandoned." Facts without falsity, without prejudgment, without carelessness, without blindness, without rumour, without slavish habit; always and everywhere the mere fact. *This happens*—that, exactly observed, is the necessary fundamental of the whole work. The Third Part, therefore, was to be a gathering of such facts—facts of nature " free and at large " and of nature forced and constrained by man; facts of all operative arts and crafts; of bodies and virtues (" original passions or desires of matter," as Density and Rarity, Heat and Cold, and so on); facts already severely examined, all received falsehoods proscribed, but yet to be more closely and exquisitely examined by others; and among them, continually interspersed, exhortations to " eject, repress, and as it were exorcise every kind of phantasm."

The Fourth Part was to consist of examples of the method in action; inquiry conducted into certain of the most noble and most different subjects, by which the whole range of its process should be exemplified, from the first instances to the final philosophical decision on the very nature of that particular nature, whereby approach should be made to the true and just philosophy which was to crown the whole work.

The Fifth Part was but accidental—things the Lord Verulam had noted on his way and in his work, though not tested and judged by the strict method, and therefore not to be held binding on him; possibilities, provisional conclusions, lesser " degrees of assurance." He would offer them not as springing from any belief in his own mind but as from his continual occupation with nature ; they might, so, have a value beyond his own wit and serve as interim stations for the exploring mind.

But the Sixth Part the Lord Verulam declared that he never hoped to write. It was to hold the philosophy which in its discovery was the end of all as by its existence it had given impulse to the beginning of all. The whole of nature being explored and understood, the whole of its operations lying open, truth (so far as the nature of things was concerned) being flagrant and ostensible, the final declaration of that philosophy would be achieved. The Lord Verulam looked to humanity to complete the work.

Such was the august Plan. Francis Bacon had begun it ; mankind was to end it. Mankind was to correct him, continue him ; he asked for nothing but that they should judge things and himself and themselves by, at bottom, the only certain rule. " Keep your eye on the object " ; " clear your mind of cant "—those two later counsels were the two directions of his spirit. A thousand errors in experiment, a thousand mistakes in judgment, a thousand negligences or carelessnesses, cannot smother the immortal crying which his energy loosed on the world ; as a thousand superfluities or falsities cannot cloud the sincerity of his spirit.

The Plan then was fully declared ; the declaration was immediately followed by the Second Part. Even that did not claim completion ; it proposed on its title-page to exhibit " the Art of Interpreting Nature, and of the truer existence of the Intellect ; not, however, in the form of a regular Treatise, but only a Summary digested into Aphorisms." In that complex style of pride and humility the Lord Verulam went on with the work. As in his private notebook he had scribbled of Sir Henry

Hobart, " Solemn goose," so in his public print he now dismissed the professors of received philosophy. The new method of learning would not be any good to them ; " it does not lie in the way. It cannot be caught up in passage. It does not flatter the understanding by conformity with preconceived notions." But, on the other hand, as he gave offices to his gentlemen without taking any fee, so he now asked of mankind nothing but free and just trial. If any man would form an opinion on the work, " let him examine thoroughly . . . let him make trial of the way . . . let him familiarize his thoughts . . . let him correct the habits of his mind . . . when all this is done and he has begun to be his own master, let him (if he will) use his own judgment."

The *Novum Organum* itself was divided into two books ; the first defined the principles of the new method ; the second exhibited it in action. The very first aphorism lays down the condition of man's knowledge and power ; the second defines his instruments and the need of further instruments. " Man can understand only so much as he has observed, in fact or thought, of the course of nature ; beyond this he can neither understand nor do anything." " The instruments are the hand and the mind." Even in that swift collocation the work is, as it were, begun ; the hand, the subtle organ of intellect, its symbol, perhaps (since certainly at present we know little more than Bacon of the true nature of man's body) its image and in a sense its identity, is here related to its invisible lord. But the hand can be trusted in its service ; it is precisely its lord which has erred, flying from immediate particulars of the senses to the most general principles and thence doubling back to establish middle principles or axioms. Its business is to proceed in order—to establish middle axioms from immediate particulars and " by a gradual and unbroken assent " to pass to the most general principles of all. Those final general principles, the philosophy which mankind was to conclude, of which Bacon had already spoken in the *Advancement*, the *philosophia prima*, "the Berecynthia of knowledge," was the end of the whole business. Human power would, on the way and at the end, produce numberless new works for the good estate of man; it would extend man's empire over all things possible. Yet so much (it might be held) was but for man's happy preservation at best. His perfection would come in the final discovery of the Laws of the Universe. The rest would be for profit and magnificence; these for honour and magnanimity; though indeed they could not so be separated, since "human knowledge and human power meet in one. Nature to be commanded must be obeyed"; it is this law of obedience which was to be proclaimed as the index of and way to the law of command.

But man's mind was lost in other obediences; there swelled over it the four great groups of Idols which Bacon named and defined for us lest we should worship them ignorantly or deliberately—of the Tribe, of the Cave, of the Market-place, of the Theatre. The first group are the shadowy reflections of the uncivilized mind itself, feverish, unquiet, incapable of repose, imposing its desires for regularity in nature, for aids to preconceived opinions and the things it desires to believe, for violent and impressive imaginations, for forms other than the laws of nature in action. These Idols of the Tribe have their being from the nature of the mind of man. But the Tribe exists separately in the caves of individuals, and in those separate caves loom other Idols, emanating from each man's constitution, education, or habit—as in those minds which excessively admire antiquity or those again which passionately desire novelty; those which study the trees instead of the wood, and those which contemplate the wood without distinguishing the trees. But to emerge from the caves into the market-place of human intercourse does not free man from his false idolatry, for there (exalted by that very intercourse) are the Idols of the market: words. Words, turned into Idols, entrancing and deceiving the mind, reduce everything into formal arguments about themselves; as if gods refused to men all concern but uncertain disputes about their own nature. And even if men escape they do so too often by falling under the dominion of some scheme of words, and taking refuge in theories, philosophical, religious, scientific; theories " compact and elegant," representing worlds of their own creation, as in stage-plays; the neat authoritative Idols of the Theatre. Here throng the worshippers of systems—Aristotelian, alchemical, Pythagorean, Platonic; natural philosophies finding systematic statements in Genesis or Job; and many more which are not yet but will certainly come to be. They are checked a little, these Idols and their credulous creators, by civil government, especially monarchies, which are "averse to such novelties . . . so that men labour therein to the peril and harming of their fortunes." Bacon was perhaps a little wrong there; the Commons were searching after a philosophical system which had not any adverse effect on their fortunes. But he felt in the Prerogative a greater system, a more original power, than could inhere in the Commons. That the power and knowledge of the State inhered in the Families he would have needed our experience to believe.

It is tempting to play with his definitions and with the acquaintances, hostile or amicable, of his life. Did he think that Cecil adored the Idols of his Cave, or his mother the Idols of her Theatre? The sacred Majesties of Elizabeth and James he would have believed to be above all Idols, unless perhaps drawn in a moment's weakness by their Favourites to that unwise worship. But did not Coke dispute about words and names, Idols of the Market-place? or was he, too, chanting liturgies in his own cave to the giant forms of his own nature ? It is more likely he did not think of them ; he was away now in the top of his beanstalk, looking down—with what most admirable lucidity !—on the world of men.

Of the relation of his own mind to those cloudy giants, at the top or at the bottom of his Igdrasil, it is more difficult to speak. The Idols of the Theatre he did not serve ; the stage-play (since, to judge rightly, we must call it so) of the Christian dogmas he reduced in his mind to the simpler but most necessary scenes, and he would not allow that its characters, gods or idols, had anything but a creative and final relationship with the world. The echo at Pont Charenton was not to be explained by the operation of the supernatural powers whom his sincere belief adored. The Idols of the Market-place he expelled from the top of the tree, making his words in the process of the great work substantial with truth, but when he came down to the market-place itself he was a little careless about them, doing obeisance to the language of his day. He was ostentatious of devotion, and no one but he knows how far his devotion was sincere. The Idols of the Cave he combated with all his power, knowing their deceptive danger. " No man," he wrote to Lancelot Andrewes, " can be both judge and party, and when our minds judge by reflection of ourselves, they are the more subject to error." His peculiar vision did not help him there ; in its nature it could not, for it contained the touchstone of no other decision but his own. In Physics this was desirable ; in morals not so desirable. The reflection of himself was therefore to be shattered, and only himself left ; in the sudden desolation —for the removal of that singular reflection leaves a man desolate—he was to abandon the Idols of the Cave. *Cogitata et Visa*—things thought and seen—was the name of the MS. he was sending to the bishop ; *cogitatum et visum*, he was left to see himself if he could.

## THE "NOVUM ORGANUM"  251

Of the earliest, most catholic, Idols of the Tribe he had his share. His mind also was sometimes in lesser things feverish, desirous of infinity, incapable of repose. It belonged to the Tribe and was agitated by the Tribe; even Francis Bacon had the nature of man, and could often only ensue and not possess lucidity. But he bequeathed his rebellion to his children in the very definition of the tyrannies under which he suffered, in the effort " to enlarge the bounds of Reason."

Beyond the Idols he came to lesser hindrances. The *Novum Organum* proceeds to point out the weaknesses of preceding philosophies, the causes of the error of thought in past history; it encourages itself and its readers with one-and-twenty Grounds of Hope; and it closes its first book with an epigram which reconciles him to all later doctors of science: " *nos qui mentem respicimus . . . artem inveniendi cum Inventis adolescere posse, statuere debemus,*" " we who behold the mind . . . ought to hold that the art of discovery will grow in proportion as discoveries themselves increase." It is his acceptance of all future improvement and alteration of his own methods.

In the Second Book he passed on to explain those methods more fully. He came to the definition of Forms. He proceeded to give an example of discovering a Form—choosing the quality of Heat. It is no use merely collecting all examples of Heat without any selection, and then playing with unchecked — probably metaphysical — fancies. Metaphysics, in the old sense, have nothing to do with it. What are wanted are Tables—a Table of Instances of Heat with their circumstances; a Table of similar circumstances lacking in Heat; a Table of instances of Comparative Heat. The mind has then to find " a nature " which is present when heat is present, absent when heat is absent, and increases or decreases in just proportion with heat. We must therefore deny and exclude all natures which according to this rule are inapplicable, and the result will be a Form affirmative, solid, true, well-defined. He provides these Tables of Instances of Heat, and suggests that the cause of Heat is motion, "expansive, restrained, rapid, and striving amongst the smaller particles of bodies," much, though he would not have approved the comparison, as he had seen it operating in the House of Commons, or, even earlier, between Essex and the Queen.

But this definition is but a First Vintage of the Understanding, a hypothesis drawn from the Tables given. There are other helps which the Understanding must use, in order certainly to discover the inerrable Form; nine in all, of which the *Novum Organum* proceeds to deal in detail with one only; the rest were postponed to that convenient day which never came. The single aid explained is that of Prerogative Instances. Prerogative Instances are remarkable facts; facts which, for one reason or another, exercise a certain power upon the mind, and impress it in relation to the nature "which is under investigation." They are, in a sense, royal among facts; they possess a dignity because of their peculiarity, and yet that dignity is but part of the whole operation of nature, as the royal prerogative in civil affairs is part of the whole operation of law and social life.[1] The understanding must be cautious in its contemplation of these instances, or it will find itself running away after a false opinion. It must, again and again, have recourse to Exclusion. But, with this caution, it does well to consider the characteristics of these Instances.

There are, in all, twenty-seven Prerogative Instances, and we have taken some of their titles into common speech. There are Solitary Instances, Crucial Instances, Striking Instances, and Parallel Instances. There are titles which have about them a lovely fancy—Instances of the Twilight, Instances of the Lamp, and Instances of

---

[1] The likeness is not, so far as I can see, Bacon's.

the Door. But they were not meant as lovely fancies, any more than the titles of the Majesty of England were meant as luxurious sensations without any relation to government. A Travelling or Migratory Instance, for example, is as follows : Let us suppose that we are inquiring into the nature of Whiteness. Now whole glass and plain water are transparent and not white, but powdered glass and foaming water are white and not transparent. The powdering of the glass and agitation of the water have produced whiteness ; they belong to the class of Instances migratory towards the generation of whiteness. Singular or Monadic Instances are phenomena which seem " extravagant," " out of the usual order." Such are the sun and moon amongst stars ; the magnet amongst stones ; quicksilver amongst metals ; the elephant among quadrupeds ; the letter S among letters. The use of these is to assist the inquiry, because these apparent marvels are also to be reduced to some fixed law ; and their singularity will but lie in their rarity and not in themselves. Whereas now man thinks them, as it were, without cause, exceptions to general rules. The elephant is a curious example to select, but the Elizabethans had three centuries less of association with the elephant as with romanticism in love.

The Lord Verulam completed his twenty-seven Prerogative Instances, and stopped. One would give something to have his account of the moment of that conclusion, as, a century and a half later, we have Gibbon's. In fact, however, it is in that sentence which told how Francis of Verulam determined to publish his thoughts, however fragmentary, because he thought they might be of interest to the living and to the yet unborn, because he had never found any other who had applied his mind to like things, because if he died all trace of the work studied through so many years and such differing chances would be lost, and because all other ambition had seemed poor in his eyes compared with this unutterable thing which his Fortune had given into his hands and bidden him carry out in loneliness. "*Neque eum fugit quanta in solitudine versetur hoc experimentum.*"

He published; he sent copies abroad; he presented copies to the Majesty and the great ones of England. Only one letter acknowledging it appears to remain, but that emanated from the Majesty. James promised to read it, even if he had to sit up late to do it; he promised to ask questions where he did not understand, and to commend " such places as in my opinion shall deserve it. In the meantime," the mortal god told his learned servant :

" I can with comfort assure you, that you could not have made choice of a subject more befitting your place, and your universal and methodick knowledge; and in the general, I have already observed, that you jump with me, in keeping the mid-way between the two extremes; as also in some particulars I have found that you agree fully with my opinion. And so praying God to give your work as good success as your heart can wish and your labours deserve, I bid you heartily farewell.

" JAMES R."

But in the end report said it was too much for the King; not even the Prerogative Instances could reconcile his learning and the Lord Verulam's.

## CHAPTER IX

### THE REMOVAL OF PRESERVATION

"BUT the quincunx of heaven runs low, and 'tis time to close the five ports of knowledge." The "ordainer of order and mystical mathematicks of the city of heaven" had ordained that the quincunx of Bacon's brief day under the heaven of the favour of Majesty should by now run low, but through the night that followed neither God nor himself closed for him the five ports of knowledge. The gate of the Monarch was neglected, the gate of mankind less peopled; he stood as a beggar in the gate of his own fortune; but the gate of nature lay open still to the coming of all light-bearing experiments; and crowds more frequent and more large began to throng the gate of the uttered word.

There is, it seems, a law in things that if a man is compelled to choose between two good actions, mutually exclusive, the one which he chooses to neglect will in course of time avenge itself on him. Rightly considered, this is a comfortable if chastening thought, for it implies that the nature of good is such that it can never, not even for some other mode of itself, be neglected. If ever it is, for whatever admirable reasons, set on one side it will certainly return. No virtue can be followed at the expense of another virtue without injury to the actor. But if that personal harm is a consequence of impersonal justice, the condition of man is not without nobility, so only that his imagination is strong enough to see and understand, love and embrace, the suffering which it involves. Otherwise good could be damaged with impunity. This is perhaps the complement of Christ's command to be perfect, and perhaps is related to that doctrine of purgatory where something other than sin is expiated by enlarged and comprehending souls.

Bacon had, in the case of Essex, followed the good he held chiefly desirable. Generations have held that he ought to have set private friendship, however faded, private gratitude, however unnecessary, private service, however futile, in front of his duty to the Majesty and State of England. An age intensely loyal in its friendships, passionately faithful to private attachments, which should canonize the fanatics of dead love, and hold love to be unalterable whatever alteration it finds, might certainly have a right to blame Francis for that; as an age intensely careful of its public purity, passionately devoted to lofty simplicity of conduct in its governors, holding the integrity of its courts (including the High Court of Parliament) to be of the first importance to the Republic, might have a right to blame him for the lack of candid sanctity in his legal life. We may judge whether this is such an age and how far our perfection may rebuke his.

Francis Bacon, in his great places, professed much—devotion to the King, devotion to law, devotion to truth. What he had never thought it worth while to profess was integrity. He knew he might be suspected of intrigue and self-advancement; that he could be suspected of corruption, and the sale of justice, does not ever seem to have occurred to him. If it had, we should have heard protestations and assurances—honest assurances and true protestations, but to a more fastidious age both a little unnecessarily loud. The standard of assurances has altered more than the standard of values. Our public men do not continually assert their purity, because it is bad taste on our part to suspect it and they will not allow themselves to be suspected of worse taste than our own.

Nowadays our governors and we vie with each other in outward behaviour. The thing itself—corruption in high office—may or may not exist ; we never come anywhere near the public discussion of it as a possibility, let alone a fact. Our age is therefore relieved of the necessity of watching its rulers. Bacon, Churchill, Walpole were corrupt ; but Gladstone, of course, was not, nor Balfour, nor whoever now holds public place. It does not happen. Or if it does happen it would be ungentlemanly to suggest it. But Bacon was entirely free from this modern notion of the gentleman, as he was from the notion that the gentlemen of England were the safest champions of freedom. One reason is perhaps that he was thoroughly well acquainted with the gentlemen themselves. He had sat on the Commission which tried the Earl of Suffolk. But himself in that thing he did not doubt. He, who would not take a forfeiture unfairly, who refused a nomination to the Chancellorship because it would be an indelicacy between him and the then Chancellor, never thought it worth while to profess integrity. But later he noted in the *Essays*, " avoid not only the fault but the suspicion." " Bind the hands of suitors from offering." A professed integrity " with a manifest detestation of bribery " is to do this. We have gone more wisely to work ; we have made the mere profession of integrity suspect, by our development of good taste. This saves trouble all round —to men in great place, to their suitors, and to us. Suspicion is officially banished, and the unofficial cannot be supposed to exist.

All his life " perfection and preservation " had gone together. The excuse he found for Essex had been true of his own Fortune. He had sought perfection by following preservation ; he had found preservation in desiring always the utmost perfection visible to him. He had followed both in standing by the Queen ; he had followed both in his devotion to the law, the Prerogative, the

State. But it is not given to any man to possess both at all times. Sometimes he chooses deliberately, sometimes ignorantly; sometimes, without his choice, the universe divides. It was so now. Perfection and preservation split apart, " in a moment, in the twinkling of an eye." " Things rather of magnificence than of magnanimity " separated from the place of magnanimity, and left him to be magnanimous if he could. He could.

The *Novum Organum* had been published just over four months when on 27th January 1620/1 the Majesty of England raised my Lord Verulam to be Viscount St. Alban. His magnificence was fulfilled. On his birthday, 22nd January, he could experience his own achievement, long delayed, often thwarted. In the time that remained he looked for it to be enlarged and expanded on every side : so far as he was concerned he would illuminate the thoroughfares of the world. God's first creature, light, was to show, yet more clearly, the relations of all things possible to be known.

But the laws of that aboriginal light are not possible to be known. We guess them only. Light was certainly to shine upon him : the light of that strange and dreadful crisis in which a man becomes a mockery to himself, in which annihilation is his only desire and in which the whole power of the universe denies him annihilation and sustains and nourishes his imagination that it may be at the same time more terribly destroyed ; the crisis of which the Athanasian phrase " perish everlastingly " is the only satisfactory definition, in which death eats the heart, the blood becomes living venom, and the wise spirit sits in its tabernacle girding at its own pain. This crisis approached him. Destiny concealed it from him, playing its usual trick. It was to overthrow not merely his glory in his life but his reputation afterwards. He was to be attacked by Suffolk and patronised by Buckingham ; and afterwards he was to be libelled by Pope and rebuked by Macaulay and pitied by Dean Church.

The astonishing, the great and immortal glory of Bacon, the magnanimity which, deprived of magnificence, he showed to the future ages to whom he appealed, is that, beyond all his accusers, in that moment he beheld justice. He had written of the desire for " purification of the understanding," and destiny took him at his word. The phrases he used of his own fall are rather beyond us than behind us. His knowledge of truth rose like a star over the tumult; in the chaos the spirit of God moved upon the face of the waters. No one but himself could have blamed himself so far as to say, in one of the few sentences, outside the poets, which deserve meditation and still pierce to the heart of all meditation : " I was the justest judge in England these fifty years. But it was the justest sentence these two hundred years."

His fortune amused itself a little in its preparation for the catastrophe. It began, remotely enough, with a small split between the Lord Chancellor and the Attorney-General. Sir Henry Yelverton had been friends with Bacon and had done him service in the unexpected affair of Coke's daughter's marriage. But during 1619 Bacon remarked a certain slackness in him, and by the beginning of the next year wrote that " Mr. Attorney groweth pretty pert with me of late, and I see well who they are that maintain him. But be they flies or be they wasps, I neither care for buzzes nor stings, most especially in anything that——" and so forth; the rest was always being said. Yelverton had never got on with Buckingham. Whether there were any that " maintained him " we do not know; if there were, they failed him soon after. In June 1620 Yelverton had in charge to draw a new charter for the City of London, in doing which he included certain clauses to which objection was taken. There was no real difficulty; the City was ready to return its charter,

Yelverton was ready to make submission, the King was ready to be gracious. But it was held that the King's honour required public clearing, and that both the Attorney and the City should make answer to the Star Chamber, the charter being returned as by their own motive, after which the King could show such mercy as pleased him. The Council advised James to this effect, and the hearing was fixed for 27th October. Between June and October preparations began to be made for the calling of a Parliament. The expenses of the proposed war for the recovery of the Palatinate would be heavy; all the retrenchment possible of the Crown's expenditure and all the raising of the Crown's income, all the benevolent offerings of peers, gentlemen, and burgesses, would not make up the yearly £500,000 at which the maintenance of the army was reckoned. It was necessary to call the Commons together in the hope that the Commons would do enough in the way of subsidies, and to take all possible measures to see that the Commons did.

In both these matters Bacon acted and advised in accordance with the principles he had laid down years before. When he took his seat as Lord Keeper he had announced that if there were anything doubtful or unusual in the letters patent to which he had command to affix the Great Seal he should stay them till the King's further pleasure be known. It was Yelverton's carelessness in a matter of a similar kind which he criticized in delivering judgment in November. "If the King's counsel be suffered to practise by multiplication on their warrant, the Crown will be undone in a short time. My Lord Chief Justice told of a fault in a Chancellor that was too forward to put to the Great Seal: but it is a greater in the Attorney that leads it. . . . He had the former charters, he went as far as they, and also further; he kept the rule by him and yet he transgressed. For extenuation of the fact, I am satisfied there was no corruption of reward." So Yelverton was fined £4000, sentenced to imprisonment during the King's pleasure, and declared unfit for his place. That was on 10th November.

On 29th November Bacon alluded to the case again. Parliament was summoned for 16th January, and Bacon with Coke, the two Chief Justices, and Sir Randolph Crewe, the King's Serjeant, sent Buckingham a letter of advice for the King. Among the points likely to be raised in the Commons were the Patents of Monopolies. Some grievances Bacon held ought to be left and remedied only by grace in reply to the humble request of the Commons, " some grave discreet gentlemen of the country such as have least relation to the Court " being put up to make a motion to this effect. But he did not think it wise to leave Monopolies to the chances of grave discreet gentlemen. In general he did not approve of monopolies; they interfered with trade. But there were economic or social exceptions. They were matters of policy, not of principle, and so was the abrogation or continuance of any of them. He knew that many of the existing patents were unpopular. He advised the King to have them raised in the Council at once, on some pretext or other—one that he named was the fresh example, " as in Sir Henry Yelverton's case," of the abuse of patents. The King and the Council could pretend to discover that such Monopolies were abused in execution or otherwise burdensome, and proceed to revoke them as of his Majesty's mere natural goodness and greatness before the Commons had a chance of getting at them. There would thus be a nice feeling all round, and there ought to be a glow of gratitude and loyalty in Parliament. But the Majesty was not to seem to do it merely to please Parliament. He added, in a private letter to Buckingham, that three of the Monopolies concerned his Lordship's special friends, but that since these three were of the highest importance he recommended Buckingham to make the most of getting thanks for " ceasing them " rather than run the risk of maintaining them. " Howsoever," he added, " let me know your mind, and your Lordship shall find I will go your way." There was a good deal of discussion on the question. Rather doubtfully Bacon yielded to the opinion that the Monopolies had better be left for Parliament to deal with. Buckingham was not anxious to do anything unless compelled, and Bacon was not anxious to press the Favourite to a disagreeable course. What he told Buckingham was that he argued against delay, but as one that would fain be convinced. He allowed himself to be convinced, in deference to the Favourite, and when he rose from the Council Table he went ignorantly out into a changed world. Between vigil for the King's greatness and deference to the King's Favourite, the Lord Chancellor was to proceed under the ironic contemplation of the universe towards the opening of Parliament. He had acted on high principles of State and those principles were to swallow him; he had acquiesced in a personal desire, and that desire postponed action till action was too late.

On 7th January 1620/1 Norroy King-at-Arms was warned of the Chancellor's investiture as Viscount St. Alban; on the 13th, writing to the King of Denmark, Bacon signed " Fr. St. Alban " ; on the 22nd he kept his sixtieth birthday ; on the 27th he was raised to his new dignity with all " ceremonies of robe and coronet," during which he thanked the Majesty for his seven-fold advancement—Solicitor, Attorney, Privy Councillor, Keeper of the Seal, Chancellor, Baron Verulam, Viscount St. Alban. In a letter to the King he made it an eightfold gratitude by inserting his establishment as one of the Learned Counsel at the beginning, and moving all the rest accordantly. " So this is the eighth rise or reach, a diapason in music, ever a good number and accord for a close. And so I may without superstition be buried in St. Alban's habit or vestment." The *Novum Organum* had been published just over three months. The accord of his five movements reached its climax. In the glorious sound of that climax he stood up on 30th January, after the King, to speak to the assembled Houses. Among the peers and gentlemen who listened to him were Buckingham and Southampton, Coke and Yelverton. "May it please your Majesty——"

The Higher and Lower Houses were attending. They had heard of the duty of Parliaments, of the advice they might offer, of the supplies they might offer, of the distracted state of Christendom and the invasion of the Palatinate, of the King's trust in their good offices. They heard the Chancellor saying how wonderful the King was, and bidding them behave modestly and helpfully to so good a sovereign. And now let them choose a Speaker. They did so on 3rd February; on the 5th the Commons appointed a Committee of Grievances and themselves went into Committee of Supply. On the 15th they heard of the £500,000 per annum; on the 16th they voted for two subsidies, amounting to £164,000, "but not . . . concerning the Palatinate." On 16th February they discussed economies, and the scarcity of money, and on that day—exactly a week after that first meeting—some one mentioned the Monopoly of Gold and Silver Thread. This was held by Sir Giles Mompesson; he also held the Monopoly of Inns, which came up in a few days. He was accused of having corruptly and shamefully administered his power. By the 23rd he and Sir Francis Michell, another monopolist, were at the bar of the House, Michell defiantly, Mompesson submissively. On the 27th Michell was in the Tower, and Sir Edward Coke was laying down as a legal maxim that : " If any one accused for a grievance do justify it in this House of Parliament, it is an indignity to this House, and for this the House may send any one to the Tower."[1] It seemed, however, after investigation, that the House had no power by the precedents to judge or sentence offenders against the State, so that Mompesson could not be touched by the Commons alone ; they would have to join with the Lords. And meanwhile Mompesson had been questioned about the Patents he held. The Commons were not anxious to attack the King directly—they were perhaps remembering the Lord Chancellor's advice and carrying themselves modestly. But before any patent for a monopoly had been issued the King had referred it for approval of its legality and convenience to his advisers, " the Referees " as they were called. Mompesson's patent had been referred for legality to the Lord Chancellor, the Lord Chief Baron, and two other Judges ; for convenience, to Suffolk, the two secretaries, and a lawyer. The House at first thought of calling all these Referees before them, and if they appeared guilty, of punishing them. For this, however, in spite of Coke's legal maxim, it now seemed they had no precedent. On Wednesday, the 28th February, they decided to pray a conference with the Lords, to discuss the whole question of Monopolies, rights and administration and all. The Prerogative was again on its defence.

At midnight on that Wednesday the Lord Chancellor received a letter from the King telling him to consult with the Treasurer and Prince Charles on the best answer. A little after seven on the first March morning, both the great officers of State came secretly to Charles at Whitehall, and agreed to desire of the Commons some time for the Lords' preparation. From Whitehall, the Chancellor went on to the House, and saw the Archbishop. For by

---

[1] Therefore any one who, in the King's service, committed an act afterwards felt to be a grievance, might be condemned unheard by the House, and if he sought to defend himself flung into prison.

a happy chance the Archbishop had a personal wish that the Lords should not sit on Wednesdays and Fridays because those were Convocation days.[1] He was encouraged to propose it. The only business for the Lords was the reading of two bills. They were read; the Archbishop made his motion. Bacon adjourned the House till Saturday, and "it was no sooner done but came the message from the Lower House." It was too late. When it came again on Saturday it had an addition. Mompesson had escaped through a window; would the Lords help to catch him? The Lords would; orders for his arrest were sent out; the conference took place.

Bacon, though he had managed a delay—presumably to give the Government a chance of consultation—was not disturbed. He did not think, according to his information, the Referees would be named, though he did think Sir Edward Coke would make trouble if he could. He wished the King would give Coke a round *caveat*; "a word from the King mates him." He was still anxious that this Parliament "by its sweet and united passages" might impress foreigners with the King's fame; questioning of great counsellors would be misunderstood. There were indeed to be "sweet and united passages," and Bacon was to be the cause of them. So exquisitely was he given the chief part of his will, and allowed to be the cause of the concord he so heartily desired; in payment, the rest of his prayer was "whistled down the wind."

The conference was disappointing to the Commons, not because of the Lords but because of their own speakers. It had been generally expected that these would, in presenting the subject, name the Referees, but

---

[1] In the heat of the Commons it was proposed among other things that requests should be sent "to the Convocation House to draw a curse" against all future procurers, advisers, or countenancers of patents. Certainly it was a more ostentatious age than our own.

they did not, and for sufficient reason.  When it came to
the point, the only evidence they had of the great persons
to whom the King had referred the patents was Sir Giles
Mompesson's, which (i) only covered his own and (ii) was
at best hearsay ; and Sir Henry Yelverton's, who had
been concerned with the gold and silver thread.  The
King had not officially told any one available, nor had
the Favourite.  Nor could members of the Lords be
cross-questioned.

There was a great hubbub, Parliament being " never
so out of order " ; the Speaker was blamed, the speakers
were blamed—and apologized.  At last it was decided to
hold a second conference, at which, on the testimony of
Mompesson and Yelverton, the Referees were to be named,
and there was added another matter concerning the imprisonment of certain tradesmen who had refused to
enter into a bond not to make the thread.  Yelverton had
committed them, with the confirmation of the Chancellor,
who had afterwards on their appeal examined them and
sent them back to prison.

The King on that next day, Saturday, 10th March,
came down to the Lords, and made a general speech,
rather putting the blame on his advisers ; he sent a
message to the Lower House deprecating any delay in
the Subsidy Bill.  At two in the afternoon, the second
conference opened.  The Referees were named.  The Lord
Chancellor and the Lord Treasurer made some effort to
justify themselves, for which afterwards (as having gone
beyond the orders of the House) they were compelled to
apologize to the Lords.  All the unfortunate Referees
must have spent a restless Sunday.  But the Chancellor
must have been more disturbed than most.  Yet the
real attack which the nature of things was to loose upon
him was not disclosed.  His consciousness of integrity
was untouched.

But for a man who liked a quiet life and the appreciation and praise of his fellows the growing possibility that he would be the centre of the Commons's hostility was bad enough. He had always got on well with the Commons, while yet honestly serving the Crown in his passion for the Crown : easily a Parliamentarian while " peremptorily a Royalist." He knew he had given his best judgment to the King. But he could not be quite certain that he ought not to have urged his own judgment more strongly, though certainly the King knew best. He had yielded to the Favourite's wishes in the matter of postponing the correction of the Monopolies. He had desired that the Houses and the King should meet in generous interchange. But it began to look as if that generous interchange might be over the heart of the man who proposed it. And Bacon's own political principles, carried out with that touch of lavish phraseology, that slightly facile emotion which had distinguished them in action on, say, Yelverton, now drove him to recognize his own risk. Could he, if things got really bad, wish the King to maintain him against the Houses ? But things were not yet as bad as that, and perhaps they would not be.

There was, it is true, one other matter. The universe was swerving in its movement ; and the curve which it was following was approaching him from another side. On that same Wednesday, the last day of February, before the Lord Chancellor had been called at midnight to receive the letter from the King, another witness had appeared before the Commons' Committee of Grievances. A clerk, by name John Churchill, who had been dismissed from the Chancery for malpractice, and was in danger of further punishment, determined that he would not " sink alone," that he would perhaps not sink at all if he could take advantage of the Commons to protect himself by involving others, and he came before the Committee with a full confession. He was referred to a Committee

which had been set up to inquire into the Courts of
Justice, as to which the Lord Chancellor had, ten days
earlier, on the seventeenth, offered "that any man might
speak freely concerning his Court." He expected no
evil there, more than any slightly hostile examination of
the working of any department must bring to light. But
he cannot, on the Sunday, have been altogether unaware
that the examination was proceeding, and that all sorts
of things might be shown in an unfavourable light.
There was yet another suggestion of other and more
dangerous discontents. A Mr. Christopher Awbry was
being tiresome. He had had a case in Chancery and
through his counsel, Sir George Hastings, he had sent
the Chancellor a hundred pounds. The hundred pounds
had disappeared, and yet the business had gone on but
slowly. Awbry wrote letters to the Chancellor to expedite it, until Bacon said sharply that if there were any
more importuning Awbry should be "laid by the heels."
It was not what Awbry expected for a hundred pounds;
he also would petition the Commons. Bacon heard of it;
he went so far as to have Awbry fetched and promise him
redress, to ask Hastings to keep quiet, and even to say
that if Hastings affirmed the giving of the money he
himself would and must deny it on his honour. Or so
the story went later. Money had poured in and poured
out; Bacon had never particularly bothered about where
it came from, but it would look bad to have such a tale
put forward. Besides, he certainly did not want Awbry
on his heels as well as John Churchill and Sir Edward
Coke. The Referees business was bad enough by itself;
the question of the administration of the Chancery was
an additional nuisance; and if the discontents of litigants who wrote importunate letters were to be added.
. . . However, he was still comparatively at ease. The
week opened gloomily but not dreadfully. But by the
next Sunday something like fear had entered; he

knew by then not the worst but the coming of the worst.

On the Monday the Commons finally passed the Subsidy Bill; the Lords busied themselves with considering the complaints of the Lower House, whom they invited to come with their full proof to a third Conference with a Committee; they agreed that any of the Lords of the Committee might question the Commons, and they appointed the Attorney-General to assist the same Lords. The Conference was fixed for Thursday. But on the 14th, Wednesday, Mr. Awbry, unappeased, petitioned the Commons, and was immediately referred to their Committee for the Courts of Justice. The troubles of great place began to throng about the Chancellor. Worry made him ill, and that would look bad at such a time of stress. He wrote to Buckingham :

" MY VERY GOOD LORD,

" Your Lordship spake of purgatory. I am now in it, but my mind is in a calm; for my fortune is not my felicity. I know I have clean hands and a clean heart; and I hope a clean house for friends or servants. But Job himself, or whosoever was the justest judge, by such hunting for matters against him as hath been used against me, may for a time seem foul, specially in a time when greatness is the mark and accusation is the game. And if this be to be a Chancellor, I think if the Great Seal lay upon Hounslow Heath, nobody would take it up. But the King and your Lordship will, I hope, put an end to these miseries one way or other. And in troth that which I fear most is lest continual attendance and business, together with these cares, and want of time to do my weak body right this spring by diet and physic, will cast me down; and then it will be thought feigning or fainting. But I hope in God I shall hold out. God prosper you."

He was at the Conference on the Thursday, and heard the Declarations of the Commons concerning Patents. He then made a special speech dividing the matter into five points—concerning the patents, the parties to be charged, the proofs, the punishments, and the precedents for punishments. Southampton moved and Bacon seconded the reference of each Patent to a separate Committee, which should consider first the execution of the Patents ; the Lord Chancellor also moving that the Lords' Committees should confer with certain members of the Lower House who had been most concerned. Nothing on that day was said about the Referees, and in fact the charges against them were not pressed any further. The Commons were now off after a single offender.

For further matter had been brought before that other Committee. In a pause between two suits, Mr. Edward Egerton had presented the Lord Chancellor with four hundred crowns, and then the decision had gone against him. He had sent it ostensibly as a present to buy a set of hangings for York House ; the obtuse Lord Keeper had not done his part of the bargain ; we do not know whether he bought the hangings. It was soon after he had received the Seal, " a time when I was presented by many." But this particular one out of many had no idea of not getting his money's worth, and now this matter also was reported, with Awbry's, by the Committee to the whole House on the same day when the Lord Chancellor was talking about Patents. He heard of it soon enough ; he heard that the Committee had found matter for a charge of corruption, and that the Commons were on the Monday to bring request for a fourth conference, no longer on patents or referees, inns or gold and silver thread, but on " abuses in eminent persons." The whole truth, fantastic as it must have seemed, broke over him. He was to be denounced as corrupt. Any one who had ever sent him a present and ever had a case in Chancery might swell the list of offences. He had no idea who might appear or what might be charged. Out of two thousand orders and decrees in a year who could possibly remember whether some one litigant might some time have sent a suit of hangings or a diamond ring, a dozen gold buttons or a bag of a hundred pounds ? Which, out of all these presents, whose bearers had received guineas and half-guineas, might now prove to have been meant as a bribe ? His enemies were hunting up accusations ; the Commons were in a state when they were determined to make somebody suffer. The whole thing was maniacal ; it was outside any clear intelligence. And yet, of course, it was *not*. He might, so easily, have done precisely that —have taken a gift while a suit was pending. He had been exactly that kind of fool. Folly within and practice without. And he had meant so well all the time ; he had meant to be just ; he had always, as far as in him lay, *been* just. The whole world had turned completely over. The Lord Chancellor—*Novum Organum* and all—was a mark for spite and despite. And now what was to happen to the Great Instauration ?

It is impossible he should not have thought of it, though it may have seemed part of the general horror.

In Sir Edward Coke's library there was a copy of the *Novum Organum* which Bacon had presented to him. To the inscription Coke, dropping into Latin and English verse, had added the following lines :

> Auctori concilium
> Instaurare paras veterum documenta sophorum ;
> Instaura leges, justitiamque prius.[1]

There was then a little drawing of a ship with the further lines :
> It deserveth not to be read in schools,
> But to be freighted in the Ship of Fools.

---

[1] (Roughly) you desire to reform the lessons of the wise men of old ; reform the laws, and justice first of all.

On such a ship, fantastically labouring on a wild ocean, manned with imbeciles, and captained by a blind self-credulity, the Lord St. Alban saw himself dwelling.

On the Monday he was too ill to attend the Lords. Buckingham, at the King's command, came twice to see him, and on the Tuesday presented a letter from him to the Lords. In this the Lord Verulam said (almost in so many words) that he felt as if he was going to die and go to heaven, and that in consequence he had largely "sequestered his mind from worldly matters"; however, he requested their Lordships to let him advise with counsel, take exception to and (through the Lords) cross-examine witnesses, and produce his own witnesses. He added a hope that they would not allow the mere number of complaints to prejudice them, but permit him to answer each separately. The Earl of Southampton moved in answer that they would proceed according to the rule of justice; they would be glad if his Lordship should clear his honour; they prayed his Lordship to provide for his defence. This their Lordships agreed to do, and sent the answer verbally. Bacon thanked them, adding, however, that he would presently remind them of the points in his letter to which they had made no reference. He was obviously thinking of the possibility of examining the witnesses; that was his chief concern, for witnesses examined and unexamined might prove quite different things. He was preparing to fight.

The Majesty, having sent the Favourite to inquire, remained aloof except for one movement—perhaps as much as could be expected. It offered to grant a commission to six members of the Lords and twelve of the Commons, with power to examine witnesses upon oath. But the Houses were not inclined to allow any such subtle inroad of the Crown; acting together, they could do all they wanted without the smallest suggestion that the King was permitting or helping or distributing Justice.

The Lords proceeded to examine witnesses upon oath. There were to be three Committees engaged on the business, and four questions were to be put to witnesses; whether they had given, or advised or directed to be given, or known of any that had given or advised or directed to be given, or intended, attempted or contracted to be given, any money or other gratuity to the Lord Chancellor, his friends, or servants? And whether they or the parties so advised and directed, or heard to have been so advised or directed, had or intended to have any cause before the Lord Chancellor? No witness was to accuse himself, no witness was to be asked if he had himself received anything, " but only what bribes were given to the Lord Chancellor "; no testimony taken in this Court was ever to be used in any other case or in any other Court.

No more admirable or more entire method of discovering all possible accusations against the Chancellor could be imagined. Any one who had ever heard of any attempt to give a gratuity to any servant of the Lord Chancellor was invited to say so, with a promise of complete amnesty and oblivion. Pure desire of the abolition of every kind of corruption—so far as the Lord Chancellor was concerned—could hardly have gone further in Utopia or the New Atlantis. It is all but a noble testimony to the incorruptible spirit of English public life, the conscious freedom of the Judiciary, Parliament, and all Governments from any kind of stain. The glorious fact had not perhaps been generally recognised up to then; it has been more generally recognised since—has, in fact, been entirely and universally recognised since. To this recognition, and the law of libel, we owe our freedom from public scandals. But " the price of liberty is eternal vigilance," and it is our part to watch closely that no such scandal is ever given the opportunity to arise. To do us justice, it is not. It could only be (owing to the law of libel) if the scandal-monger were a rich man, and rich men do not encourage scandal of that kind. That, it has been well said, is why they are rich men.

Before the adjournment for Good Friday and Easter three more cases were brought forward. On the 25th March Bacon wrote once more to Buckingham and the King.

"MY VERY GOOD LORD,

"Yesterday I know was no day; now I hope I shall hear from your Lordship, who are my anchor in these floods. Meanwhile to ease my heart a little, I have written to his Majesty the enclosed; which I pray your Lordship to read advisedly, and to deliver it, or not to deliver it, as you think best. God ever prosper your Lordship.

"Yours ever what I can,
"FR. ST. ALBAN, *Canc.*
"*March* 25, 1621."

"It may please your most excellent Majesty,

"Time hath been when I have brought unto you *gemitum columbæ* from others. Now I bring it from myself. I fly unto your Majesty with the wings of a dove, which once within these seven days I thought would have carried me a higher flight.

"When I enter into myself, I find not the materials of such a tempest as is comen upon me. I have been (as your Majesty knoweth best) never author of any immoderate counsel, but always desired to have things carried *suavibus modis*. I have been no avaricious oppressor of the people. I have been no haughty or intolerable or hateful man, in my conversation or carriage. I have inherited no hatred from my father, but am a good patriot born. Whence should this be? For these are the things that use to raise dislikes abroad.

"For the House of Commons, I began my credit

there, and now it must be the place of the sepulture thereof; and yet this Parliament, upon the message touching religion, the old love revived, and they said I was the same man still, only honesty was turned into honour.

"For the Upper House, even within these days before these troubles, they seemed as to take me into their arms, finding in me ingenuity which they took to be the true straight line of nobleness, without crooks or angles.

"And for the briberies and gifts wherewith I am charged, when the books of hearts shall be opened, I hope I shall not be found to have the troubled fountain of a corrupt heart in a depraved habit of taking rewards to pervert justice; howsoever I may be frail, and partake of the abuse of the times.

"And therefore I am resolved when I come to my answer, not to trick up my innocency (as I writ to the Lords) by cavillations or voidances, but to speak to them the language that my heart speaketh to me, in excusing, extenuating, or ingenuous confessing; praying to God to give me the grace to see to the bottom of my faults, and that no hardness of heart do steal upon me, under show of more neatness of conscience than is cause.

"But not to trouble your Majesty longer, craving pardon for this long mourning letter; That which I thirst after, as the hart after the streams, is that I may know by my matchless friend that presenteth to you this letter, your Majesty's heart (which is an *abyssus* of goodness, as I am an *abyssus* of misery) towards me. I have been ever your man, and counted myself but an usufructuary of myself, the property being yours : and now making myself an oblation to do with me as may best conduce to the honour of your justice, the honour of your mercy, and the use of your service, resting as clay in your Majesty's gracious hands.

"FR. ST. ALBAN, *Canc.*

"*March* 25, 1621."

The King on the next day made a speech to the Houses, thanking them for the subsidy, promising to abolish the three most objectionable monopolies, and promising to leave judgment to them and to be guided by them. The Houses adjourned for Easter, leaving the Committees at work. Bacon made his will and prepared to " make his soul." He left " my body to be buried obscurely." He left " my name to the next ages and to foreign nations " ; so far at least he was still royally certain of himself. He had not oppressed the poor ; he had hated cruelty and hardness of heart ; he had sought to do good to all men. He had sought it all his life. Burleigh had despised him ; Essex had turned from him ; James had used him in politics, which was good, but not his supreme good. His heart had been a coal on God's altar—he drew up a prayer " or psalm " in which he said so. And he was right ; only six months earlier it had seemed as if other wood might catch fire from that coal. There followed a sentence incredible but for its sincerity : " ever as my worldly blessings were exalted, secret darts from Thee have pierced me, and when I have ascended before men I have descended in humiliation before Thee."

Secret darts—what strange remembrances did that cover ? Bacon was no religious mystic ; he speaks of God everywhere almost as a politician must. The great war of the Churches left him unmoved. But secretly through that busy life the universe reminded him of its end ; it reminded him of his sole business, and he grew remorseful even over political callings and State affairs. " I confess before Thee, that I am debtor to Thee for the gracious talent of Thy gifts and graces, which I have neither put into a napkin, nor put it (as I ought) to exchangers, where it might have made best profit ; but misspent it in things for which I was least fit ; so as I may truly say, my soul hath been a stranger in the course of my pilgrimage. Be merciful unto me, O Lord, for my

Saviour's sake, and receive me into Thy bosom, or guide me in Thy ways."

He accused himself perhaps unjustly. It is not so easy, between the clanging moral uproars of existence, to decide with what exchangers the divine talent makes profit. By the end of life all that we know is that it has gone. It is only then that the long error of our actions becomes clear, and had our actions been wholly other still their long error would have been clear. That extreme error is the only revelation vouchsafed to normal man, and that error (since man acts always here and now, and never there and then) is inevitable. Francis Bacon repented of the inevitable as we all do; that perhaps is man's greatest hope, for in that his submission and his defiance are curiously one.

However, action was still possible and necessary. He looked up precedents; they were hopeful. There had been a Chief Justice whom a King had pardoned, in spite of the fact that he had taken a very strict and specially devised oath, and that the King, Edward III, had sworn to hang him if he took bribes. There were examples of really great offenders, whose honours had not been touched. He worked out, in that exploring and formulating mind, the various degrees of bribery: (1) reward taken for perversion of judgment, the case still pending; (2) gifts taken, the Judge supposing the case to be ended, but not inquiring diligently after it; (3) gifts taken, the case being really ended, and no possibility of fraud. He did not yet know of what he was accused, but he was clear of what he might be guilty. Of the first, he was as innocent "as any born on St. Innocents' day." Of the second, he thought he might "in some particulars" be faulty. Of the third, he thought it no fault; if it were he would be glad to know and to be sorry. "For," he wrote unexpectedly, "I had rather be a briber than a defender of bribes." Probably he would. The one would have meant only obliquity of action ; the second, obliquity of mind. Bacon would rather have committed almost any sin than deliberately abuse his mental clearness. He had known long since that there was something in him kindred to truth.

He pleaded to see the King, and by consent of the Lords of the Council James admitted him to a private interview the day before the Houses reassembled. The burden of the conversation was that Bacon wanted to know what the charges were, and to have an opportunity of denying them or defending or extenuating himself. James referred him to the Lords. The Houses met ; on the 19th the three Committees reported ; the thirty or more examinations were read, and it was decided that the Committees should draw up one general report. The House adjourned for five days to let them do it.

When they met again Prince Charles rose. He had a letter for the House from the Lord Chancellor. It was read. It was a submission that he had understood enough of the particulars, not from the House, but by his own recollection and conscience, to prefer to abandon the defence " and to move your Lordships to condemn and censure me." He would not trouble about those charges which might fail of proof ; he would not comment on the credit of the witnesses. He would leave an intelligent understanding to the intelligence of the Lords. He petitioned that the King would take the Great Seal again, and he thought that might serve in expiation. He begged that his penitent submission might be his sentence and the loss of the Seal his punishment, and that their Lordships would spare him further sentence. He thought this example of his fall would purge the Judges, and this purgation of guilt would be the beginning of a golden world. So far at least he would be glad. He was their humble servant and suppliant.

Quite suddenly therefore he abandoned defiance and

# THE REMOVAL OF PRESERVATION 279

even defence, and left no explanation to tell our inquisitive minds why. It is possible that he thought defence unlikely to prevail; such were the customs of the time that if any great person were accused of corruption he was almost certain to be guilty. It is possible that he saw that defence must involve the Majesty in appearing to support or abandon him; he would not, for high reasons of State, have wished the King to contend with the Commons on his behalf, nor would he have desired that the King should have to deal with him as a convicted criminal. But always he had dreaded " change rather than continuance "; he had mistrusted the world, and now when his mistrust was justified he could not bring himself to contend against the universal violence of the world. Change was at last upon him; his spirit was defeated even before it could take arms. But it was not defeated merely by its fear but by its lucidity. He saw at once his innocence—" I was the justest judge in England these fifty years "—and his fault—" but it was the justest sentence these two hundred years." He would not fight. A holier spirit would perhaps, on that revelation, have abandoned for ever all effort to alter or diminish the world's judgment.

> 'Tis very just they blame
> The thing that's not.

Francis Bacon was not a Francis of Assisi. But that was, after all, God's decision; it was enough for him—it is enough for us—that in his catastrophe he remained Francis Bacon. He submitted to the agony of his nerves but no less to the lucidity of his mind.

"No Lord spoke . . . after it was read for a long time." No one presumably quite knew what to say. It was unexpected; it was all very fine, only—— The fact was that the House was thinking of one kind of thing and the Lord Chancellor of another. They were thinking of corruption; Bacon of follies. They were thinking of one kind of wickedness; Bacon of another. What he admitted was nothing like all that they expected him to admit. They had all the articles of corruption read. The Earl of Suffolk said the confession was not what they expected. The Lord Chamberlain said he had confessed nothing in particular. The Earl of Southampton said he was charged with corruption and had not confessed corruption; the honour of the House demanded a particular confession or a particular answer.

It was decided, as was natural, that the submission was not a confession to particular charges. Virtue demanded exactitude, and whatever besides virtue may have moved in the hearts of any of the Lords demanded something more than general contrition for its trouble. The charges were ostentatious; there must be an ostentation of reply. It was determined that the charges should be sent to the Lord Chancellor, and it was so done. The proofs—that is, the depositions of the witnesses—were not, however, sent. The answer to his letter announced that he had not confessed any particular bribe, nor did he explain how he had come to know of the charges, and even that submission (such as it was) " extenuated " the confession. The Lords expected his answer to the particulars of the charge sent herewith.

He asked for time to consider; they gave him five days till the thirtieth of April. On that day the Bishop of Bangor moved for a Bill to provide a remedy against women Recusants who returned "scoffs, flouts, and taunts when the Bishops offer to instruct them "; the Bishop of Bath and Wells moved for a Bill against the abuse of sacred things, as in christening of dogs, etc. Between these episcopal troubles the Lord Chief Justice, acting in the place of the Chancellor, offered a sealed roll from the Chancellor, which was opened and read. Of the twenty-six separate charges (three were reckoned as one), Bacon admitted eleven cases of receiving presents after judgment ("after" meaning anything from a few days to nine months); he denied any kind of wrong in three cases; the remaining twelve he admitted to various extents. There were only four which he allowed to be "*pendente lite*," and even of these two were sent to him as New Year's gifts. One of the other two, he asserted, was sent in a case where there were two decrees, "one for inheritance, the other for the goods and chattels," and that the money was sent after the first decree and before the second. The fourth was poor Christopher Awbry's—" I do confess and declare, that the money was given and received, but the manner of it I leave to the witnesses." That is the most extreme of Bacon's admissions. In three cases sums which were held to be bribes were afterwards claimed by the "bribers" from Bacon's estate as debts. That is the most charming touch in the whole business.

It is certain that at any time a judge making such a confession would be removed; it is certain that any dream of justice among mortal men would demand that so dangerous a practice should be stopped. The chastity of that divine virtue goes in arms, like Milton's severe young angels sitting in the bright cold about the purity of the Holy Child. All human integrity has in it something of that angelic snow and steel. It is by trial of snow and steel that we ought to test, preserve, and nourish the servants of justice. The honour of a thing almost inconceivable by man is in peril, and (what is perhaps the wildest hope of our race) the possibility that right can be determined and executed between man and man.

Perfection had its way, and destroyed Bacon. But preservation—at least, the preservation of our sense of proportion—ought to have its own whisper. He had been Keeper or Chancellor for four years. He asserted that he had issued two thousand decrees and orders in a year. It is true that the time of examination took only from 14th March to 19th April, and it may be that many who had sent gifts had no opportunity of bearing witness; it is true also that some or many who had sent gifts intended corruptly and then lost their cases may have seen no point in bearing public witness to their failure. But the most extreme safety had been promised to witnesses; the most remote testimony invited. It was very proper; the propriety, however, rather emphasizes the result. The result was four charges in a degree confessed; the result was, more remarkably, that no decree was changed, no decision altered. The Lord Chancellor's judgments were final and to this day remain final. So long as one man may judge, and the judge may himself be judged, the trial of the Lord Chancellor could and ought to have no other result. But if four years' labour in any occupation leaves us with no worse record of sin there are few who would not be—except by high laws of sanctity—content.

 The Lords sent twelve peers to ask if he would stand to this confession. He answered: "My Lords, it is my act, my hand, my heart. I beseech your Lordships, be merciful to a broken reed." They petitioned the King to sequester the Seal. He sent four peers to receive it, who found him "very sick." They wished him better. He answered: "The worse the better. By the King's great favour I received the Great Seal; by my own great fault I have lost it."

 That was on 1st May; on the 3rd the Lords proceeded to sentence. "They were of opinion that he was in a general way guilty of whatever the charge contained." They did not go into particulars again: "the question being put, they all agreed that the Lord Chancellor is guilty of the matters wherewith he is charged, *nemine dissentiente*." So that was that. On the sentence they disputed for some time. They decided, naturally, that he was unfit to sit among them any more, and unfit to hold any office, place, or employment in the State or Commonwealth. Of all the clauses of the sentence and notes of the speeches those two are perhaps the most exquisitely satisfying to the observer. The irony which closed all Bacon's own young belief in his being called to serve the State by this decision of other servants of the State is equalled by the irony which declared that he was not fit to sit with Southampton and Suffolk and Buckingham. Such an irony is in the nature of things, unescapable, welcomed in their own experience by the wise. They added to this decision the minor matters of a £40,000 fine, of imprisonment in the Tower during the King's pleasure, of banishment from the Court. They passed the sentence all but unanimously. There was one dissentient—George Villiers. It was a little thing enough, and yet a great and pleasant thing that—for one moment—the exalted Favourite stood by his early adviser.

The Lords then sent for the Commons, put on their robes, and, the Commons arriving, informed them of the sentence, and entreated the Prince's Highness to deliver the sentence to his Majesty. " His Highness was pleased to yield unto this request." The trial of Bacon was concluded ; the next person of so great place to be challenged by the Parliament was a person even nearer the Throne, the magnificent Favourite himself.

To the trial the universe allowed itself in the Lords one *postlocutum*. On 3rd May the judgment was pronounced. But ten days later the Lord St. Alban was still not in the Tower. On the 12th Southampton drew the attention of the House to this ; he wished something done, that " the world may not think our sentence vain." Buckingham said that the King had respited him during his illness. There was some talk of a warrant from the House to commit him to the Tower. But it was dropped. By the 31st he had been conveyed thither on the original sentence; from there on that day he wrote to Buckingham:

" GOOD MY LORD,
"Procure the warrant for my discharge this day. Death, I thank God, is so far from being unwelcome to me, as I have called for it (as Christian resolution would permit) any time these two months. But to die before the time of his Majesty's grace, and in this disgraceful place, is even the worst that could be; and when I am dead, he is gone that was always in one tenor, a true and perfect servant to his master, and one that was never author of any immoderate, no, nor unsafe, no (I will say it), nor unfortunate counsel; and one that no temptation could ever make other than a trusty, and honest, and thrice-loving friend to your Lordship; and howsoever I acknowledge the sentence just, and for reformation sake fit, the justest Chancellor that hath been in the five changes since Sir Nicholas Bacon's time. God bless and prosper your Lordship, whatsoever become of me.
" Your Lordship's true friend, living and dying,
" FR. ST. ALBAN.
" TOWER, 31st *May* 1621."

By 4th June he had been released at the King's direction, and after a short stay in London he was compelled to retire to Gorhambury.

On Twelfth Night in that year Ben Jonson had made for the entertainment of the Court the *Masque of Gipsies*. He was then near the centre of things; the gossip and the news came to him. He was not a man who easily flattered, and he wrote of the Lord St. Alban: " My conceit of his person was never increased towards him by his place or honours; but I have and do reverence him, for the greatness that was only proper to himself, in that he seemed to me ever, by his work, one of the greatest men, and most worthy of admiration, that had been in many ages. In his adversity I ever prayed that God would give him strength, for greatness he could not want. Neither could I condole in a word or syllable for him, as knowing no accident could do harm to virtue, but rather help to make it manifest."

"Neither could I condole in a word or syllable for him." It is the only proper tribute to the faults, the greatness, and the ironical Fortune of Francis Bacon.

## CHAPTER X

### THE FINAL ENERGY

PERFECTION and preservation had been separated at last. They no longer presented themselves to Bacon as a single light shining within and without, a glory of intellect manifesting within and through a glory of great place. Preservation no longer meant a rise beyond the eightfold degrees for which he poured his gratitude at the feet of the Majesty of England; it now meant something much more like literal preservation from poverty and distress. It meant the effort to free his character from the decision by which the Lords had defined it. Mortal perfection was gone; but immortal perfection remained always the same.

He believed that in some sort he was nearer it, that he had undergone some interior change. He called himself *nova creatura*, " a new creature to God." But that change and new creation were produced—in so far as they were produced, and not Bacon nor we can tell how far that was—not merely by the fall but by the five years that followed the fall. He had to experience, not only catastrophe but that more trying and longer period during which catastrophe exposes itself to a man in its full extent and consequences; in which he realizes (how slowly ! how painfully !) that it has happened, and that, very exactly, nothing will ever be the same again. For such a realization five years is not too long a period, especially to a man who had always had to ask often for what he wanted. He was not treated abruptly or brutally; every one—or almost every one—was always—or almost always—polite. But he was " out of use and out of sight "; he was not *there*, and he faded, and the care and recollection of him faded. He had some hopes of recovering what he had lost; it is permissible to believe that, if he had had none, as at last he must have had almost none, still his astonishing energy would have driven him on, as in fact it drove him, though he found personal reasons for it. Perhaps all Bacon's ostentations of flattery were never much more than superficial excuse for his own energy, as they were certainly its superfluity. It occupied itself now with continual efforts at the service of the State; it loosed itself in little feverish appeals; it busied itself—it had to—with his financial disasters; it sought to retrieve all that could be retrieved of every kind. But also it wrote books; it translated its earlier books, revising and enlarging; it planned a serial monthly investigation and account of natural facts; it proposed laws; it proposed recompilement of laws; it toiled, expounded, and elucidated. By 4th June the Lord St. Alban was freed from the Tower. Three months, practically, had covered the whole bewildering change. By 8th October—another four months—he had completed and sent to the King the fair manuscript of his *History of Henry VII*. They say (not without excuse) it is the beginning of modern history in England. He produced a portrait, and yet (as in all Bacon's writings) it is not so much a portrait as an image, and a living image. It is neither a flattering nor a scandalous interpretation, and in it sometimes the nature of its maker leaps out. " He coveted to accumulate treasure, and was a little poor in admiring riches "; " riches are for spending," say the *Essays*, " and spending for honour and good actions "; and again, " I cannot call riches better than the baggage of virtue." " In him, as in all men (and most of all in kings) his fortune wrought upon his nature, and his nature upon his fortune "; in all men, perhaps, but perhaps in none less—now, in his catastrophe—than in Bacon.

He had written it partly as a proof of his capacities, a plea for continued employment. In some of the letters he sent to James during that dreadful March and April he had spoken of it; in a pathetic effort at a painful humour he had written, "Because he that hath taken bribes is apt to give bribes I will go furder, and present your Majesty with a bribe. For if your Majesty give me peace and leisure, and God give me life, I will present your Majesty with a good history of England, and a better digest of your laws." But it is not so much the motive as the execution which marks, in this book, the triumphant appearance of his undefeated mind.

As early as June the King condescended to ask his fallen Minister for advice; he consulted him—of all things in the world—on reformation of the Courts of Justice. It is one of the most tactful things James ever did. The Lord St. Alban answered in a letter which is full, as it were, of the cloud of the glory of Majesty. The Star Chamber is the highest court of judicature ordinary, the mount upon which when the King appears his garments shine before he goes off. Let the King then so appear and announce his determination, now Parliament is gone, to pursue reform by his own regal power and care; in course of which the memorials of what has been passed in both Houses are to be considered, and the learned counsel are to search for precedents of what kings have done in this matter, and resolutions shall be taken what shall be done by commission, what by council, what by proclamation, what prepared for Parliament, what left to Parliament; so that many grievances may be answered by deed, and the King's care be better than any committee in this interim between the meetings of Parliament. In all things, as in music between one voice singing the greater part and then the choir sweetly and solemnly consorting, the harmony between the King and his Parliament is to be preserved. But for more particular advice it was not for him, as he then stood, to send for entries or search for precedent, lest any—even his Majesty—should think his counsel busy or officious or relating to his present fortunes.

Nothing came of it. Bacon was not asked for further advice, and the King made no public announcement. Meanwhile the inevitable troubles of disgrace thickened. Some one told Buckingham that the Lord St. Alban must have received, since he became Lord Keeper, a hundred thousand pounds in gifts—" an abominable falsehood. . . . I praise God for it, I never took penny for any benefice or ecclesiastical living, I never took penny for releasing anything I stopped at the Seal, I never took penny for any commission or things of that nature, I never shared with any servant for any second or inferior profit." Buckingham may not have believed the slander, but Buckingham spoilt his lonely stand in the Lords by falling into a personal spite against the fallen minister on a matter almost contemptible ; if any human desire can be so. He wanted York House, and Bacon did not want to part with it. The Lord Marquis became distant. The new Lord Keeper (John Williams, Bishop of Lincoln—" I thought I should have known my successor," Bacon said when he heard the name) was very averse from the King doing anything in the way of pardon that might offend the Parliament, and almost anything (he thought) might offend the Parliament. Access to the King was not to be had. One thing only James did, fairly quickly ; he assigned the £40,000 fine for administration to persons chosen by Bacon ; thus putting the money at his disposal and keeping it, since it still nominally belonged to the Crown, from the creditors who were pressing him. Sooner or later he also signed a general pardon for all offences and for restitution of all lands and goods forfeited by such offences, including riots and routs, embezzling and usury, but excluding treasons, murders, rapes, and incest.

Excluding also, which was more to the point since there is no present sign that Bacon had committed treason, murder, rape, or incest, all penalties and forfeitures adjudged against him by the late Parliament. In fact the sentence was never overruled. He held out for York House until the next March. He refused it in January to the Duke of Lennox, who also wanted it.

"MY VERY GOOD LORD,
"I am sorry to deny your Grace anything; but in this you will pardon me. York House is the house where my father died, and where I first breathed, and there will I yield my last breath, if it so please God, and the King will give me leave; though I be now [in the house] (as the old proverb is) like a bear in a monk's hood. At least no money nor value shall make me part with it. Besides, as I never denied it to my Lord Marquis, so yet the difficulty I made was so like a denial, as I owe unto my great love and respect to his Lordship a denial to all my other friends; among which in a very near place next his Lordship I ever accounted of your Grace. So, not doubting that you will continue me in your former love and good affection, I rest

"Your Grace's, to do you humble service, affectionate, etc."

By then Buckingham had satisfied himself elsewhere, but that did not mean he was content to let Bacon remain in possession. If the Lord St. Alban would yield York House, then the Lord St. Alban should be granted leave to come to London. Bacon thought of offering him Gorhambury for nothing, in the hope of melting him. In London he "could have company, physicians, conference with my creditors and friends, . . . helps for my studies and the writings I have in hand." At Gorhambury he lived "upon the sword-point of a sharp air,

endangered if I go abroad, dulled if I stay within,"
without friends, discussion, books, records, and every
kind of help. But Buckingham did not want Gorhambury ; if he could not have what he had wanted then one
of his friends must have it. The King told him, after the
Lennox refusal and the Gorhambury offer, that the Lord
St. Alban " played an after-game well ; and that now he
had no reason to be much offended." But the King was
no nearer granting relaxation without the Favourite's
assent. The Lord Treasurer Cranfield was, at that
moment, a friend of the Favourite. " If York House
were gone," wrote Sir Edward Sackville to Bacon, " the
town were yours, and all your straitest shackles clean
off. . . . The Marquis would be exceeding glad the
Treasurer had it." He went on to advise Bacon to make
a motion of it to the Treasurer, yet not absolutely until
Buckingham should request it ; that would be the next
best thing to letting Buckingham have it, for which it
was now too late.

London, in the end, was worth York House. Bacon
gave in, and wrote to Cranfield in the sense indicated.
The Favourite was satisfied ; " the great Lords long to
be at York House," and graciously consented to procure
the signing of a warrant permitting Bacon to come
" within the verge." [1] One was prepared ; the Marquis
lost it ; there was a delay of twenty-four hours while
another was drawn. With his letter of thanks Bacon
sent the Lord Marquis a copy of the printed *Henry VII*.
Could the whole fantastic tale be better signified than in
those two facts ? Yet, even so, though Bacon was
Bacon and Buckingham was Buckingham, yet Bacon
looked on Buckingham as the elected Favourite of
Majesty, and " he that honoureth not the King is next
an atheist, wanting the fear of God in his heart." That
is what makes Bacon difficult to us, the mere fact that

[1] The " verge " was a distance of twelve miles round the Court.

he had the fear of God in his heart and beheld the King as a " mortal god on earth."

But in the service of that mortal god he was to do no more. The current of his mind which was concerned with the Monarch in action was dammed up. He drew up and submitted papers—on a digest of the laws, on the regulation of usury, on the proper behaviour of the Favourite after his return from Spain in great popularity, on the possible war with Spain—but they were not wanted, nor was he. The Prerogative was closing in on its last defences ; fifteen years after his death the gates of Hull refused to open to the Majesty of Charles in person. As for mankind in action, from that too, he was largely driven. He was left to his private friends, to Toby Matthew, Sir Thomas Meautys, Lancelot Andrewes ; his own action was dammed and separated from the movements of the great world. Occasionally old troubles cropped up again. In a business about the separation of the Apothecaries from the Company of Grocers and making a new Company of them, something had been said about one of the old charges. It was a case with which he had had to do, and each of the three Companies concerned had, when an agreement was reached by his means, publicly presented him with a present. And now Sir Edward Coke, busy with a new development, snapped at him again. "It may be," wrote Bacon, "he hath a tooth at me yet which is not fallen out with age." It was twenty years since Coke had said something like that, and Coke had the last bite.

Of the study of nature in action, however, Bacon was still capable, and in that he still toiled ; with himself in action he was still concerned. The years went by and nobody wanted him. He was not yet sufficient of " a new creature " to resign himself completely and happily to the mere operation of the universe as a means of living more intensely and more universally. He stil wanted his own way; he desired to be, if not justified, at least freed. He wanted more money and he wanted—above all and last of all he wanted the remission of his sentence. He desired to sit once more among the Lords. Southampton did, who had committed treason. Suffolk did, who had committed exaction. Was he alone to be an outcast? He wrote to Southampton.

"To the Right Hon[ble.] his very good Lordship the Earl of Southampton.
" MY VERY GOOD LORD,
    " It pleased your Lordship when we met last, and did not think, I dare say, that a Parliament would have been so soon, to assure me of your love and favour; and it is true that out of that which I have heard and observed of your noble nature I have a great affiance in your Lordship. I would be glad to receive my writ this Parliament, that since the root of my dignity is saved to me it might also bear fruit, and that I may not die in dishonour.
    " But it is far from me to desire this except it may be with the love and consent of the Lords: if their Lordships shall vouchsafe to think me worthy of their company or fit to do them service, or to have suffered sufficiently, whereby I may now be after three years a subject of their grace as I was before a subject of their justice.
    " In this matter I hold your Lordship's favour so essential as if God shall put it into your heart to give me your favour and furtherance, I will apply my industry and other friends to co-operate with your Lordship. Otherwise I shall give over to think of it; and yet ever rest,
    " Your Lordship's affectionate and humble servant,
                            " FR. ST. ALBAN.
" *Last of January*, 1623."

It is perhaps not strange that Southampton did nothing; a little strange that nobody else cared: not the King, nor the Marquis (now the Duke), nor the Prince, not the Prince when he became King. It may be that, in the increasing struggle around Prerogative, Bacon was remembered only as the man who had preached an unattainable reconciliation, a union of love between Majesty and the opponents of Majesty. There was certainly no likelihood of a union, nor between Mr. Pym and the new King any particular wish for union; nor between the impeached Duke and his accusers. Bacon was an old man, an old Elizabethan; on both sides they had changed all that. The old man, servant in his youth of the old woman who had once ruled England, was thought no use in these later and more bustling times. Let him lie forgotten at Gorhambury, or in those old chambers of his at Gray's Inn, which he had now taken again to save the expense of a town house. He was in fear of want—a little unduly in fear; Bacon was never quite as poor as all that. But the mistake can easily be forgiven. He was pressed; he thought of selling Gorhambury; he remembered the financial troubles of his youth; he loved magnificence. He still thought "of change rather than continuance," and change might too easily be for the worse. But there was always a chance it might be for the better. The chance lingered for four years or so and seemed to be going out. In 1623 the Provost of Eton died; Bacon asked for the appointment—" it were a pretty cell for my fortune." But it had already been promised; some months passed, owing to Buckingham's absence in Spain, before he could get a definite answer, and then it was refused. It remained vacant for a long while, owing to the number of suitors, but the Lord St. Alban at least was put out of the running. In 1624 Bacon addressed a petition to James, asking for three years' pension in advance, and for a remission during those three years of the rent of £1000 " reserved upon his farm of petty writs." He got the advance ; the remission he did not get.

" The King," wrote the King's Favourite, " may by this seem not to satisfy your desert and expectation, yet, take the word of a friend who will never fail you, hath a tender care of you, full of a fresh memory of your by-past service. His Majesty is but for the present, he says, able to yield unto the three years' advance, which if you please to accept, you are not hereafter the farther off from obtaining some better testimony of his favour worthier both of him and you, though it can never be answerable to what my heart wishes you, as
" Your Lordship's humble servant,
" G. BUCKINGHAM."

Not to G. Buckingham but to James, Bacon about the same time wrote once more, sending his last letter to the Majesty of England.

" MOST GRACIOUS AND DREAD SOVEREIGN,
" Before I make my petition to your Majesty, I make my prayers to God above, *pectore ab imo*, that if I have held anything so dear as your Majesty's service, nay your heart's ease, and your honour's, I may be repulsed with a denial. But if that hath been the principal with me, that God, who knoweth my heart, would move your Majesty's royal heart to take compassion of me and to grant my desire.
" I prostrate myself at your Majesty's feet ; I, your ancient servant, now sixty-four years old in age, and three years five months old in misery. I desire not from your Majesty means, nor place, nor employment, but only, after so long a time of expiation, a complete and total remission of the sentence of the Upper House, to the end

that blot of ignominy may be removed from me, and from
my memory with posterity ; that I die not a condemned
man, but may be to your Majesty, as I am to God, *nova
creatura*.  Your Majesty hath pardoned the like to Sir
John Bennet, between whose case and mine (not being
partial to myself, but speaking out of the general opinion)
there was as much difference, I will not say as between
black and white, but as between black and grey, or ash-
coloured.  Look therefore down, dear Sovereign, upon
me also in pity.  I know your Majesty's heart is inscrutable for goodness ; and my Lord of Buckingham was
wont to tell me you were the best-natured man in the
world ; and it is God's property, that *those he hath loved,
he loveth to the end*.  Let your Majesty's grace, in this my
desire, stream down upon me, and let it be out of the
fountain and spring-head, and *ex mero motu*, that, living
or dying, the print of the goodness of King James may
be in my heart, and his praises in my mouth.  This my
most humble request granted, may make me live a year
or two happily ; and denied, will kill me quickly.  But
yet the last thing that will die in me, will be the heart and
affection of

"Your Majesty's most humble and true devoted
servant,

"FR. ST. ALBAN."

As if his Fortune knew better than he what was in
his heart, he received no satisfaction.  There had been
something dearer to him than the King's service, or if
not dearer, then not so only because that other thing was
more himself than the service to which he gave himself.
There had been a pursuit in which his mind had not
" grown old or cooled in so great a space of time "—
"*propter ardorem et constantiam mentis nostræ, quæ in
hoc instituto non consenuit, nec tanto temporis spatio
refrixit. Equidem memini me, quadraginta abhinc*

*annis "*—" for I remember how, forty years ago, I composed a youthful work upon these matters, which I named, in great confidence and by a magnificent title 'The Greatest Birth of Time ' "—" *magnifico titulo ' Temporis Partum Maximum' inscripsi.*" But the letter in which that was said was not to the King, who had found the *Novum Organum* " like the peace of God—it passeth all understanding " ; it was to Father Fulgentio, a Venetian monk.

In fact the foreign nations, to whom and to next ages in the first will made under the dark threat of overthrow he had left his name, and to whom he was again to bequeath it in his actual will, were already beginning to gather. From Annesi the professor of philosophy and mathematics, Father Redemptus Beranzano, had written, asking about the place of metaphysics in the new philosophy, about the syllogism, about the number of Instances required. Bacon answered in detail, ending with the same cry : let men submit themselves to things. " Love me as you have begun, but truth above all," he ended ; *meque ut excipisti, maxime autem veritatem ama.*" Beranzano unfortunately died that year, being received into truth. In Tuscany, Sir Toby Matthew in an Introduction to an Italian translation of the *Essays*, had nobly described his friend's intellect and character to the Grand Duke. The Spanish Ambassador, the Count Gondomar, had used his services with King James when Buckingham was cold, and had offered to ask the King of Spain to intercede with the King of England. The new French Ambassador, the Marquis D'Effiat, arriving in 1625 with the Queen Henrietta Maria, wrote to the Lord St. Alban asking permission to address him as " father," and indeed the letters which we possess begin " Monsieur l'Ambassadeur mon fils." James's daughter, the Queen of Bohemia (among her own distresses) complimented him on his writings. That may not have meant much, but the first vibrations of his growing fame were sounding. France and Spain, Venice and Tuscany, paid their first-fruits. He gave courtesy for courtesy; he was grateful for services; but to those who turned indeed to the great work he wrote in the same strain as he had more softly used, " *quadraginta abhinc annis,*" that it was a work for the ages and the peoples—" *maxime veritatem ama.*"

Towards that greater fame and that all-dominating truth he laboured. Sixteen years earlier he had wanted to have the *Advancement of Learning* translated into Latin that it might find many readers (which, considering " the privateness " of the English in which it was written, it could not then do). He had corresponded with Dr. Playfere, Lady Margaret Professor of Divinity, and Playfere had actually made a beginning. One story declares that Bacon found the first specimen of the translation of such " superfine Latinity " that he did not encourage his collaborator to proceed. In any case Playfere died in February 1608/9, and since then the work had lain by. He now took it up again, directing the translators, of whom George Herbert is said to have been one. He omitted whatever might seem to offend men of other peoples and other beliefs than his own; he enlarged it to four or five times its early size; he published it in 1623—*De Augmentis Scientiarum*. He sent out presentation copies, and in a magniloquent outpouring of rhetoric the learning of the University of Oxford offered its thanks. He planned his natural history in monthly instalments; a new " history " each month, and named the first six. He gathered together the material for *Sylva Sylvarum*, the collection of ten centuries of facts or reported facts of natural science; it was published the year after his death. Stories and uncertainties went into it as well as truths; he knew it; he knew he would be blamed for it. But what could be done? He had shown the way; he was left also to begin the work. " I have heard his lordship often say that, if he should have served the glory of his own name, he had been better not to have published this Natural History. . . . I have heard his lordship speak complainingly, that his lordship (who thinketh he deserveth to be an architect in this building) should be forced to be a workman and a labourer, and to dry the clay and burn the brick; and more than that . . . to gather the straw and stubble all over the field, to burn the bricks withal. For he knoweth that, except he do it, nothing will be done: men are so set to despise the means of their own good." So wrote Rawley; Bacon himself called it " not natural history, but a high kind of natural magic."

He began a treatise on a *Holy War*—not the war which John Bunyan was afterwards to call by that title, but a lesser argument on the justice, policy, and possibility of the kings of Europe making war against the Turk; it was to be dedicated to Lancelot Andrewes. He published his metrical translation of some of the Psalms—not very good, but not as bad as might be feared; only neither is their badness a Shakespearean badness—dedicated to George Herbert. One morning in 1622, after he had been ill again, he spent some hours dictating a number of Apophthegms, gathered from his reading or his experience, and published them in 1624. He began a life of Henry VIII, at the reported request of the Prince. He republished the *Essays*, finally revised and enlarged, in 1625. He wrote the *New Atlantis*, in which he recounted the discovery of that most true country where the desire of his heart was fulfilled; where Sal mon's house stands, " dedicated to the study of the works and creatures of God . . . for the finding out of the true nature of all things (whereby God might have the more glory in the workmanship of them, and men the more fruit in the use of them)." It was never finished; how should it be?

He laboured, and the years went by. He was sixty-six in the January of 1625/6, and he was staying in London. Charles had been already crowned: the Parliament was proceeding to impeach Buckingham. The Crown was being pressed as the Chancellor had been. It was twenty-four years since, in February, the earlier Favourite had died by the will of the Minister and the decision of the Queen. In another twenty-four years, in January, the King himself was to die. Snow was to fall over London then as it had fallen now when the Lord St. Alban drove out from London to Highgate. For the King it was to do no more than provide an adequate and picturesque background. But the Lord St. Alban, reclining in his coach, remembered that he had wondered if snow would preserve flesh from putrefaction. He stopped the coach, so the tale goes, at a cottage, and there procured the body of a hen. He helped to stuff it with the snow; he had it taken to the coach; as they drove on he felt the cold seize him. The coach was stopped again at the house of the Lord Arundel, and the great visitor (the host being absent) was received by the servants and duteously attended. But the bed they gave him, the finest bed, was unused, cold, and damp. He lay there for some days; he dictated a letter to the Lord Arundel:

" MY VERY GOOD LORD,

" I was likely to have had the fortune of Caius Plinius the elder, who lost his life by trying an experiment about the burning of the mountain Vesuvius. For I was also desirous to try an experiment or two, touching the conservation and induration of bodies. As for the experiment itself, it succeeded excellently well; but in the journey (between London and Highgate) I was taken with such a fit of casting, as I knew not whether it were the stone, or some surfeit, or cold, or indeed a touch of them all three. But when I came to your Lordship's house, I was not able to go back, and therefore was forced to take up my lodging here, where your housekeeper is very careful and diligent about me ; which I assure myself your Lordship will not only pardon towards him, but think the better of him for it. For indeed your Lordship's house was happy to me ; and I kiss your noble hands for the welcome which I am sure you give me to it.

"I know how unfit it is for me to write to your Lordship with any other hand than mine own ; but in troth my fingers are so disjointed with this fit of sickness, that I cannot steadily hold a pen."

The experiment was succeeding excellently well. But the cold had a greater victim. All his life he had felt the necessary cold of his vocation ; he had been a stranger in his pilgrimage. And now the cold of an earthly winter struck him. The illness turned to bronchitis ; in the early morning of Easter Sunday, 9th April 1626, he choked, and struggled, and died.

## CHAPTER XI

### FRANCIS BACON

THE *Essays* which the Lord St. Alban sent to the French Ambassador, the last edition in his own life of his first book, had nothing directly to do with the Great Instauration. Bacon does not seem, perhaps for that reason, to have thought very highly of it, yet it has been his most popular. That is natural, for it is about man. At the beginning of the seventeenth century three books concerning man were created from and received into English literature—the Authorized Version of the Bible, the collected First Folio of Shakespeare's plays, the *Essays Moral and Civil* of Francis Bacon. The first differed from the others, for it contained as an hypothesis and endeavoured to explore and imagine in words the secret place in man's being where the supernatural dwells, and to discover clearly the operation of that supernatural both in the world and in the soul. The second differed from the others, for it endeavoured to measure by the rule of the decasyllabic line the utmost pits and the farthest heights apprehensible by the natural human mind. The third differed from the others, for it implied as an ideal a certain self-possession and self-knowledge where they had accepted self-destruction; it considered rather man in society than man in solitude. Bacon has been called " the Father of English prose." It is true in the sense that he was among the first to make direct and easy communication of his private meditations, but the prose of solitude is hardly his. That, even during his lifetime, was being shaped again by one who in past years had been secretary to Sir Thomas Egerton, afterwards the Lord Ellesmere whom Bacon succeeded, and had in York House itself known an experience of young love which Bacon (it seems) never knew, by the interpreter of death whose name was John Donne. Donne's public sermons at Paul's Cross were more private than Bacon's secret meditations ; they were more private because they entreated, and agonized, and wrestled with God, and because in such a wrestling God imparts something of his infinite secrecy to each ardent combatant. God, in Bacon, is the father of lights. He may be secret in himself but his concern with man is manifestation. Man has to strive with nature to discover truth, but nature is passive to his endeavours. Donne and the Authorized Version knew of no such passivity ; they pursued God into His recesses ; they fled into the mountain alone to see the rearward of His glory.

Mankind in action, then, is the subject of the *Essays*, and mankind in action in the world. Mankind in the desert was not Bacon's business. It is the sense of the desert indeed, and only the desert, which is lacking in his writing. The wilderness into which Christ was driven, the heath upon which Lear underwent dissolution, are not in that other prose. It would be rash and foolish to assert that there is any moment in Bacon's life when any other man can certainly say he himself would have acted differently. It would be rash and foolish to assert that he more than any of his—or of any—time and place sought preservation at the expense of perfection, or magnificence at the expense of magnanimity. It is still rash, but not quite so foolish, to assert that men have seemed to feel in him a certain cheapening of integrity, a lack of capacity for detachment. He did not make haste to deny himself everything but finality ; he lingered in the world and the Court. He had even so the best of reasons ; God, he thought, meant him to be a summons to men, and whom could he summon in the wilderness ? But we, with St. John Baptist pre-eminent in our minds, are anxious to see him feeding on locusts and clothed in camel's skin ; we expect so great a wind of marvel to come to us rather from the deserts than the towns. Certainly those warring and persecuted Puritans and Papists moved, one feels, to a mightier dance than he until he rode out to Gorhambury from the Tower, until (after five years of separation and neglect) he sent his last appeal to the King's Majesty. Yet he must have known more of the desert than we easily guess. His mother knew how he lay awake at night thinking strange things. We know how all those busy years he hid his vocation in his heart ; the letters that are full of so much remind us that he could never release his mind to any of the men he wished to serve and to use ; the prose itself witnesses that such sentences come only from thought intensely concentrated in loneliness. He also knew— "*neque eum fugit quanta in solitudine versetur hic experimentum,*" "my soul has been a stranger in her pilgrimage." But there is a distinction even in solitudes, and Bacon's loneliness, however lonely, was yet for society ; he purposed to do social good to man. It was not loneliness that pursued farther loneliness ; it did not presume to imagine Gethsemane or Dunsinane, where credible supernatural Good or imagined natural evil walked in their separate and self-chosen exile. It was neither his need nor his privilege ; in that sense he is indeed the first of the modern world, the first great English mind fully escaped from the paths of the hermitages, the doors of the convents, or the mystical sepulchres of the saints. Shakespeare, though he called them by other names—Hamlet or Lear or Imogen— knew more of them than he. He has none of the irrational transcendencies which mark the poets nor the sharp and terrible comforts of the holy ones. To the lights and heats of youth, as of spiritual seers, the wisdom of the *Essays* often seems a poor thing. Blake dashed down " Atheist ! " as he read, and scribbled that if what Bacon said was true what Christ said was false. But greater men even than Blake have hastily supposed they knew what Christ meant and what He did not, and Blake's negations are not as certain as his affirmations. He was wrong ; he himself wrote that Creation was the Mercy of God, and the Mercy of God is a wider thing than Blake supposed. Poets do not write like Bacon nor perhaps do the prophets read him. But, poets and prophets having gathered their congregations, there still remain some who listen to that other bell calling men to know themselves as they are to know all other natural things.

In the *Novum Organum*, speaking of his beloved Forms, he had defined their nature. " In nature nothing really exists beside individual bodies, performing pure individual acts according to a fixed law." But " in philosophy this very law, and the investigation, discovery, and explanation of it, is the foundation as well of knowledge as of operation. And it is this law, with its clauses, which I mean when I speak of Forms." Mankind also consists of individual bodies performing pure individual acts, and though Bacon and his great religious contemporaries would alike have denied that man always acted according to a fixed law, yet in the generality of his actions man does so act. It is man in his actions, and the law that controls them, which are the continual subject of the *Essays* ; they investigate and discover the law which is the Form, and determines knowledge and operation. Neither here nor in the *Novum Organum* is the Form anything like the great Platonic archetypes. Bacon himself had told us in the *Advancement of Learning* how Plato—he said " erred " ; let us rather say, " differed." Plato had half-freed his Forms from matter ; he had mingled theology with physics, and into his theology his physics had escaped, nobly but unreliably transmuted on the way. Those Forms were after the style of the poets; because things in their nature disappointed Plato, he too would exalt the mind of man to some sphere outside known facts. It is not surprising that Platonism has so attracted and affected the English poets. But that Elizabethan Englishman would have nothing of these fantasies. Theology and the supernatural set aside, man was subject to his Form. " I form a history and tables of discovery for anger, fear, shame, and the like; for matters political; and again for the mental operations of memory, composition, and division, judgment and the rest; not less than for heat and cold, or light, or vegetation, and the like." For as regards man also he was concerned to build in the human mind a model of the world as it truly is, " and not such as man's own reason would have it to be." " Atheist! " wrote Blake. Bacon need not even write his comment; the works of his antagonist supply it. He has but to point to those shadowy giants, Los and Enitharmon, Orc and Rintrah, Thel and Palambron, Urizen and Oothoon; hardly with such companions is a man led accurately to know his preservation and perfection, the contemplation of true knowledge and the operation of true power. It is impossible to play hide and seek with such ghosts.

The *Essays*, then, are the definition of the Form, of the law, which controls the pure individual actions of the individual bodies of men. It is the sudden and compressed statement of some clause or other of that law which makes their greatness; it is the misapprehension of a clause of that same law which allows their mistakes. But the mistakes are few, and the successes many, and the final success of all those successes is greater still. Experience of the *Essays* is something more than the separate experiences of their many detached phrases.

It seems to grow within us to something like a discovery of man's nature ; to define something which is " present where man is present, absent when man is absent, and yet has a specification of a more generic nature "— perhaps the creative energy of the word. In the strength of the word it is possible, reading the *Essays*, to feel that we stand at some centre where, by the application of their knowledge and power, we can alchemize one kind of man into another, purifying, debasing, transmuting. The style which produced that sense of knowledge and power presents itself to us as itself a universal form. Its author is characteristic of man's knowledge ; he is a principle of life, and in his sentences there is a definition of mankind. This is what we do ; this is how we carry ourselves among our fellows. It may not be noble—it looks at man as he is. But neither is it ignoble ; never, assuredly, while goodness, that is, the affecting of the weal of men, " of all virtues and dignities of the mind, is the greatest " ; while envy " is the vilest affection and the most depraved " ; while " truth, which doth only judge itself, teacheth that the inquiry of truth, which is the love-making or wooing of it, the knowledge of it, which is the presence of it, and the belief of truth, which is the enjoying of it, is the sovereign good of human nature. . . . Certainly, it is heaven upon earth, to have a man's mind move in charity, rest in providence, and turn upon the poles of truth." Nowhere perhaps has man been more accurately yet more generously defined, with more intelligence and charity at once, a sometimes victorious, often defeated, but always excelling wonder of the universe.

It is his possession by the word in action that has imposed him on us, directly and indirectly. His reputation has been affected by the accidents of his concern. The six parts of the Natural History which he proposed to issue separately were to be called : *Of Winds ; Of*

*Density and Rarity ; Of Heaviness and Lightness ; Of the Sympathy and Antipathy of Things ; Of Sulphur, Mercury, and Salt ; Of Life and Death.* Almost in the old alchemical method he named them ; almost the great titles sound as if something more than Natural History were there investigated, as if he hid under veils the making of the *nova creatura* which he seemed to himself to have become. But it would be doing Bacon ill service to pretend he was occupied with such solemn occultisms, however saintly. The fascination of his person and devotion has drawn around him the wildest clouds of fable. Men have made him royal in his birth, the son of Elizabeth ; they have clothed him with the more awful sovereignty of the poetic genius of Shakespeare ; they have cast on him all miracles of words in that age, as in the Middle Ages the tales of many miracles were cast about one saint ; they have attributed to him the knowledge of antediluvian wisdom and the foundation or nourishment of schools of secret science and spiritual mysteries. In his honour they have wrested, not insincerely, things to their thoughts ; in his who all his life declared the necessity of submitting the thought of man to the fact of things.

Even when they have despised they have magnified him ; if they cannot name him John they will call him Judas. There is imposed on them the fact of himself. Pope touched him with superlatives—" the wisest, brightest, meanest of mankind " (" the meanest "—Pope !). Macaulay—so unnecessarily—lamented over him as over a fallen archangel ; even Lytton Strachey, in the midst of his dainty jests at the Trinity and the Earl of Essex, at the death-agony of Philip of Spain and the life-agony of Elizabeth of England—even Lytton Strachey, in a phrase perhaps caught from Macaulay, who perhaps caught it from Bacon himself, was compelled to turn him into an exquisite and terrible evil. He must be beyond belief subtle in wickedness, lest he should be merely honest, and, on one side, human. The other side, we know, is that of a god ; touched with immortality, diffusing light. By a myth more terrible than that of any Greek legend they will have his divine clarity interfused with putrefying flesh and cancerous sores. He has been made to want what he never wanted, to believe what he never believed, to transpose his own professed fidelities, to deny his profoundest decisions, in order that he may be suitably denounced by an outraged world. They have made a myth out of a man who desired nothing but to keep myth in its small and remote place, so great has been the sorcerous glamour of his labour and his vision. But glamour was not for him. Something more or less than glamour is in the *New Atlantis*. There beyond the ocean, in the country of Bensalem, lies the College of the Six Days' Work of God, the house of Salomon, where justice and simplicity dwell, with its galleries and furnaces and gardens and libraries and terraces and cellars, its laboratories and studies, its halls and places of statuary ; whence the ships go out to the rest of the wide world to bring back all knowledge, all merchandise of truth, and for ever the experimentalists labour and the rationalizing students toil, and the Masters of the whole work judge and decree, and for ever the Father whom the travellers met declares to ages and peoples their great purpose— " the knowledge of the secret causes of things and the extending of human empire over all things possible." The Lord St. Alban was Chancellor of England and held great place, but his greater place is that in which he is one with the Father of Salomon's House and the visionary master of man's mortal scope.

It must be admitted that he took his revelation solemnly, and perhaps himself solemnly as its means. How he might have lived and written without the Great Instauration it is, unfortunately, impossible to judge.

That solemnity may have been one of the elements which rendered him capable of the Great Instauration ; a too vivid self-mockery would have thwarted his energy and blinded his vision. Yet sometimes a little would be grateful. Of pretended laughter, of mock humility, of the detestable mannerism by which a man fawns on the self he adores, Francis Bacon was incapable ; prophets are not made of such metal. But of that other irony which thrives on the impossibility both of workman and of work, the laughter in the midst of labour at a complete overthrow of the labour, the enjoyment of universal absurdity, of this too he was senseless. There again is that little extra reach of Shakespearean greatness ; could the playwright ever have taken *Macbeth* quite as solemnly as the Chancellor took the *Novum Organum* ? This extra reach, this doubling in upon itself of genius, this beholding of their proper worlds from an infinite depth of sceptical delight, is not in the founders of missions. It was not in Milton or in Wordsworth ; it is not in Bacon. He, as they were, is a dedicated soul, and such an experience of dedication, excluding scepticism, tends to exclude laughter also. If Bacon was indeed a concealed poet, it was not *Twelfth Night* and *Antony and Cleopatra* and *A Winter's Tale* that he wrote, but *Paradise Lost* and *Paradise Regained*.

Nevertheless, laughter and irony were not lacking ; the universe took the burden of those enjoyments upon itself. In the preface to the *Novum Organum* Bacon had chanced upon a rare lightness—" Even as though the divine nature took pleasure in the innocent and kindly sport of children playing at hide-and-seek, and vouchsafed of his kindness and goodness to admit the human spirit for his playfellow at that game "—" *non aliter ac si divina natura . . . puerorum ludo delectaretur . . . atque animam humanam sibi collusorum in hoc ludo . . . cooptaverit.*" (The kindness and goodness of the divine

nature might perhaps have excluded medicine from its
play ; we should have enjoyed the rest of it so much
better.) The unusual sweetness of the metaphor makes
one wonder if the universe or perfection or the divine
nature or his Fortune—whatever name we give to that
perpetual otherness—wrote that sentence for him ; and
with a peculiar appropriateness. For such a game of
hide-and-seek it assuredly played with Bacon. The
amusement which, it seems likely, he never found in his
great task, it discovered for itself at his expense. It
produced him in fortunate circumstances, a child of a
man close by the Throne ; it gave him in his early years
every prospect of a satisfying career. It allowed him to
take the first necessary steps of that career, and before
they were ended it communicated the vision of something
of its own perfection to his mind and heart. It showed
him " what he was born for," and having shown him
that, which was itself, it hid itself. At first it seemed to
be immediately before him, but suddenly his father died
and there was no direct way. He supposed it had fled
to the Cecils, and sought it there, himself the while
diligently recording the vision in the *Temporis Partus
Maximus*. But the years passed, and after having
diligently examined all the Lord Treasurer's purposes he
determined that it was not hidden there. Again it
seemed to be with the brilliant and intellectual Essex,
and to Essex Bacon went, to see if he could discover
there both preservation which is the search for perfection,
and perfection which is the end of the search. Anthony
returned, and the rooms of Essex House and the corridors
of the royal palaces became full of much business ; and
Francis toiled patiently and drafted instructions and
was quarrelled over and waited in antechambers and
heard loud voices within and saw the raging exodus of
the Favourite, and feared that if perfection had ever
hidden there it had fled, and found himself gradually

dropped. Then for some months perfection altogether disappeared, while the Queen talked to him and rumours were spread and Cecil deprecated hostility to the Earl, and Francis saw his very preservation in danger; until the Earl went mad altogether and the whole episode closed in blood, and there was a clear world again with only Cecil and Coke and a strange King. Perfection this time might, he thought, be hidden in retirement, not after all in great place, and thither he proposed to follow her. But, lest he should believe his early assignation false, she suddenly showed herself in the House of Commons, and ran in front of him to the royal throne, and sat at the table of the Commissioners for the Union. She even let herself leave the *Advancement of Learning* with him for encouragement, before she gleamed at the window of the office of the Solicitor and then of the Attorney. And now the game was very near an end; preservation and perfection were almost one. In York House and Gorhambury she waited for him, sat with him, talked with him, watched over the final revision of the *Novum Organum*—the second part of the great work; how much more remaining yet to do! And then, when he thought he had securely found her, when his interest and his advancement and his loyalty and his duty and his vision were almost one, she vanished in the days of a sudden March, and he found that he had been tricked again. His accusers were everywhere; in that moment he accused himself, but not of earthly corruption, only that he had not sought rightly for Perfection, he had not followed quickly enough on the flying feet of that divine nature, he had misspent his talent. As if in recompense, when the noise was over and he flung away, while he still looked back and thought she lingered in London, she came to him, quietly, almost secretly. She renewed his energies, she thrilled his style, she preserved in him the vision of the *New Atlantis* and the secret causes of things. In the time of his humiliation he had still believed in truth—

> This
> Stands as a child laughing to see the sun,
> Immortal, incorruptible, sovereign truth;
> Blessed be God who hath made our souls for truth!

The vitality of truth remained with him. As if in a wild symbolism his Fortune closed upon him, meeting him on Highgate in the experiment of preservative snow. By some such coldness she had preserved him, because through all mistakes and faults his own preservation had sought her; in a celestial and happy irony she sent, as it were, from his dying form, during that final Holy Week, a message such as he himself dictated to his secretary, and while the Lord Arundel read his letter, future ages and other nations turned to hear the lofty cry of the perfection that had summoned and charmed and eluded and led him: "The experiment succeedeth excellently well."

# A BRIEF CHRONOLOGY

1560–1 Francis Bacon born.
1573–5 At Cambridge.
1576 At Gray's Inn.
1577 Goes to Paris.
1579 Death of Sir Nicholas. Francis returns from Paris.
1582 Utter barrister.
1584 *Temporis Partus Maximus.* Enters Parliament.
1589 Promised the reversion of the Clerkship of the Star Chamber.
1592 Letter to Burleigh. Friends with Essex.
1593 Offence in the Commons. Attempt on the Attorneyship.
1594 Coke Attorney. Attempt on the Solicitorship.
1595 Fleming Solicitor.
1596 Warning to Essex.
1597 *Essays.* " Discontinuance of privateness " with Essex.
1599 Essex's return from Ireland.
1601 Rebellion of Essex.
1603 James I. Francis knighted.
1604–6 The controversy on the Union.
1605 *The Advancement of Learning.*
1607 Solicitor-General.
1608 Receives the Clerkship of the Star Chamber.
1610 Failure of the Great Contract in Parliament.
1612 Death of Robert Cecil.
1613 Attorney-General.
1615 Fall of Somerset. Promotion of Coke. Failure of " Undertakers."
1616 Removal of Coke. Bacon Privy Councillor.
1617 Lord Keeper.
1618 Lord Chancellor. Baron Verulam.
1620 Publication of the *Novum Organum.*
1621 Viscount St. Alban. Accusation, submission, imprisonment, and retirement.
1622 History of Henry VII. First parts of the *Natural and Experimental History.*
1623 *De Augmentis.*
1624 *Apophthegms.*
1625 *Essays.*
1626 Death.
1627 The *New Atlantis.*

# INDEX

Advancement of Learning, 119–21, 130, 138–40, 142–50, 160, 243, 248, 298, 305–6, 312.
Andrewes, Lancelot, Bishop of Winchester, 46, 178, 235, 250, 292.
Apologie concerning the Earl of Essex, 42, 85, 89, 119–20.
Awbry, Christopher, 268–70, 281.

Bacon (Barnham), Alice, 116 and n.
Bacon (Cooke), Lady Anne, 3, 5–7, 9, 21, 29–32, 56, 58, 65, 69–70, 104, 249.
Bacon, Anthony, 2, 6–7, 21, 29–32, 38, 39, 56, 58–60, 70–1, 80–1, 104, 107, 113, 311; relations with Essex, 42–6, 80, 96–7, 100–1, 151.
Bacon, Francis, birth and childhood, 1–3; first interviews with the Queen, 2–3; at Cambridge, 7; his vocation, 7–11; at Paris, 11–14; return to England, 14; and Burleigh, 15, 33, 35; in London, 31–2; *Temporis Partus Maximus*, 33, 297, 311; meeting with Essex, 38, 42, 46; gives offence to the Queen, 47–56; put forward for the Attorneyship, 57–60; for the Solicitorship, 60–5; and Shakespeare, 1, 64–5, 104–6; warnings to Essex, 67, 77, 83, 85; money troubles, 69–75; examination of prisoners, 75–6; proposed marriage, 79; *Essays*, 81, 104, 299, 302–7; interviews with the Queen concerning Essex, 87–98; slanders, 93; at the Star Chamber court, 95; at the trial of Essex, 99–102; share of the fines, 103; his perfection and preservation, 106, 237–8; his letters, 107, 235; quarrels with Coke, 108, 177, 292; interview with James, 113–4; letters to Southampton, 115, 293; proposes to retire, 117, 121; his *Confession of Faith*, 117; *Sacred Meditations*, 119; *Apologie concerning the Earl of Essex*, 119; on himself, 120; prominence in the House of Commons, 122–7; and the Union, 128, 133–5; *Advancement of Learning*, 130, 138–50, 298, 312; and the Gunpowder Plot, 130–2; Solicitor-General, 137, 151; flattery of James, 142–3; five concerns of his mind, 153, 162; his notebooks, 154–61; and Somerset, 163–4, 168; and the Blagrave case, 165; and the Great Instauration, 166; vision of Majesty, 167, 175–6, 291–2; and the Overbury case, 168–71; his *Advice to Villiers*, 171–4; *Cogitata et Visa*, 178; letter to Lancelot Andrewes, 178; and Toby Mathew, 179, 222, 297; *De Sapientia Veterum*, 179–80; disapproves of the Great Contract, 182–3, 184; opinion of Cecil, 186–9; offers himself for the Secretaryship, 187; advice to the King, 189–90; and the Benevolence, 192–3; prosecutes St. John, 194–5; and the nature of love, 195–9; proposes to promote Coke, 201; Attorney-General, 203, 204; *Descriptio Globi Intellectualis*, 204; *Thema Cœli*, 204; and duelling, 204–5; and cases of treason, 205; and Peacham, 206–8; dealing with Coke, 207–8, 209, 210–12; Lord Keeper, 212, 213–6; Lord Chancellor, 216; Baron Veru-

# 316                         INDEX

Bacon, Francis (*continued*)—
lam, 216; mode of living, 216–21; his servants, 219–20; his clearance of suits, 221; and the Judges, 222; and the Hatton marriage, 223–35; angers Buckingham and the King, 230–3; and Raleigh, 236; and Suffolk, 237; political and social views, 237–40; the *Novum Organum*, 240–54, 271, 305, 310, 312; the King's opinion, 254, 297; and Yelverton, 259–61; and the Monopolies, 261–2; Viscount St. Alban, 262; and the attack on Monopolies, 264–7; malpractice, 267–70; accused of corruption, 270–4; letter to the King, 274; his prayer or psalm, 276; his own judgment, 277, 279; his submission, 278–81; the sentence, 283; in the Tower, 284; retires to Gorhambury, 284; *Henry VII*, 287; consulted by the King, 288; refuses York House to Buckingham, 289, 290; then yields, 291; last letter to the King, 295; *De Augmentis*, 298; *Natural History*, 298, 307–8; *Sylva Sylvarum*, 298–9; *Holy War*, 299; translation of the Psalms, 299; *Apophthegms*, 299; *Henry VIII*, 299; *New Atlantis*, 299, 309, 312; last experiment, 300, 313; illness and death, 300–1, 313.
Bacon, Sir Nicholas, 1–7, 11, 14, 38, 63, 176, 187, 239, 284, 311.
Buckhurst, Lord, 12–13, 130.

Carr, Robert, Earl of Somerset, 19, 163–4, 168–70, 203–4, 208, 233.
Cecil, Robert, Earl of Salisbury, cousin to Bacon, 2; promotion, 15, 37, 43; and Anthony, 45; in Parliament, 50–3; and Bacon's promotion, 57–63; Secretary, 59; Chancellor of the Duchy, 81–2; and Essex, 82, 88; warning to Bacon concerning Essex, 90; rumours, 93; destruction of Essex, 98, 99; use of Bacon, 99, 102; at the trial, 101; in power, 102, 108; Bacon's relations with him, 110–11, 112, 136–7, 177, 235; proclaims James, 111–12; Earl of Salisbury, 112; Treasurer, 112; and Goodwin, 124; and the Gunpowder Plot, 130, 132; Bacon's opinion of, 157, 158, 186–9; and the Great Contract, 178, 181–2; death, 185–6.
Cecil, Sir Thomas, 58, 79.
Cecil, William, Lord Burleigh, uncle to Bacon, 2, 3; and Sir Nicholas, 4; promotion of Robert Cecil, 15, 37, 59; and Spenser, 16; and the Queen, 18, 42; Master of the Wards, 21; rebukes Bacon, 33, 140; assists Coke, 34; and Bacon's career, 35–8, 311; Anthony and, 43, 45; appoints Bacon to Parliament, 47; angry with him, 53; and his promotion, 57–63; death, 84.
Churchill, John, 267–8.
*Cogitata et Visa*, 178, 250.
Coke, Sir Edward, 7, 24, 49, 123–4, 152, 237, 249, 312; helped by Burleigh, 34; and the Attorneyship, 57, 59, 60; marriage, 79, 223–35; and Essex, 95, 99, 101; antagonism to Bacon, 108–10, 130, 136, 177, 292; and the Gunpowder Plot, 132; Chief Justice of Common Pleas, 137, 201; and the Overbury trial, 169, 170; and the Benevolence, 191–2; and the Crown, 200, 207–12; Chief Justice of King's Bench, 203–4; suspended, 212; and the Villiers marriage, 223–35; and Raleigh, 236; and the monopolies, 261, 263–5, 268; on the *Novum Organum*, 271.
*Colours of Good and Evil*, 81.
*Confession of Faith, A*, 117–8.
Coventry, Sir Thomas, 21.
Crewe, Sir Randolph, 261.

Davies, Sir John, 113.
*De Augmentis Scientiarum*, 298.

# INDEX

*De Sapientia Veterum*, 179-80.
*Descriptio Globi Intellectualis*, 204.
Devereux, Robert, Earl of Essex, 16, 22-4, 38-9, 75, 111, 114, 141, 233, 235, 252; and Elizabeth, 18-19, 22, 39-42, 54, 57-60, 65-9, 76-103, 170; and Francis Bacon, 38, 42-4, 54, 57-69, 76-80, 82-3, 85-102, 141, 171, 177, 256-7, 276, 311-2; and Anthony Bacon, 42-6, 80, 96-7, 100-1, 151; and Ireland, 82, 84-9; trial of, 94-5, 100-2.
Drake, John, 131-2.

Echoes, 3, 12-13, 250.
Egerton, Edward, 270.
Egerton, Sir Thomas, Lord Ellesmere, 75, 77, 88, 130, 137, 165-6, 200, 204, 212, 303.
Elizabeth, Queen, 143, 151-2, 166-7, 199-200, 252, 308, 312; Bacon presented to, 2-3; flattery of, 17-22, 41-2; and Essex, 18-9, 22, 39-42, 57-60, 65-9, 76-103, 106-7, 170; death, 111-2.
*Essays, the*, 3, 9, 39, 46, 81, 104, 118, 162, 204, 239, 257, 287, 297, 299, 302-3, 305-7.

Faunt, Nicholas, 31-2, 34.
Fortesque, Sir John, 123, 126.

Goodwin, Sir Francis, 123-4, 126, 128.
*Greatest Birth of Time*, 33, 297, 311.
Gunpowder Plot, 130-2.

Hatton, Lady, 79-80, 225-6, 231, 234-5.
Hickes, Sir Michael, 71, 104, 112, 155, 159.
*History of Henry VII*, 287, 291.
Hobart, Sir Henry, 137, 158-9, 201, 203, 246-7, 264, 280, 283, 293.
*Holy War, The* [Bacon's], 299.
Howard, Lord Charles, 16, 45, 82-3, 93-4.
Howard, Lord Thomas, Earl of Suffolk, 258.

James I, and Somerset, 19, 168-70; Essex's letter to, 23; his learning, 64, 138; and Essex, 95, 99, 114; accession, 105, 111-12; Bacon meets, 113-14; his first proceedings, 116-17; and the Commons, 124-5, 126-7, 181-5, 189-90; Bacon's first speech to, 125; and the Union, 128, 129, 132, 135; Bacon's relations with, 139-40, 142-3, 156, 214; and the Overbury murder, 168-70; and Villiers, 169, 171; and Coke, 200-3, 207-12, 265; and the Hatton marriage, 228-35; and Raleigh, 237; and the *Novum Organum*, 242, 254, 297; and the Monopolies, 264, 266; and Bacon's fall, 272, 274-6, 278, 284, 289, 291; consults Bacon, 288; Bacon's last petition, 294; and last letter, 295, 304.
Jonson, Ben, 130-1, 197, 214, 284.

Killigrew, Sir Harry, 71.

Lawson, Mr., 7, 30-1.
*Letter of Advice to a King's Favourite*, 39, 171-5.

Matthew, Toby, 179, 222, 235, 292, 297.
*Meditationes Sacræ*, 81, 118.
Merrick, Sir Gilly, 104.
Michell, Sir Francis, 263.
Mompesson, Sir Giles, 263-6.
Mountjoy, Lord, 85-6, 92, 99.

*New Atlantis, the*, 106, 273, 299, 309, 312.
*Novum Organum, the*, 13, 179, 204, 240-54, 258, 263, 271, 297, 305, 310, 312.

O'Neill, Sir Turlough, Earl of Tyrone, 86, 89.

Paulet, Sir Amyas, 11, 14, 28.
Percy, Sir Henry, 9th Earl of Northumberland, 113-4, 160.
Prerogative, the, 152-3, 163, 180-1, 183-4, 188, 201-2, 209, 212, 222, 249, 252-4, 257, 264, 292, 294.
Purveyance, 128, 181.

Raleigh, Sir Walter, 16, 42, 51, 101, 103, 236–7.
Reynolds, Mr., 131–2.

Sandys, Sir Edwin, 135.
Shakespeare, William, 1, 12, 16–17, 20, 33, 41, 56, 64–5, 104–6, 108, 116, 146, 156, 162, 167, 174, 193, 197–8, 215, 302, 304, 308, 310.
Shirley, Thomas, 126–7, 129.
Southampton. *See* Wriothesley.
*Sylva Sylvarum*, 198, 298–9.
Sympson, Mr., 74, 126–7.

*Temporis partus maximus*, 33, 297, 311.
Tenure, 181–2.
*Thema Cæli*, 204.
Trott, Nicholas, 71–2.
*True Greatness of Britain, The*, 168.

Tyrone. *See* O'Neill.

Villiers, George, Duke of Buckingham, 39, 64, 163, 169–75, 208, 215–16, 221, 223–5, 227–37, 258–9, 261–3, 266–7, 272, 274, 282–3, 289–91, 294–7, 300.
Villiers, Sir John, 223–7, 230–1, 234.

Waad, Sir William, 46, 74.
Walsingham, Sir Francis, 16, 28, 37, 46.
Wardship, 128, 181–4.
Wriothesley, Henry, Earl of Southampton, 101, 103–5, 114–15, 263, 270, 272, 280, 283, 293–4.

Yelverton, Sir Henry, 125, 203, 227, 232–3, 259–61, 263, 266–7.

www.ingramcontent.com/pod-product-compliance
Lightning Source LLC
Chambersburg PA
CBHW031325230426
43670CB00006B/246